3D Graphics

Tips, Tricks, & Techniques

David J. Kalwick
San Diego, CA

AP PROFESSIONAL

Boston   San Diego   New York
London   Sydney   Tokyo   Toronto

AP PROFESSIONAL
1300 Boylston Street, Chestnut Hill, MA 02167
World Wide Web site at http://www.apnet.com

An Imprint of ACADEMIC PRESS, INC.
A Division of HARCOURT BRACE & COMPANY

United Kingdom Edition published by
ACADEMIC PRESS LIMITED
24–28 Oval Road, London NW1 7DX

ISBN 0-12-394970-X

Printed in the United States of America
96 97 98   IP   9 8 7 6 5 4 3 2 1

Contents

Contents

Chapter 8

Chapter 9

Chapter 10

Chapter 11

Animation — Giving Objects Life

Chapter 12

Deformation Tools

Chapter 13

Product Reviews

Glossary

Index

To my lovely wife Marilyn,
only through her unwavering inspiration,
and endless support, was this book possible.

Acknowledgments

I would also like to thank the following companies for their support in a variety of ways; including technical support, software, and general help:

AP Professional—I would like to thank everyone at AP Professional, Boston; especially Jenifer Niles, Barbara Northcott, and Jacquelyn Young who have been extremely helpful in the creation of this endeavor.

Strata Incorporated (Strata StudioPro Blitz)—Many thanks to Jeff Lewis over the past year for the support he has given me through Strata Inc. I would also like to thank the many wonderful people at Strata Inc.; including Joe Fox, Mike Ditmire, and Heidi Rosenberg.

Electric Image Incorporated (Electric Image Animation System 2.5.2)—Special thanks to Wendy Keough Bozegan for all of her efforts.

auto•des•sys Inc.

AutoDesk

Avid Technology

Caligari Corporation

Ray Dream, Inc.

4D Vision/Schrieber Instruments

Specular

The Valis Group

Preface

You've seen it on television and in the movies, as well as in some of the most popular computer games, and now you too would like to enter the exciting world of 3D graphics. Whether you are an artist, engineer, game developer, into special effects, or just love to tinker and draw, the world of 3D graphics holds many exciting, new ways to express yourself visually.

In the past, books on computer graphics have been written by computer progammers who disclose endless pages of computer code, just to create the infamous reflective sphere over a checkerboard plane. With today's graphical user interfaces and more user-friendly computers, there is no need to pore through tons of code to produce pretty pictures. With *3D Graphics: Tips, Tricks, and Techniques* you will not find a single line of computer code. All lessons and techniques are easily understood by the most computer illiterate person as well as your local C++ guru.

Since creating 3D graphics without high-end equipment is a relatively new art form, many of the techniques used are not readily available. With *3D Graphics: Tips, Tricks, and Techniques* you can begin creating realistic 3D graphics right away. You'll learn from a professional how the tools of this trade can be applied through a three dimensional thinking process.

You can begin your adventure armed with knowledge of how to use the tools you need to succeed. Creating 3D graphics is an exciting adventure into the unknown because, although the medium is not physical, the product looks very real. While many of the skills needed to be successful are derived from other disciplines; such as illustration, sculpture, and cinematography, there are also new disciplines that are unique to the 3D graphics world. These new concepts are discussed in easy-to-understand terms, so that even if you are not computer literate, you will be up and running quickly.

Whether you prefer the Macintosh, PC, or other platform, *3D Graphics: Tips, Tricks, and Techniques* is there to guide you through the intricate world of creating realistic 3D graphics. This platform independent book shows you how to use the same techniques used by professionals to build your own library of shapes and get you jump started into the world of three dimensional graphics.

It starts you off with an introduction to 3D modeling and the various platforms available, as well as navigation through three dimensional computer space. You will learn about the 2D and 3D primitives, which are the basis of all models, and how to build other models through the use of these tools.

Since there are many tools used in model creation, this book provides an in-depth look at the various tools in a variety of software packages. Tools such as lofting sweeping, object deformation, splines, and many others are discussed in platform independent terms, so that they may be applied to any program or machine on which you choose to develop.

This book was written to help you along the normally steep learning curve associated with creating 3D graphics and animation. Because there are so many tools and programs to choose from, a CD-ROM is included to allow you to try out some of the more popular 3D programs before you buy. There are also models and textures included for your use. Many of the models are used in examples, so that you can study how they were built, or refer to them while working on a similar project.

Since you have already decided that you are interested in 3D computer graphics, you can side-step some of the learning curve by using the professional hints provided here. You too can create stunning 3D graphics and animation in no time with *3D Graphics: Tips, Tricks, and Techniques*. Now you have your own personal 3D tutor at your desk whenever you get caught between a spline and a polygon.

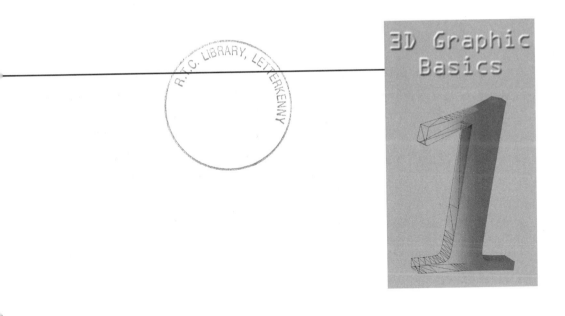

3D Graphic Basics

What Is 3D Modeling?

There is a visual revolution on the rise. Soon it may be impossible to discern the real from the imaginary in the theaters or on television. On television, advertisers use images of animated candy and mouthwash bottles to make their products known, while across town, engineers use the same technology to design and analyze stress on jet engine components from images such as the one in Figure 1-1 before they are ever built.

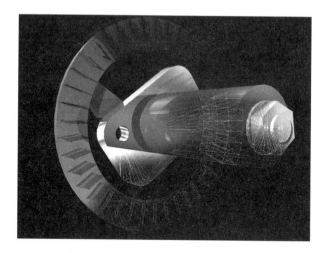

FIGURE 1-1 Using computer-generated images of engine parts, engineers can analyze stress on the component using sophisticated software and high-end computer technology.

What makes this type of animation possible is an emerging phenomenon known as three dimensional computer modeling and animation. It facilitates the most realistic simulation in the world and is called 3D animation or 3D for short. This relatively new form of visual communication is taking the world by storm. Due to faster and more powerful computers, 3D animation is gaining wide acceptance in many visual applications. Because of its convincing portrayal of real-life objects, 3D animation is becoming a legitimate tool in object prototyping, courtroom litigation, boardrooms, engineering labs, and Hollywood's special effects industry.

This technology is now found throughout the advertising industry and high-budget action films. Even the military is using virtual reality settings to simulate flight during battle situations.

In a courtroom environment, computer modeling and animation can reconstruct a traffic accident by using data obtained at the scene. This type of modeling provides a more objective and precise reenactment than actors can. This type of objectivity and flexibility is a prime concern when trying to convince a jury or a judge.

From an engineering or architectural perspective, computer modeling can be used to hypothesize about what might happen with a potential structural failure. It allows engineers to simulate the effects of various changes, or what will happen if no changes are made. These types of events are excellent examples of how useful computer modeling can be.

TECHNIQUE: Steps to Creating 3D Graphics

- *Modeling:* A computer model of a desired object is built. The objects are constructed from primitives that have been worked into the desired shape using graphic tools. The models are then given a surface texture for a more realistic look.

- *Scene layout:* During the scene layout or scene building phase, objects which are to be part of the image are positioned in 3D space. During scene layout, the 3D objects are like the actors on a movie set in that they must be positioned on the set. Cameras and lights are also added at this time.

- *Animation:* When the scene is going to contain animation, some or all of the objects in the scene must be animated. In the animation phase of 3D graphics, objects are choreographed to move about the scene by means of keyframes.

• *Rendering:* The rendering phase is the process of producing the final image. Object geometry and surface texture and their reaction to the simulated light is taken into account to produce shadows and different types of surfaces. This is where the strength of the computer is most appreciated as it calculates the seemingly endless flow of data created by the computer models.

3D Features

Three dimensional animation is not like the old 3D movies that require special, two-color glasses, although new stereopolarized glasses can make some three dimensional animation seem to jump right off the screen. Instead of using two-color glasses and offset images to produce 3D objects, 3D animation uses proper perspective to give a true sense of an object. It is the type of perspective seen in Figure 1-2 and the ability of the camera to view the object from any angle that gives computer-generated 3D models an advantage over traditional 2D imaging. Since perspective is an important part of how we view objects, images or pictures with no perspective tend to look flat. On the other end of the spectrum, images with too much perspective tend to look unrealistic. In computer modeling and animation, once the lens size and perspective have been chosen, a consistent perspective is handled mathematically by the computer, thereby creating an animation, which if animated and built correctly, can be very convincing.

FIGURE 1-2 3D graphics are in high demand in virtually every facet of visual communication because of vanishing points and perspective, and the ability to display images from any angle.

Another aspect of 3D animation that sets it apart from traditional animation is that all objects within a scene have the potential to react to other objects and conditions present within the scene, such as lighting, in a realistic manner. Some of the benefits of 3D modeling which make it seem so realistic include shadowing, reflected or refracted light, and simulated gravity. A virtual camera's ability to move through the scene as if the objects really existed adds to the realism of 3D animation.

Although some of the benefits of 3D animation are not always apparent to the general public, the implications are phenomenal. We can now use computer animation to simulate delicate surgery or commercial flight, or we can entertain ourselves with interactive worlds of futuristic fantasy. And it is all done through 3D animation and computer models.

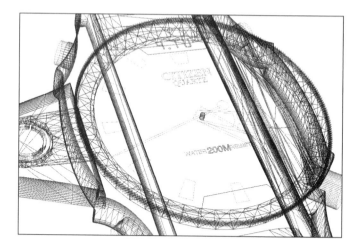

FIGURE 1-3 3D computer-generated graphics are created through the use of computer models that describe an object's shape on all sides.

They Are All Models

Within a computer animation, all of the created objects are called *computer models*. A computer model is really just a series of mathematical matrices that describe, among other things, the object's shape and position in 3D space (see Figure 1-3). The computer model is primarily a bunch of points in space which, when connected like a connect-the-dots puzzle, form the shape of an object. The major difference is that some objects can easily contain many thousands of points.

TIP: Try before you buy. Different modeling types require a different technique to build the models. There are polygonal modelers and spline-based modelers. Some will use NURBS and Bézier patches; others may not. It is always a good idea to thoroughly check out all of the features, limitations, and requirements of the software before purchasing. If you are unsure, request a demo version of the software before buying. Many companies will comply with your request.

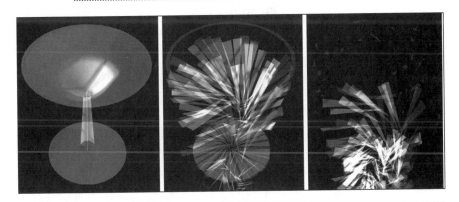

FIGURE 1-4 Through the use of special effects software, you can change the shape of an object over time by means of effects such as morphing, exploding, and atomizing. This effect was created using Strata Studio Pro's shatter feature.

Special Effects

Although the computer model is the foundation of computer animation, it is special effects that are the most desirable. Being able to take a group of points and splines and turn it into an animated object that can dance, fly, or react to physical properties is nothing short of amazing. Special effects, such as the one in Figure 1-4, make use of shattering and morphing techniques, which can change one object into another.

Because the physical properties in the real world are mathematical, they can be quantified. Using these formulas in computer software allows the computer to simulate lighting and other physical effects such as gravity. This practice is easier explained than practiced since these physical effects are math intensive, and only recently have production line computer systems been able to handle the workload necessary for production of quality 3D animation.

The creation of special effects such as fire and flowing water is very difficult because of their organic nature. Some of the extremely high-end software packages such as Alias PowerAnimator (Silicon Graphics) make these types of effects more manageable than the standard desktop computer software.

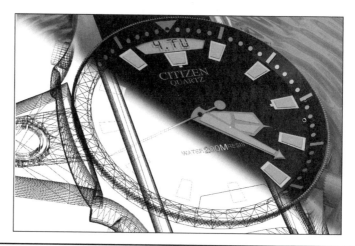

FIGURE 1-5 To complete a computer-generated image, the scene must be rendered. Rendering is the process of applying the given attributes and processing the light as it interacts with the objects within the scene.

Rendering

After the models have been built, the objects animated, and the surface textures applied, the process of rendering begins. Rendering is the process by which the computer interprets all of the information contained in the computer model. This includes lights, surface textures, deformation areas, and environmental data. This process, although handled by the computer, is more math intensive than modeling. The computer needs to analyze all data and render the correct image from its interpretation of the parameters set in the model and environment.

During the rendering phase, each ray of light must be calculated and each point in every object's geometry must be accounted for. In this process, every reflection on every polygon and every shadow is calculated. If this does not seem like a big enough task, imagine models containing tens and hundreds of thousands of points and polygons. All this needs to be recalculated for every single frame in a typical 30 frame per second animation. Since a 10 second animation at 30 frames per second adds up to 300 frames, it is easy to see how the rendering process can quickly grow to become an enormous job.

The simplest solution to the rendering process is to have the fastest process available and the most random access memory (RAM) the machine is capable of handling. Also, using a number of machines connected through a network to farm out the rendering process will dramatically cut down on the rendering time by dispersing subsequent frames to each computer.

TIP: When rendering large images or animation, it is best to render at a time when the computer is not needed for other tasks, especially if only one computer will handle the job. Since rendering is CPU intensive, rendering an animation while using the computer for other tasks slows down the rendering process and any other processes running concurrently.

Storage

In addition to having the horsepower to render an animation in a timely manner, there is also a need for permanent storage. Depending on the type of compression/decompression algorithm (Codec) you choose and the resolution of each frame, the final movie size can become quite large. It is not unlikely for a short animation (under 30 seconds) to be over 100 megabytes. I recommend a minimum of one gigabyte of hard drive space, with four gigabytes being comfortable. Disk space is utilized very quickly, due to the amount of trial and error, previews, image maps, and test animations required for building final animation.

TIP: When configuring a system for 3D modeling and animation, buy a system that is capable of handling large amounts of RAM. The very bare minimum to do 3D modeling is about 20 megabytes. If you plan on creating animation, you will need a minimum of 40 megabytes to handle the demand. A tip for buying RAM—buy as much as you can afford; you can never have too much RAM. Typically, more money is spent on RAM and hard drives than on the computer itself.

Simulators

Although the money invested in hardware and software may seem substantial for an individual, the real investment comes when commercial companies decide to use 3D animation for simulators and multimedia. 3D animation is beginning to make a big impact in multimedia, but the perfect home for 3D animation is in procedural simulation.

By performing with sophisticated simulation hardware and software, people in all types of professions benefit by learning their trade in repeatable and controlled environments. To the casual observer, some of these simulators may seem like toys, but in reality there are millions of dollars of research and engineering involved in the software, called *reality engines*.

Reality engines are required to produce the graphics that change dynamically as the situation within the simulator changes. These extensive and realistic simulators cost well into the millions of dollars, but can save many more lives and countless dollars in design and engineering costs. Because any situation or environment can be created or recreated using 3D simulation, buildings and other physical structures such as bridges and tunnels can be analyzed for stress while still in the design phase.

Unlike desktop game simulators, high-end simulators allow the operator to experience the total environment. Not only do the simulators have realistic graphics and controls, but in the case of flight simulators, they may also be attached to hydraulics that give the pilot the sensation of flying by banking and dipping as the pilot encounters various hazards of the sky.

Currently, the number of commercial jetliners that have experienced a crash landing and survived is relatively low. If pilots could train and practice landing a commercial jetliner under emergency conditions, they would be better prepared for a real emergency.

FIGURE 1-6 Versatility makes 3D modeling worth the effort. Once the model of the ancient Egyptian boat was created, only the camera angle needed to be changed to create a different perspective.

3D Versus 2D

Since the initial cost of producing a 3D animation is very high, what is the advantage of using 3D animation over traditional art? Although there are many reasons to choose computer models, versatility is the key in visualization. Although the both views of the boat in Figure 1-6 are of the same model, only one view was created by the artist. Once created, models can be used over and over without the duplication of effort found in two dimensional artwork. Changing the camera angle is a trivial task compared to the work the traditional artist would have to do to recreate the same image by hand if the perspective needed to be changed.

Typically, when using 3D animation to recreate an accident scene or demonstrate product design, the scene needs to be viewed from many angles. Since computer models are built in three dimensions, the animation may also be viewed from any angle with relative ease. Once an animation has been constructed, changing the camera angle is a trivial matter. It then becomes a matter of rendering the animation again.

Anytime an attribute of a computer model is changed, the change will propagate throughout the animation automatically (unless otherwise isolated). In traditional cell animation or 2D art, one change would mean an entire rework on every affected piece of art. In an animation that spans thousands of frames, this quickly becomes a costly change. The use of computers and layers has made a dramatic impact on 2D line art, but each individual frame in traditional cell animation would still need to be changed. Producing traditional cell animation is also moving to computers to solve this very problem.

Whether you are using 3D graphics in animation or still form, there is no question that the presentation will have a higher impact on the audience. Three dimensional graphics offer more realistic renderings than any other type of visualization available.

Animation

Motion is simulated very much like that of traditional animation, but with a slight twist. Instead of just moving across the page, 3D animation can take the object anywhere in space. Since the model does not exist anywhere physically, except in digital media, animating the object can get very complex. To aid in complex animation, tools have been created that help isolate or group objects. Bones, nulls, hierarchical object trees, inverse kinematics, and motion capture are all tools that can make complex animation somewhat easier. These tools may have a steep learning curve, but in the end they make the task either easier or possible.

Once the object has been modeled and textured correctly, the animation possibilities are endless. Since the model is mathematical, the object can be viewed, manipulated, or animated into any possible scenario. Viewing the object from another angle merely means adding a camera with a different viewpoint to the scene and rendering the scene through that camera. When recreating an event, or in product engineering, this is the major benefit of 3D animation compared to cell animation.

Also available to 3D graphic animation are special real-life attributes and effects, such as weight, gravity, collision detection, and object metamorphosis (known as morphing). Since traditional physics is based on mathematics, a formula could be applied to an object to make it appear to have realistic qualities. Although adding a realistic bounce to a 3D beach ball may sound simple, complex equations are applied to recreate nearly any physical attribute. It is these physical attributes that make simulators very accurate and realistic.

For manufacturing, the value of a 3D computer model or animation can far outweigh the cost. By testing a component using 3D computer models and real-world simulation, a product can be tested thoroughly to ensure a safe and efficient design before committing to its production and finding out later that there was a design flaw. Any design flaws will be revealed in the 3D simulation testing. More complex and accurate testing can be performed with a computer model than can be done in the field. This type of testing can prove most valuable in product safety and liability cases.

For a 3D animation company, once the model has been built and animated, it may be used over and over again for many animations. Because a library of objects can be created and inserted into any scene, animation companies can reuse existing models and animation paths. From a business standpoint, this means higher productivity when producing multiple animations that contain similar objects.

Whether for use in engineering, litigation, or the commercial arena, the world of 3D animation and simulation is an ever-increasing industry. As computers become more powerful, simulations will become more realistic and beneficial. We have only begun to harness the power of computer simulation, and exciting adventures and uses are the destiny of emerging technology.

FIGURE 1-7 Using different types of lenses, we can create illusions of different perspectives with the click of a mouse. Perspective is what gives the image depth and realism.

Perspective

In the virtual 3D world *perspective* refers to the camera lens used to render a scene. Changing the size of the lens will change the perspective of the scene, much like the lens of a real camera. Typically, most rendering software will use values for camera lenses that duplicate the effect of a real camera lens of the same size. Camera lenses range from panoramic fish-eye lenses, to large telephoto lenses used to zoom in on minute details.

We know that different lens sizes create different perspectives, but how does perspective make 3D animation three dimensional? Being able to view an object in proper perspective gives the object depth and a sense of mass. As the camera moves around the scene, the viewer is afforded a sense of depth and spatial relationships that is not easily created using traditional cell animation.

So what is perspective? In the 3D world perspective is illusion of depth and spatial relationships between objects in virtual space. In other words, objects that are very close will appear larger than objects of the same size that are farther away. Perspective also creates a vanishing point for objects on the horizon.

Perspective is a very powerful tool. Without perspective, 3D modeling would not have the impact it currently does. In fact, without perspective, 3D would just be 2D. Adding perspective to the scene affords the viewer information which would not be apparent in a two dimensional perspective.

To recreate perspective on a computer involves a phenomenal amount of mathematical calculations, due to the geometry of the objects, the lighting, and the physical and surface characteristics given to the objects. That is one of the reasons why realistic computer-generated images have only recently begun to become part of an artist's portfolio. Personal computers in the past few years have struggled with the number crunching required to create these math-intensive animations. It is not that the technology is new, but, more important, that it is possible with desktop computers, instead of rooms full of high-cost equipment. As computers become faster and more powerful, computer artists will become less constrained by equipment and software and limited only by their imaginations.

The calculations involved in creating a computer model can quickly add up to a massive mathematical nightmare. In addition to the object geometry, lighting, textures, reflectivity, object interaction, and other attributes need to be calculated. To give you an idea of how complex the operations are that create and animate computer models, here is an example. During the sixties, a computer equivalent to an IBM 286 processor with one megabyte of RAM was used to land a man on the moon. That same computer today would be unable to create the animation possible with today's desktop computers.

It is important to remember that 3D modeling is simulation. Because of the sheer quantity of mathematics involved in creating realistic 3D graphics, even the most powerful computers may bog down as the models and animation become more complex. Although number crunching is what a computer does best, don't be surprised if your new whiz-bang high-speed computer drags along while rendering an intense scene or complicated object morph.

17

From Home to Hollywood— Are You Ready?

With 3D graphics being the hot topic in the graphics world, many art students are looking to become the next great 3D artist. Although a different type of art form, artists of all types can find a niche in the 3D animation world. Computer animation requires the talent of many people, such as illustrators, storyboard artists, modelers, and animators.

3D modeling is a different mind-set from traditional art, because it requires a learning curve associated with producing realistic images. General knowledge of perspective and artistic ability will give the beginning 3D artist a step up on those with no computer or artistic experience.

TIP: For a first 3D modeling package, decide how much is affordable. Buy the software with the most features you can afford. Buying a product because it has amazing particle systems and deformation areas before you can even model may not be the best bargain. Start small and work up to the high-end package.

If you are a beginning 3D artist, do not let the learning curve get you down. How many other activities require you to be an engineer, sculptor, artist, animator, cinematographer and computer hacker all at the same time? All of the concepts can be learned and mastered by putting in the time. Even the world's greatest artists were beginners at one point in their lives. There is no doubt that computer graphics demand a lot of time to learn and understand, but that is what makes it so special. If anyone could click a mouse on the screen and create Hollywood-caliber graphics, the job would become a mundane chore for undergraduates working their way through school.

In a traditional Catch-22, while you are learning today's tools, more tools are being created all the time. While the tools are definitely making some of the tasks easier, this also allows more experienced and talented artists to really push the limit of object creation and animation. As with any other talent, one must constantly exercise his or her skills to keep up with the rapidly changing technology behind the most exciting art form in the world.

Choosing the Platform

During the past few years, a number of new computer manufacturers have touted their product as being "the fastest machine alive." For the most part, there are only a few different platforms available for desktop use. Within each of the most popular platforms, however, there are many different configurations of machines. Each can have myriad slots for expansion boards, graphics cards, RAM, and boards for many other devices, both internal and peripheral. By and large, the most commonly used platforms today are the Macintosh, Silicon Graphics workstations, PC Pentiums, and the Commodore Amiga. Although Commodore went out of business in the mid-1990s, the European market is strong enough that manufacturing may continue through another company.

Each of the platforms has its strengths, and building the perfect machine is both an investment in time and money. If you plan on using your machine for 3D production, get

19

the fastest processor, the biggest hard drive, and the most RAM that you can buy. Buying too little RAM in the beginning may cause you to lose the money invested in that RAM when trying to purchase additional RAM.

The world of computer graphics is a world full of memory hogs. High resolution images and astronomical polygons account for the never ending desire for more RAM and permanent storage such as hard drives. As 3D animation and modeling continue to become more complex, a computer's unquenchable thirst for more and more memory will have to be satisfied.

Permanent storage is the easiest problem to solve. Buying larger hard drives and storing completed animations on CD-ROM or digital tape are simple solutions to the problem. When rendering, precious time could be lost if you run out of space in the middle of rendering an animation. Likewise, it is self-defeating to delete previous animations to make way for new ones, without saving the old animation to film, videotape, or digital tape.

Solving the RAM problem is not quite so simple. Because of the characteristics of the computer system, deciding how much RAM to buy initially is very important. The motherboard may come with up to 16 megabytes on board, but will that be enough? If you plan on doing 3D work, the answer is no. Before you buy your system, be sure you have factored in the cost of the RAM. Additional RAM will be placed in your RAM slots. Your computer may have up to four or more slots in which additional RAM may be placed. If you fill the slots with 1-megabyte SIMMs (standard in-line memory modules), you will have to replace them when you decide to add more RAM. A good rule of thumb is to research how much RAM you will need for your modeling software and at least double it.

TIP: The golden rule of RAM is "you can never have too much." For a minimum, I suggest 40 megabytes of RAM when doing 3D animation. It is typical to work with a paint program while modeling to produce textures and maps for surfaces. If memory is low, you may not be able to create any test renders without exiting other programs. Quitting and having to restart applications can quickly become a drag.

Amiga

Although the Amiga is no longer being manufactured by Commodore, they still have a very strong presence in the 3D animation arena. When the technology was first invented, they were ahead of their time and had amazing power and grace for broadcast and Hollywood-style animations. Until recently, the Amiga, equipped with the Video Toaster, Personal Animation Recorder (PAR), and Lightwave 3D, had been unsurpassed in fulfilling the majority of professional 3D animator's needs at a reasonable cost. Its main drawback was its lackluster acceptance by the general computing public in the United States, although there was acceptance in the European market.

There are still many Amiga users providing quality 3D animation for many uses. Motherboards are being produced for these machines which are faster than the old version, but still do not compete with the Power Macintosh RISC chip or the Pentium 133-MHz chip. In some cases, the Amiga is still used for postproduction effects, while many Amiga modelers and animators have migrated to PC Pentiums running at 90 MHz and higher, because of the port of Lightwave 3D, which had a stronghold on Amiga animation.

Macintosh

Known for its user friendly interface, the Macintosh line of computers has been a major player in the 2D graphic design industry. With its intuitive graphic interface and plug-and-play peripheral support the Macintosh has gained wide acceptance with companies and individuals looking for a powerful and easy way to use computers for production. With the advent of the Power Macintosh RISC processor, the new-generation Macintosh will be even faster and better than ever.

In the past, the single drawback for the Macintosh had been its price. With a price tag higher than that of a typical PC, the Macintosh line cost more than the average person was willing to spend on new technology. All of this may change since Apple began licensing its operating system. The first Macintosh clones may help establish the Macintosh as a computer for all budgets.

With CPU speeds reaching over 130 MHz, the new Power Macintosh series is offering graphics speed never before seen in a desktop computer with such eloquent tools. Since the Macintosh's acceptance by a wide majority of graphic houses, there have been many very powerful and top-quality graphic tools written for the Macintosh.

The Macintosh, having a jump on most other systems in the graphic market, has many excellent programs for creating 3D animation such as Strata's Studio Pro, auto•des•sys' s form•Z, and ElectricImage's ElectricImage Animation System (EIAS). Electric Image was the first desktop computer software used to create animation effects for network television and, retailing at less than $7500, is by far, the best animation system for the Macintosh, if not all desktop computer systems.

PC

Of all personal computers in the world today, the PC is the most widely accepted and used. This does not necessarily mean they are better. The main reason for their success, is that the PC platform has been available to the public longer than any other computer in production. Generally, a typical PC can be purchased for less than the average Macintosh or Amiga system. As pricing trends continues, the difference in price between the Macintosh and PC is becoming nominal, compared to the difference in features.

Although the PC has in the past shown poor performance in the graphic industry, that too is changing. The PC boasts some excellent 3D software with Autodesk's 3D Studio 4.0, Newtek's Lightwave 3D 4.0, and Caligari's trueSpace 2.0. With image manipulation software such as Adobe Photoshop and Illustrator available on the PC, as well as graphics cards and accelerators, the PC is beginning to make a mark in the graphics and animation industry.

Silicon Graphics Workstations

Although too expensive for the casual user, the Silicon Graphics line of computer systems is worth mentioning. Silicon Graphics workstations such as the Indy or the Extreme 2 are very powerful graphics computer systems. These powerhouses are specifically designed for 3D computer graphics and have the processing power to prove it. The Silicon Graphics line includes machines that are capable of handling many processors and decadent amounts of RAM to produce some of the finest animation in the world. For the casual graphic enthusiast, the SGI workstation may prove financially on the steep side. Although prices on the machines vary, they will easily cost over $30,000. If you were to choose software such as Alias PowerAnimator or Wavefront, you could easily add another $35,000 to the price tag. If someone else is going to foot the bill for your computer, these are the computers to look into.

Modeling Basics

Surface and Solid Geometry Modeling

The data used to create the shape of an object are referred to as its object geometry. Object geometry can be created using a number of methods, such as points, splines, or polygons. The two types of geometry are solid and surface geometry. In most basic terms, solid geometry is that in which the geometry constitutes a 3D form, while surface geometry represents two dimensions. Figure 1-8 illustrates solid and surface geometry.

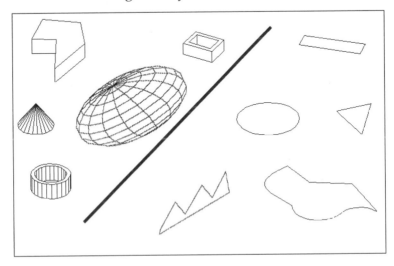

FIGURE 1-8 Solid geometry incorporates volume into each object. Having volume, the model can also have other physical characteristics attached to it. Surface geometry is typically two dimensional, yet 3D shapes can be constructed of 2D faces. Surface geometry does not have volume.

Model geometry is the collection of data points used to create an object. These points are also called *vertices*, which are used to create edges or segments, which in turn create polygons or splines. It is not unusual for an object to contain many thousands of points. The points alone, though, do not completely describe the object. The point is just a location in space. The data points also need data that describe which points are connected and the direction of the connection.

Points and the
World Coordinate System

Due to the fact that all computer models contain geometry data, and geometry is made from a series of points, all computer models use a World Coordinate System to plot the data points for each model. Since a point is merely a position in space, every data point used to build a computer model must be positioned using a coordinate system. Before creating, transforming, or manipulating objects, one must first understand the 3D universe. The three dimensional environment is based on a coordinate system which uses X, Y, and Z axes and is notated as such (x, y, z). A coordinate of (minus 1, 2, 3) means that an object is located at the position $x=$ minus 1, $y=2$, and $z=3$. Each of these axes is used to measure the distance from the center of the modeling universe to a point along that axis. The center of any modeling universe is (0,0,0).

FIGURE 1-9 In 3D space a coordinate system is used to position objects in space. As objects move in the direction of the arrows, coordinate values increase.

Axes

As the image in Figure 1-9 shows, the X axis is parallel to the horizon, while the Y axis is perpendicular to it. The Z axis represents the distance in depth. All axes can be referenced in the positive and negative direction. Positive values for the X axis start at the right of the universal and increase as you move to the right. The Y axis has positive values above the universal center with values increasing as you move up. The Z axis has positive values moving away from the front of the universe. When looking at the directional arrow from an isometric view, we notice that all values to the right of universal center are increasing in value, while values to the left are decreasing in value.

Regardless of whether an object moves from negative to positive or vice versa, there is still distance. When calculating how far an object is away, or how far it has to be moved, be sure to use the coordinates in absolute values. Moving along the X axis from -3 to 2 is just as far as moving along the X axis from 4 to 9.

Because the computer environment is comprised entirely of numbers, we are able to assign a location for any position within that space through the use of decimals. In actual practice, the number of positions available in any computer model is limited to the precision of the data that stores point positions. This means that the distance between two points can become very small or very large. Some modeling environments may go from over 100 miles down to 1/10,000 of an inch within the same scene. Of course, a range of this size may not be practical. In reality, the range may be much smaller depending on the size of the objects and the amount of memory (RAM) installed.

TIP: In some cases, you may find that the Y and Z axes have been reversed. Some software runs with Z "up" while others use the more common Y "up" mode. There is no significance to either one, but it may lend to confusion if the user is not aware. Some software even allows the user to change the configuration of Y "up" or Z "up."

Topology

Topology is a term used for the data that tell the software how to connect the points. A group of points is really like a connect-the-dots drawing, and only one configuration is the correct (or desired) way. When the topology data become corrupted, the object appears completely unrecognizable and may be referred to as a haystack (see Figure 1-10). The informal term haystack accurately describes inaccurate topology because the object looks like an unorganized group of line segments. A *haystack* contains all of the correct points of a model, but the connectivity or topology has been corrupted, thereby causing points to be connected to their incorrect counterpoint.

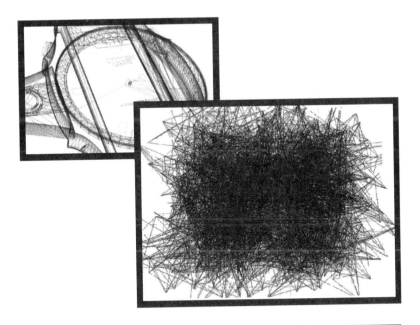

FIGURE 1-10 Without the correct topology, the object on the left could end up looking like the object on the right. Topology is a means of "connecting the dots" correctly.

Segment

A *segment* is the connecting "tissue" of the model. By itself, the segment is nothing. It has no three dimensional form, yet the connecting of segments is the basis of building polygons. Three or more segments can be used to create a polygon or face. Segments are also known as edges and may be referred to as such. The purpose of a segment is to delineate the edge of a polygon by connecting vertices. By connecting vertices with edges, polygons are built that are used to form shapes out of the geometry.

Face

A *face* is a collection of outlines used to describe planar geometry. Faces can be a single polygon or a collection of polygons. A face is sometimes used to refer to a facet of geometry. Although this term is used in many ways, typically it is within reference to a planar segment of geometry. **Faces are the visible geometry that creates the object (see Figure 1-11)**. When an object has a shader applied to it, it is the faces which receive the shader information and the faces which are rendered.

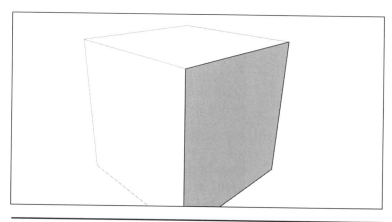

FIGURE 1-11 The face is a collection of polygons that make up an entire side. The polygons on a face are all planar and all are on the same plane.

Viewing the Models

Since current computers cannot handle the viewing of all models in a fully ray-traced mode, options are available to control the various levels of detail visible when viewing a model. These levels of detail do not change the way the model is rendered, but they are helpful when modeling complex objects or building complex scenes. The different levels of detail allow the artist to distinguish geometry between different objects which are in proximity. **Notice the difference between the wireframe, hidden line, and shaded views in Figure 1-12**. The shaded view offers more detail as to the placement of objects. From the wireframe view, it is impossible to detect whether the olive is in the martini or somewhere above or below it.

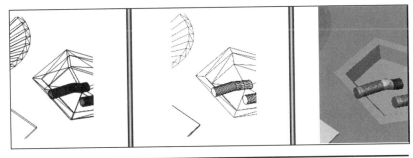

FIGURE 1-12 Different view types show the same object with different degrees of information.

At the very lowest level of detail, objects are viewed strictly as bounding boxes. The bounding box can be described as the smallest boundary that can be drawn completely around an object. By viewing objects as bounding boxes only, every object is comprised of only eight polygons. **Figure 1-13 shows objects viewed as bounding boxes**.

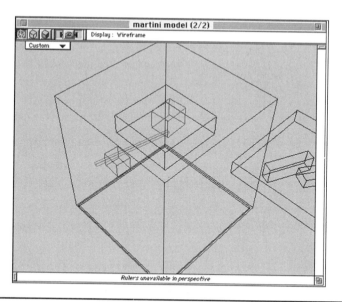

FIGURE 1-13 Viewing an object as a bounding box greatly increases the speed of the redraw. Animations can be rendered in preview mode using wireframes to view motion, yet they will render very quickly.

Choosing a View

Since any view used to visualize a model is a rendering, choose a view type that portrays the model accurately, while producing quick screen redraws. View types with slower screen redraws will become annoying once you notice that every time you make a change it takes 15 seconds or more to redraw the screen. During the model building process, it is often ideal to change the view type as well as the view angle many times to see that the object is indeed what and where you intend it to be.

TIP: Every view type is a rendering of the data associated with a model. Since the scene must be rendered, the more detail viewed in a particular view, the longer it will take to produce the image. Choose a view with enough detail to build a model accurately, without having to wait each time you make a change to the model.

Wireframe View

The wireframe view is the most basic view and it shows actual geometry. The wireframe view does not show object textures, shadows, or any lighting effects. Some wireframe modes will display object geometry in a color representative of the texture color, using the most common color in the object's texture. Wireframe mode does show the object close to actual geometry, although some modelers will decrease the detail to enable quicker screen redraws.

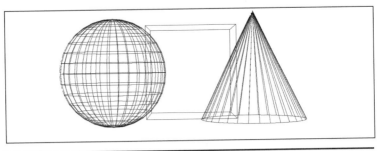

FIGURE 1-14 Wireframe images show all of an object's geometry, but do not show textures, environmental lighting, or object interaction.

One drawback of the wireframe mode, especially with organic shapes, is the inability to distinguish object orientation correctly. **The object in Figure 1-15 is a standard cube**. In wireframe mode, it is difficult to distinguish the orientation of the cube. The object could be above or below the camera.

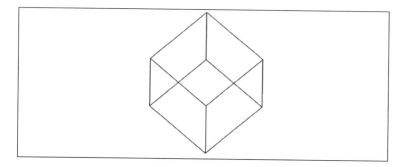

FIGURE 1-15 This wireframe image can be confused as either one of the objects in Figure 1-16.

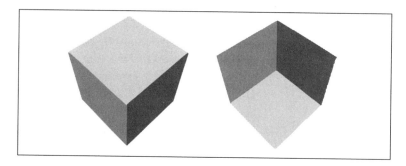

FIGURE 1-16 Depending on how the image in Figure 1-15 is shaded, it could be either one of the objects in this image.

Although this case is oversimplified with the object shown above, in very complex models it may be necessary to change the view type instead of the view angle to assess an object accurately.

Advantages of the wireframe mode include:

- Quicker screen redraw.

- All geometry lines are visible.

- Objects behind or inside other objects are visible.

Disadvantages of the wire-frame mode include:

- Geometry lines can become confusing in complex scenes.

- Difficult to distinguish which surfaces are in front or behind.

- Texture and lighting data are not displayed.

Hidden Line Removed View

A hidden line removed view shows all of an object's geometry that would be visible if all surfaces were solid and opaque. It does not take into account any transparency or other texture attributes that have been assigned to the object. The hidden line removed view is very similar to the wireframe, except that any line that is behind a polygon is not drawn.

Using the hidden line removed view when modeling may at times be more ideal, but again this view will require more time to redraw the screen since it contains more detail (removing hidden lines constitutes more accurate detail since the hidden lines must be calculated, then removed). **Figure 1-17 shows objects viewed in a hidden line removed mode.**

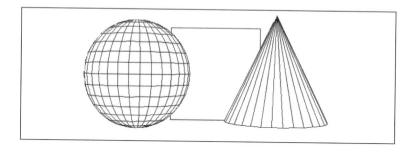

FIGURE 1-17 Hidden line removed images show only the geometry lines that are not behind other polygons. Like the wireframe view, textures and environmental lighting are not visible. Objects which are blocked by another object are not visible.

Advantages to the hidden line removed mode include:

- Hidden polygons and hidden lines are not drawn.

- Less confusing due to less geometry being visible.

- All objects are viewed as solid.

- Objects behind other objects are not visible.

Disadvantages to the hidden line removed mode include:

- Slower screen redraws than in wireframe mode.

- Object attributes are not rendered, so objects behind transparent objects are not visible.

Shaded View

Currently there are two types of shaded views used while in a modeling mode, flat shading and smooth shading. The two shaded modes are similar in many ways, but their differences are worlds apart.

In most modeling software, a flat shaded mode is the best mode you could find while in a modeling window. A flat shaded mode provides the artist with a view of solid models, not wireframe. The surface textures are not visible, but models are also given a single color derived from the surface shader applied to the object. The object is not smooth, and has a faceted appearance, but will display the effects of lights on an object's surface. Shadows from other objects are not provided in this view. Modeling in a flat shaded mode will cause the screen to redraw slower than in wireframe mode, but the detail provided may be worth the wait, even if it may take more than twice as long to redraw the screen. **Figure 1-18 shows an example of objects in a flat shaded mode**.

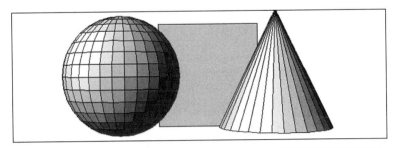

FIGURE 1-18 A shaded view shows objects closer to what they would look like in a rendered environment, without the textures or shadows. Lighting is associated with this type of view and the polygons are shaded accordingly.

Advantages to the shaded mode include:

- Hidden polygons and hidden lines are not drawn.

- Objects are shaded according to light sources in scene.

- All objects are viewed as solid.

Disadvantages to the shaded mode include:

- Slower screen redraws than wireframe and hidden line removed modes.

- Object texture is not rendered, so objects behind transparent objects are not visible.

Shaded Graphics Modeling

The latest advance in modeling is shaded graphics modeling (SGM). Using the Macintosh QuickDraw GX and QuickDraw 3D routines or the Pentium's OpenGL, modeling software is now able to model in a smooth shaded view. Objects can be created, edited, and manipulated while displayed in a real-time, smooth shaded rendering. Objects appear smooth, not faceted, while their surfaces display accurately the shader applied to them.

Whether in wireframe or SGM, objects remain true as they are manipulated or edited. This facilitates more accurate modeling and scene building. While building scenes, adding lights also update the rendered view instantly. With SGM, you can place a light in a scene and watch in real time how the light affects objects as you move the light around in the scene.

TIP: Use SGM as well as wireframe when creating objects and building scenes. Building or manipulating organic objects will benefit most from SGM, due to their nonlinear shapes. SGM is also best served when adding lights to a scene. Due to real-time lighting, immediate effects on objects can be spotted using SGM.

While SGM is the newest breakthrough in modeling environments, only a few software packages employ this technique. Currently on the Macintosh side, Strata's StudioPro Blitz (1.75) is the only Macintosh modeler that provides this type of modeling view. On the PC side, Caligari's trueSpace 2.0 and Autodesk's 3D Studio 4.0 are the only modelers that offer any form of SGM that I know of.

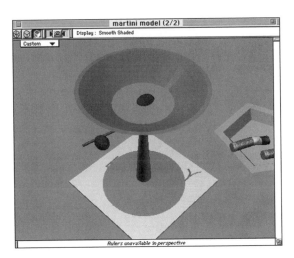

FIGURE 1-19 Shaded graphics modeling allows for immediate feedback when editing or modeling an object. Until recently, SGM was not available on desktop systems.

TECHNIQUE:

Advantages of using SGM:

- SGM has all the features of a non-SGM mode in addition to some additional benefits.

- Objects are viewed as they would be rendered.

- Prevents self-intersecting geometry by displaying accurate surfaces.

- Real-time surface rendering requires less trial and error. SGM is more visual than mathematical.

- Real-time lighting enables more accurate placement and intensity for light sources.

Disadvantages of SGM include:

- Although SGM provides real-time surface rendering, complex models may slow it down. When the scene gets to that point, wireframe or flat shaded displays will redraw the screen faster.

- SGM requires more memory (RAM) than non-SGM systems.

- SGM is not available on older systems that do not contain code libraries for QuickDraw GX, QuickDraw 3D, or OpenGL.

Manipulating Views

Every model or layout program affords the user various views (as explained earlier). Although there are a set of standard views, these views may also be changed, by zooming in or out (dolly in or out), rotating, or resizing the view. By changing the view, the user may see different parts of a model or may look at the part from a different angle.

Dollying/Zooming

To more accurately create objects, modeling software allows the user to zoom in or out of a scene. Zooming, also referred to as "dollying," moves the viewport either closer or farther from objects. When the viewport camera "zooms in" or "dollies in", the object will appear larger. When the viewport camera "zooms out" or "dollies out," objects appear smaller (see Figure 1-20).

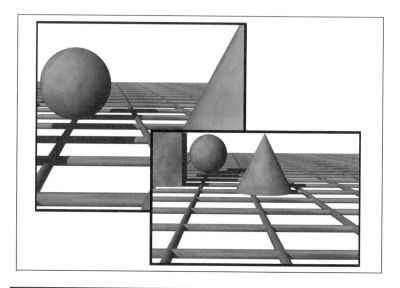

FIGURE 1-20 Use a dolly or zoom command to move the camera closer or farther away from the subject.

When a view is zoomed or dollied, the objects themselves are not moved, only the camera from which the objects are viewed. Zooming in and out is essential for working with smaller objects within a scene.

Typically, a zoom feature icon in a modeling or layout program appears as either some sort of magnifying glass, near and distant mountains, or some other similar icon or text.

TIP: Use the Dolly-in or Zoom-in command to line up perfect corners. Some objects, due to their organic nature, will not align properly when using an alignment command. This is due to the bounding box used to represent the object. When this is the case, use the Zoom-in or Dolly-in command to isolate the smallest possible region to include portions of both surfaces. Align the surfaces. Repeat this method until the objects are perfectly aligned or until zooming in no longer helps in alignment.

Rotating the View

As well as dollying, rotating the view is absolutely necessary for many reasons. From a modeling perspective, rotating the view is helpful when the position of an object needs to be checked, and one of the standard views (top, front, side, perspective) is not helpful.

By using a rotating view tool, one can change the angle of the modeling camera so that an object may be viewed from any angle. This is done without moving any objects within the scene. By rotating the view and not the object, scene integrity is preserved. It is far better to change the view, than to try to realign the object.

Some programs (such as Lightwave 3D) do not have viewports that can be rotated. There is however an alternative to viewing an object on any side without moving or rotating the object. Lightwave 3D has a perspective window in the modeler which, if turned on (under the Display Options menu) will show a preview of the object. By clicking and dragging on the object in the perspective preview window, the object is rotated until the mouse button is released. With this method the object may be viewed from any angel.

If the software you are running does not have either the rotate view function or the preview window with object rotation, there is still hope. One way to fix the problem is to add another camera to the scene and view the object through the new camera, placed in the correct location and rotated so that it points directly toward the object you are trying to view.

One of the benefits of dollying, zooming, or rotating a view is that viewports may see objects from any angle. Even after the view has been changed, it can always be brought back to

43

one of the standard views. The standard views are normally the top, front, side, and a perspective view. The side view may be either from the left or the right, but normally from the right. Some programs also include standard views equivalent to all sides of a cube (front, back, top, bottom, left, and right). You can tell the orientation of the view from the number line or coordinate indicators located in the modeling or layout windows. Figure 1-21 shows what a typical number line may look like. This one is from Strata StudioPro Blitz 1.75

TRICK: If you are unsure as to whether your modeling or layout program's side view is from the left or right side, here is a simple trick which tells you. Decide which side is increasingly negative in value. When viewing from the right side, as you move toward the left, numbers will become increasingly negative (or smaller), while numbers on the right will be increasingly positive (or larger). When viewing from the left side, the reverse is true.

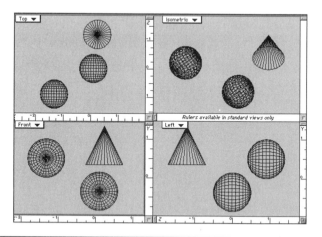

FIGURE 1-21 Using the number line can help orient objects, cameras, and lights. It is also useful when rotating around an axis. The axis not shown is the one which runs from front to back like a skewer through the object.

Manipulation Tools for Surfaces and Objects

A three dimensional computer model can be made through geometry creation or through geometry deformation. Points, polygons, surfaces, and objects can be manipulated by various means to produce different shapes. The simplest type of object, polygon, or point manipulation is to move, rotate, or scale it (with the exception of the point, which cannot be scaled). More complex object manipulation features may include rounding, sweep, bevel, or triangulation of objects. The art of computer graphic modeling is really an art of point manipulation.

Whether the points make up a polygon, spline, or mesh, the objective is the same: arrange the points so that the desired object is formed. Although this may sound simple enough, it is no trivial task. Many tools have been developed to make the job of manipulating points easier, and this chapter explains the most basic of these tools.

Each 3D artist has his or her own preferences when building models. Some like to have a four-view window, while others prefer a single view at a time. Some like working in wireframe, while others use hidden line or the newly implemented shaded graphics modeling (SGM) mode. Whatever your preference, the one important aspect of modeling in three dimensional space is to always build an object from at least two views. Using at least two views will better help the artist analyze where the object is in space, relative to the other objects in the scene.

TIP: When manipulating or modeling an object use an orthographic view (or one with no perspective). When rendering use a camera view or a view with perspective.

Origin—Center of the Universe

Although trivial in the real world, moving around in 3D space can be as confusing as floating in outer space, with only slightly more control. Since there is no gravity in the modeling window, any angle could be up, down, or sideways. The modeling universe, however, does have a beginning and an end. These limitations are set forth by a combination of the software and computer memory. If the memory is available, some scene layout programs can handle a universe of over 100 miles!

To reference distance properly, all virtual worlds have a center of the universe called the *origin*. The origin has a coordinate value of (0,0,0). Although the origin is created by the scene layout software, it is an important point to recognize. The origin is the point from which all other points in space are referenced.

TIP: A point to remember is that the origin does not change, while the center point of an object can reside anywhere in 3D space. Knowing where to place the center point of an object can be very beneficial during animation. See the chapter on animation for more on offsetting center points.

Where Am I?

Before we can move objects around, we must understand the virtual environment in which we are working. When moving around in 3D space, one can quickly become disoriented and confused as to which way is up. Depth perception can also become limited during the modeling phase when viewing objects in a wireframe mode. To determine which end is up, many modeling packages provide a grid as an artificial horizon.

The artificial grid, pictured in **Figure 2-1**, provides a reference when modeling or manipulating objects in 3D space. The grid is provided as reference only and will not render in the final output. Grid spacing may also be changed to accommodate very small or very large objects. While some artists prefer the grid, others do not. Typically, software that provides a grid will often provide a means for turning off the grid option.

Grid spacing is a term used to describe the distance between each line in the grid. A spacing of one meter means that the distance from any line on the grid to the next is one meter. Grid measurements may be changed from metric to English and the range is typically from inches to feet or from micrometers to meters. Decimal equivalents of smaller units may also be used.

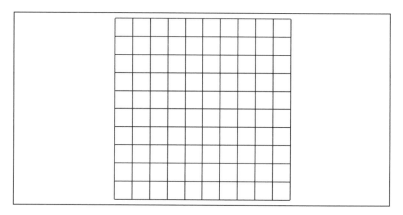

FIGURE 2-1 The use of an artificial grid can make modeling and scene layout easier when positioning objects. Many software packages incorporate a grid as a horizontal plane (X and Z axes), while other use optional grids for all major planes (front, XY; side, ZY; and top, XZ).

TRICK: If your modeling software does not provide a grid for reference, you can make a grid object to place in your models. Use this grid to align objects or to measure distance of movement along an axis. Be sure to remove or hide the grid object before rendering, so that it will not render as part of the scene. A grid object has been provided on the CD-ROM to import into any modeler or layout program.

TECHNIQUE: Building Your Own Grid

1. Create a 2D line 10 units long along the *Y* axis (vertical). Unit size does not matter since the entire grid object may be sized to fit the need.

2. Duplicate the line 10 more times with a spacing of one unit along the *X* axis. The unit must be the same unit used in measuring the object (i.e., if the line is 10 inches long, each duplicated line must be spaced 1 inch from the previous line). **The resulting object should look like the object in Figure 2-2.**

3. Group all 11 lines to form a single object.

4. Duplicate the 11 line objects and rotate 90°. **The object should now look like the object in Figure 2-3.**

5. Align both objects by their top and left sides.

6. Group both grids to form a single object and save as an object.

TIP: When producing the grid, use an open polygon tool or two points joined to create an object that will not render. You may even use more lines or multiple grids on more than one axis to get a complete grid system.

FIGURE 2-2 After creating a set of vertical lines through duplication, you should end up with the object shown above.

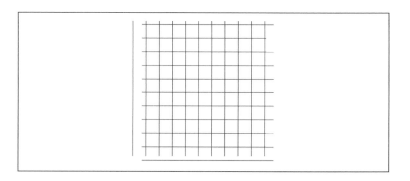

FIGURE 2-3 After the horizontal lines have been created, you should end up with this object. Simply align the left and top edges to produce a grid similar to that shown in Figure 2-1.

Multiple Views

Another aid that cuts down on the confusion factor is multiple views. By allowing the artist to view the model from more than one angle at a time, the artist gets immediate feedback on work which affects more than one axis. Typical standard views are the front, top, bottom, left, right, front, rear, or isometric (perspective) views. **Figure 2-4 illustrates a typical multiple-view window.** Some software such as Strata's StudioPro provides for the user to manipulate the current view with a view rotation tool.

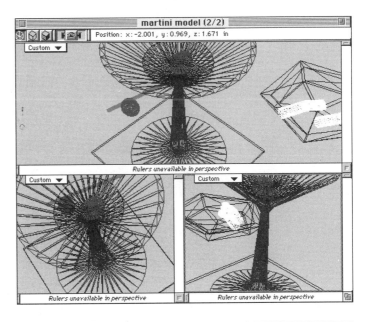

FIGURE 2-4 The use of multiple views allows the artist to view the model from many angles simultaneously, thereby aiding in the correct construction or positioning of an object.

 TIP: When modeling objects, you must use at least two views to place an object correctly. Because of the inaccurate depth perception (or absence thereof in orthographic views) in a typical modeling environment, objects that appear to be lined up in one view will be misaligned when viewed from another angle.

Axis Labeled Views

Some software uses the visible axes as the name of the view. Typical names would be *XY*, *XZ*, and *YZ*. An *XY* view consists of visable *X* and *Y* axes and a hidden *Z* axis . This naming was derived because any changes along the hidden axis are not recognized in an orthographic view (so objects will not appear to get smaller as the move away or larger as they move closer). The hidden axis is always the axis in which objects would move toward or away from the camera. **Figure 2-5 shows two windows with different axes visible.**

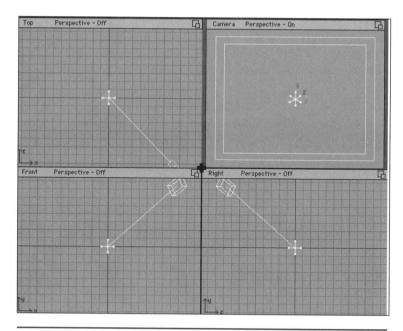

FIGURE 2-5 Using views with different axes available aids in keeping the movement constrained along the visible axes.

Moving Objects

Movement of an object is a basic task that is used often. Objects can be moved either by dragging the object or by numeric input entered through a dialog box. Both have their advantages, and a combination of both is most useful when fine tuning an object's location.

Using the drag method is useful for eyeballing an object's placement. Zooming in will allow more accurate precision when using the object drag method of movement. The advantage is that you can see exactly where an object is going by placing it at the correct location. The disadvantage is that you must zoom in and out in order to be assured that the object is in the correct location.

TIP: Remember to check an object's location in at least two views to be sure that the placement is correct on all three coordinate planes.

Numeric input is a very exacting method of object placement. When building complex models or architectural models, it may be essential to place objects at specific numeric locations. Numeric input simplifies this type of model, because the coordinates can be figured out before the model is built, or taken directly from blueprints.

Your preference, and the looseness of your scene are the true elements that will help you decide whether to use numeric input or object dragging. Both will accomplish the task and, like all tools, each is better suited for a particular situation. Like any craftsman, it may be necessary to use more than one tool to get the task at hand completed and I find that a combination of both methods works best in most situations.

Although objects can be moved while in any view and even while looking through the camera, there are some considerations to be aware of. When positioning an object, it is generally a good idea to position the object through the camera from which you intend to render. For alignment, it is imperative that an orthographic view be used to ensure proper alignment. It is for this reason that at least two views should be used each time an object is moved. Objects moved in a view with perspective may not be exactly where they appear to be. Always position an object in a perspective view, but check and make minor adjustments in an orthographic view.

 TIP: Whenever an object's location must be aligned, use either an orthographic view or a numeric input dialog to achieve exact positioning. Modeling should always be done in an orthographic view, while scene layout is best accomplished with a combination of both.

Moving with Handles

There are a variety of ways in which objects may be moved around the 3D environment. In some modeling programs, selected objects gain handles, which are used to move, rotate, or scale the object. There are typically eight handles. The handles are used for moving an object along the three dimensions. **Figure 2-6 shows an object with its bounding box and the direction on which each handle will take it.**

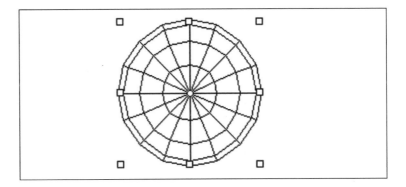

FIGURE 2-6 Bounding box and object handles. Clicking and dragging different handles affects the movement of the object.

The handles of a selected object are used to move an object smoothly along an axis. This is useful for moving objects along one axis only. The handles along the center of the bounding box move the object horizontally or vertically. In some software, the axis which the handles control may change according to the view. For instance, while in a front view, the right center handle will move the object along the X axis in the positive direction only. In an isometric view, moving that same handle will move the object in the positive X direction for that view, which if viewed from the front is a combination of equal amounts of both the X and Y axes. Depending on your need, this feature could be very useful or annoying. **Figure 2-7 depicts the object moving along the X axis in an isometric view.**

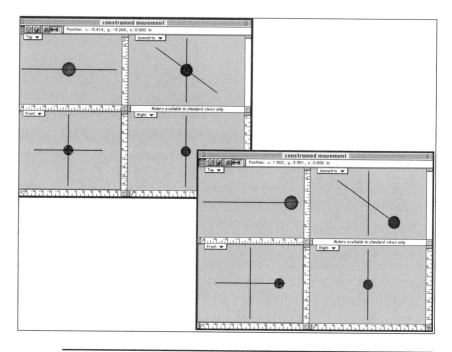

FIGURE 2-7 Notice how movement along the X axis is constrained. The object does not change position along any other axis.

Movement without Handles

While some software will use handles to move an object, other programs move a selected object through direct mouse movement and constraint buttons. Using the mouse control method, objects are first selected, then constraint buttons are toggled to restrict movement, rotation, or scale on any or all of the three axes.

The toggle buttons used for constraining an object represent active manipulation. Buttons that are activated by clicking on them (so that they appear pressed) signify that this axis is active for manipulation. Buttons that do not appear pressed are inactive and thereby constrained from changing any attributes along this axis.

 TECHNIQUE: Constraining an Object

1. Select the object to move, rotate, or scale.

2. Select the axes to be affected by modification. Buttons that are not selected will not be affected. To deselect a button that has been selected, press the button again.

3. Perform the modification.

Once the constraint buttons have been set, an object can only be affected along those axes. **The image in Figure 2-8 shows different constraint configurations**.

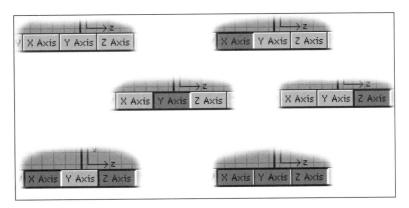

FIGURE 2-8 Using constraint buttons will allow movement only along the axes that are not constrained.

Parametric Transformation

Many, if not all programs also contain parametric transformation capabilities. This means that once an object is selected, any transformation may be edited to an exact value using the numeric input dialog for that particular transformation. A transformation includes movement, rotation, and scale. **Figure 2-9 shows StudioPro's transformation dialog box for movement, rotation, and scale of an object. Figure 2-10 shows a numeric input dialog from Lightwave 3D.**

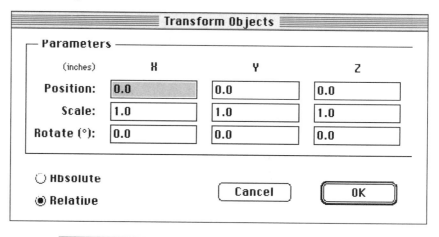

FIGURE 2-9 Movement dialog box. Most applications allow numeric control over how the object is transformed. This dialog box is taken from Strata StudioPro.

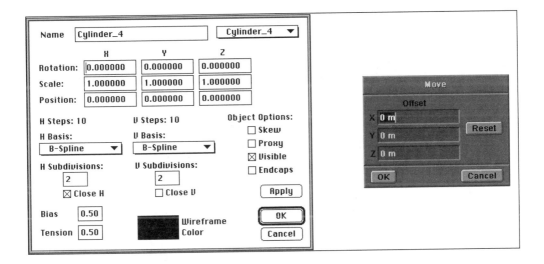

FIGURE 2-10 While some applications allow you to control all transformations through a single dialog box, some programs such as Lightwave 3D use numeric input boxes which change for each command. This image is from the Move command numeric input dialog for Lightwave 3D for the PC (right) and Pixel Putty Solo (left).

Rotating an Object— Heading, Pitch, Bank

In addition to moving objects to different locations, objects may also be rotate about any or all of the three axes. The act of rotating an object is similar to the action used to move it. The behavior of object rotation is something very different than that of object movement.

Rotation of an object may be performed along any of the three axes. While the actual rotation may go under different names, common terms are heading (Y axis), pitch (X axis), and bank (Z axis). As an object is rotated on any of the three axes, it can be thought of as being attached to that axis like a tire to an axle. The object will rotate around that axis from the object's pivot point. To describe the conditions of rotation, picture the object being rotated as a sailboat on the ocean. Using the motion of the boat as an example, rotation can be described as the following:

- *Heading:* This would be the direction in which the boat is traveling. To change the boat's heading, the boat would be rotated along its Y axis. Since the Y axis runs vertically, the Y axis could be compared to the boat's mast. The keel acts as a stabilizer by providing the boat with a pivot point to rotate around.

- *Pitch:* As the boat moves through the ocean, it is sure to encounter waves. As the boat moves up and down the swells in the ocean, the pitch of the boat is constantly changing. The pitch rotates around the X axis, or the horizon. The ocean of course is a horizontal plane, and as the boat moves across the ocean's surface, it rotates along the plane by varying amounts at different times.

- *Bank:* As the sailboat moves through the ocean and encounters bigger waves, the boat is bound to rock from side to side. This rocking is the same action as banking and it occurs along the Z axis.

Rotation along each axis individually is not very complicated. It is when rotation occurs along more than one axis that things begin to get tricky. When rotating an object along more than one axis, the order of rotation affects the final orientation of an object. Banking an object 90° then pitching it 90° would not yield the same object position if you changed the pitch first and then the banking by the same amounts.

Once an object's orientation has been changed, it may be very difficult or impossible to rotate it properly without the aid of a parent-child object relationship. Take, for example, wheels attached to a suspension bar. Typically, the wheels will not be sitting perfectly vertical with the ground. **Figure 2-11 shows the way the tires would sit if attached to a suspension bar.**

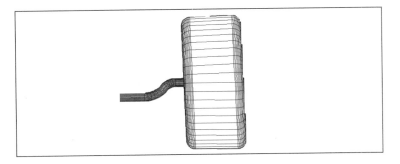

FIGURE 2-11 The order of rotation plays an important role when animating objects. If the tire had been banked on its side before the rotation, we would not achieve the effect of the tire rolling on the road surface.

Once the tire has been banked to this position, it is impossible to spin the tire smoothly, since its tire is no longer aligned along the vertical plane. To achieve a smooth rotating tire, we need to employ the parental relationship of a null or dummy object that has its axis in order to keep the tire spinning properly. Here is how it works:

- Be sure the tire and the parent object are both centered on their own pivot points. If an object is not centered on its own pivot point, rotation will be very different than if it had been centered.

- The tire must be parented to a dummy or null object before any rotation is given to either object.

- Give the tire the proper rotation to make it appear as if it were rolling on the pavement. If the tire were vertical, rotation would be around the X axis, or its pitch would be affected. Set the pitch for 360° to make the tire rotate once.

- After the tire has been given its rotation, bank the tire slightly as it would had there been a lot of weight on it.

- Now change the heading of the tire's parent object to 360°; the tire object follows the parent object. **Figure 2-12 shows how the object should look after the rotation.**

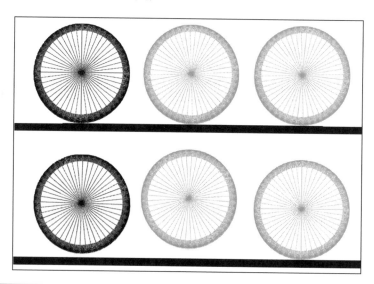

FIGURE 2-12 The tire in this image was given the correct rotation on the right and an incorrect order of rotation on the left. Notice how the tire that was rotated in the wrong order leaves the road surface after some rotation.

Had you changed the bank of the tire before the pitch, the tire would wobble as it rotated around the axle. The use of parent-child relationships is very useful for rotating objects along many axes.

TIP: To obtain a rotational value along the standard axes, use a null or dummy object as a parent for each of the three axes. You must realize that since an object can have only one parent, you must have each successive null or dummy object parented to the next on the list. This may take practice to achieve correctly.

Scaling Objects

As well as rotating and moving, objects can also be scaled. An object can be scaled to any size without losing any accuracy in data. A typical example would be something like trees or binder clips. To create a set of binder clips of different sizes, simply build one and scale it. **All of the binder clips in Figure 2-13 are the same computer model duplicated and scaled to different sizes.**

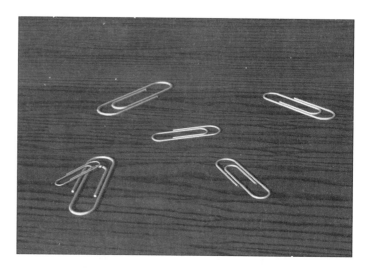

FIGURE 2-13 Scaling objects saves time when creating a group of simi-lar objects. By creating one clip, I could scale and duplicate a number of them to create a variety of clips with just a click of the mouse.

Sometimes, because objects can be scaled, computer modelers get into bad habits. A modeler may build an object without regard to size. Although this takes no more data than if the object were small, the problem comes when the model gets used in a scene. If a model of a pencil is created in the correct proportions, but is two feet long, it isn't a big problem to correct the size to a pencil of about five to seven inches. The problem begins to escalate when multiple objects need to be loaded and resized or when the relational size of the object is not known. Suppose the pieces of an engine are modeled by different modelers and animated by someone else. If all of the pieces have to be resized, the job of creating and animating the engine becomes much more complicated than it already is.

TIP: It is best to scale an object or its components during the construction phase. Building an object to proper scale during object construction will save more time than scaling it during scene layout. Scaling when inside a scene should be limited to fine adjustment of the entire object only. When scaling components of an object when it is placed in a scene, the entire object can become misaligned. It will also save many headaches and a lot of time if the proportions are correct from the beginning.

TIP: When scaling an object, scaling an object minus 100% on all axes will produce a mirror image of the original object. After creating a mirror image of an object in this fashion, you may need to flip the normals on the object, or use smoothing to flip the polygon faces.

Nonuniform Scaling

While objects can be scaled, objects need not be scaled uniformly on all axes. By scaling an object differently on all axes, variations of the original shape can be constructed. The simplest example is when using cubes. By scaling a cube nonuniformly, we can create walls, stairways, or bricks. This concept works equally well on complex objects. By scaling on only certain axes, objects can be changed to accommodate minor differences in the models. Figure 2-14 shows a sphere that has been nonuniformly scaled along the X axis.

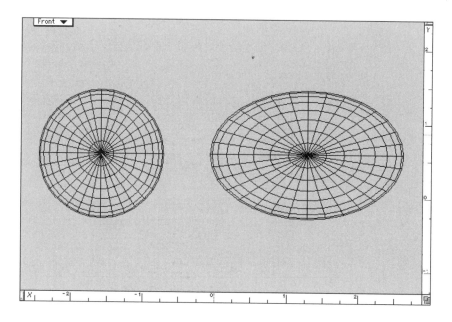

FIGURE 2-14 The use of a nonuniform scale allows you to stretch and shrink objects on certain axes only.

Object Center Points and Pivot Points

To build a scene made of many objects, one must be able to move objects through 3D space. Typically, manipulation tools are used to manipulate objects. Manipulation occurs in the form of rotation, location, or scale. Before any of these operations can take place, there must be a point of reference to the object. The reference point of every object is typically called the object's *center point* or *pivot point*.

Some software uses the center point method, while others use the pivot point method.

While the role of the center point and the pivot point are the same in most cases, where they are placed is not entirely the same. A center point is generally created at the same time the object is created and is located in the center of the object. The center of an object is derived from an imaginary bounding box, which encompasses all of the object's geometry. The center point is located in the absolute center of this box. **Figure 2-15 shows an object located at (0,0,0). The object's pivot point is located at the center of the object.**

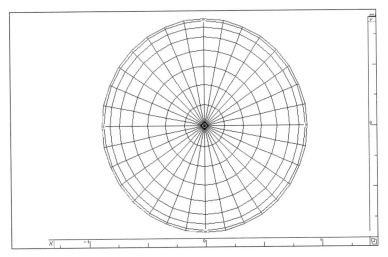

FIGURE 2-15 By locating the pivot point at the center of the object, the object's numeric location is the same as its physical location.

Instead of using the center point method, some modeling packages use the pivot point method. In the pivot point method, every time an object is created, a pivot point is also created for that object. The pivot point, however, is always located at the universal center of the modeling space, (0,0,0). Regardless of where the object is created in space, the pivot point is always generated at (0,0,0). The object will, however, still appear at the location at which it was created, but that is merely an offset from universal zero. **Figure 2-16 shows the same object created with the pivot point method.** The reference point for both is located at (0,0,0), but the actual location of the sphere is different.

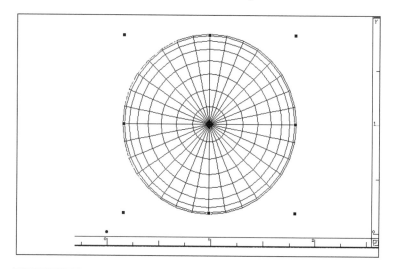

FIGURE 2-16   When the pivot point is not centered on the object, the physical location of the object is determined by its offset from the pivot point.

When objects are never manipulated, there is no difference between the pivot point and the center point, although it is rare for an object not to be manipulated in some way. While moving an object with a pivot point is typically a standard operation, the real problem comes when objects are rotated.

When an object's pivot point is not centered, rotating an object can become an interesting adventure, especially if the user is unaware that the pivot point is indeed off center. Because the pivot point is the point of reference for an object, when the object and its pivot point are offset, movement and rotation can become a problem. **As illustrated in Figure 2-16, the pivot point is located at (0,0,0), whereas the object is physically located at (1, 1, 0).**

Since the physical location and reference point are not the same, moving an object to a specific location by its reference point can produce unexpected results for the unwary user. **If we wanted to set the physical location of the object in Figure 2-16 to (3, 3, 0), using numeric input of (3, 3, 0) would not work.** The object would really be located at (4, 4, 0) because of the 1-unit offset in both the X and Y axes. **Figure 2-17 shows the object physically located at (4, 4, 0) while its pivot point is located at (3, 3, 0).**

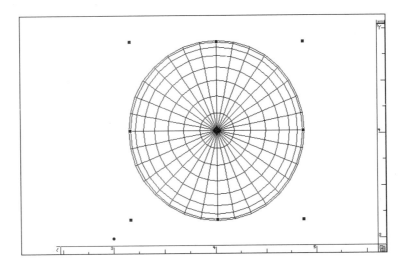

FIGURE 2-17 Because of the offset used in the pivot point when created, the object is physically located at (4,4,0), whereas its pivot point is located at (3,3,0).

When rotating an object, this problem is compounded. During rotation, any degree of rotation is from the pivot point. If the pivot point is not at the center of the object, the object will revolve around the pivot point like the moon around the earth. This is fine if this is the effect you intended, like the hands on a clock, but what about a spinning tire? To make a tire spin correctly, the pivot point must be centered to avoid a wobbly or uneven rotation. **Figure 2-18 shows how the location of the pivot point affects rotation.**

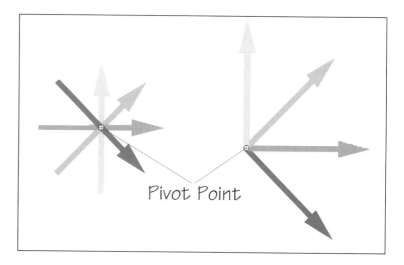

FIGURE 2-18 Setting an offset on the pivot point can create a desired effect as in the hands of the watch, whereas using a centered pivot point creates a different type of rotation.

Now that the problem of off-center pivot points has been identified, how is it corrected? Each modeling or scene layout program handles this problem differently. Depending on the software you are using, this problem may need to be corrected at the model level or the scene layout level. Since center points may also be moved for offset movement or rotation, this function applies to them as well.

The safest way to ensure that your pivot point is located at the center of your object is to center it in the first place. One way is to build your object around (0,0,0). This is not always feasible, since many times objects are built around other objects for reference of size or shape.

Another way to center an object's pivot point is to build the object wherever you want, and then use a center function. Some programs employ a macro, while others have a key command or menu item that will center an object's pivot point. In programs such as Lightwave 3D, it is best to move objects to a physical location of (0,0,0) after it is built and before saving. When the object is brought into the layout program, the pivot point is also created at (0,0,0). If the object were built at (1, 1, 1), the pivot point would still be placed at (0,0,0) when the object was loaded.

TIP: If the software package you are using uses the pivot point method, it may be a good idea to move the pivot point to the center of the object so that moving and rotation is based on the center of the object. The pivot point may be moved to another location, if an offset rotation is desired. Objects may also be built at absolute zero in the modeling space so that the pivot point will automatically be placed at the center of the object.

Layers

As a means of creating complex geometry with multiple parts, layers allow the modeler to build related parts individually, then join them when ready. The concept of layers is used in many forms of 2D and 3D graphics production. Programs such as Adobe Photoshop, Lightwave 3D, and form•Z use layers. The layer concept is very simple. Each layer is like a transparent working space located directly on top of (or below) other *layers* of the same project. Objects created in one layer are unaffected by objects created in other layers (unless specifically initiated). They are called *layers* because the working space is actually another layer located in same working environment. **Figure 2-19 shows how the objects in background layers are viewed as template color, such as grey, while objects in foreground layers are drawn in black or other default color.**

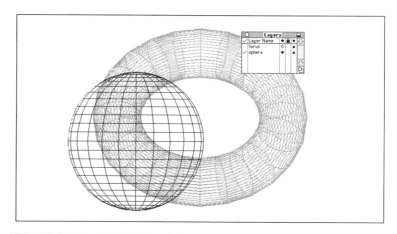

FIGURE 2-19 The use of layers allows the artist to work on one object while viewing a related object in a layer below. Background layers are not affected by changes made to the foreground layers.

Working in layers gives the artist the advantage of seeing multiple pieces of art superimposed on each other, while affecting only selected layers. When building a model, this is beneficial when building interrelated parts of an object.

Lightwave 3D and form•Z provide multiple layers, which are available in any modeling session. Any layer can be either the active layer, background layer, or turned off. Multiple layers may be active or in the background at any time. Background layers and inactive layers will not affect the geometry in the active layers during normal modeling operations.

One use for layers is to create parts of an object in separate layers and join them in the scene layout program. By separating the object in layers, they can be animated or changed more easily than if they were all part of a single object. Using the layers also ensures that objects will be in the proper position when loaded into a scene layout program. Using layers will greatly facilitate object organization and will prove beneficial during the building and animating of a scene.

Locked and Ghosted Objects

Similar to layers, locked and ghosted objects allow geometry to be seen, yet not manipulated (unless unlocked or unghosted). When an object is locked, some programs gray the object geometry to signify the object is unavailable for editing. Some programs will refer to a locked or ghosted object as a template.

When an object is locked, you may create new geometry right over it without affecting the locked object. This is great for reference objects or for building interrelated objects without inadvertently editing the wrong object. While not as easy as switching between layers, ghosting and locking provide an alternate means of templating geometry.

TRICK: Use a locked object to align objects. When there are multiple objects to be aligned, align one object and lock it in place. Other objects can now be aligned to the locked object without the locked object being moved.

Groups

Another means of organizing related geometry is through the use of groups. A group is a collection of two or more objects that have been selected and specifically classified as a group. A group of objects will share one common pivot point while each member of the group retains its own pivot point and texture attributes. The use of groups is ideal when animating objects that have similar motion paths. Each object in the group can have its own animation path, while the group as a whole may also contain a motion path. The classic example for motion paths of objects in a group is the rotation of the moon around the earth. The moon and earth are rotating on their axis, while the moon is rotating around the earth and the earth around the sun.

In the earth, moon, and sun example, there are different levels of motion. At the shape or object level, the earth and the moon each has its own axis for rotation. The next level up is the motion of the moon as it orbits the earth. In order for the earth and moon to stay together as the earth rotates around the sun, we need to group the earth and the moon. If the earth and moon were not grouped together the two objects would continue to rotate, but would soon go their separate ways.

Once the earth and moon have been grouped, the group gains its own independent pivot point. This new pivot point is then centered over the sun and given a 360° rotation so that the earth will orbit the sun while the moon orbits the earth perfectly. **Figure 2-20 shows the pivot point relationship between the earth, sun, and moon.**

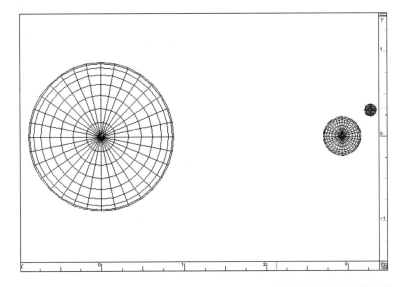

FIGURE 2-20 The use of parental chains creates pivot points between linked objects. The sun is parented to the earth, while the earth is parented to the moon.

Groups work very similar to null objects. While a null object is assigned to one or more objects through parenting, objects are selected and a new group is created by them. **For more information on null objects, see the chapter on nulls.** There is no limit to the number of groups in a scene, and groups may be grouped with other groups. This type of hierarchy is useful for object organization as well as animation.

A typical use for a group may be a bunch of air bubbles streaming from a filter in a fish tank. While each bubble has its own movement, the entire stream will move in a similar motion and direction. By creating a group that contains all of the air bubbles, you can animate the air bubbles separately, yet make the group of bubbles sway in a current as a group. This same effect can be achieved by using nulls where groups are not available.

Shapes

Another type of grouping of objects is to establish shapes. A shape object is an object or group of objects that has been established as one object. The shape object is very similar to the group, with some distinct differences. Shapes become extremely efficient when duplicated many times throughout the scene.

When creating an object or scene with a series of repetition in the scene, a shape is a better solution than a group. For example, when building a bicycle, many spokes need to be created. By creating a single spoke and classifying it as a shape, you need only insert duplicate instances of the object into the scene for as many spokes as you need. This saves memory because there is actually only one spoke object in the scene, with many instances of the spoke positioned throughout the scene.

The term *instance* is used when an object has been classified as a shape, and the shape was duplicated many times in the scene. When using a shape object, however, there are some caveats. A shape object's components may not be ungrouped and still remain a shape. To ungroup the components would mean to become disassociated with the original shape object. All efficiency advantages are lost for that instance of the shape object if it is ungrouped.

Another caveat is that any geometric or texture changes made to the shape object will propagate throughout every instance of that shape. This is good when a generic change has to be made, because it need only be made in one place, at the shape level. On the flip side, if each object needed to have slight variations, it would not be possible using a shape object.

Although changes in texture and geometry cannot be changed for different instances of the same shape object, position, scale, rotation, and motion paths can be different for each shape object. A perfect example of shape objects would be bowling pins. **As seen in Figure 2-21, each pin is exactly the same, yet the position and motion paths are entirely different**.

FIGURE 2-21 Using shapes that have been designated as self-contained shapes, you can easily import objects from various models and duplicate them just as easily. Using a shape as an instance of an object, changes made to the original (color, shape, etc.) will proliferate to all instances of the shape. If the object were not classified as a shape and the objects were copied, each one would then have to be manually changed. Scale is unaffected when using instances of shapes.

Naming Surfaces

For each object in a scene there is one or more surfaces associated with that object. The surface is the collection of polygons or triangulated mesh that contains the surface normals for rendering. Texture attributes, such as color, bump, and reflectivity, are assigned to and thereby controlled by the surface.

Some programs allow for a drag-and-drop texture application, while others use object association. Lightwave 3D supports the naming of surfaces and requires that each surface be named. Any surfaces not named will be given a default name and also a default texture shader. While this may at first seem like an inconvenience, there are definite advantages to the naming of surfaces on an object.

By assigning a name to an object's surface, objects that will be assigned the same texture or shader can all have the same surface name. If you are doing an animation of a company logo where all of the pieces of the logo are made of chrome, each object can be given the same surface name so that assigning the chrome texture to that surface name will give each object the same exact shader specifications.

Another application of the surface name property is to assign different polygons in the same object different names. Typically, an object can have only one shader assigned to it. By giving a group of polygons a different name, more than one shader can be applied to a single object. An example of this would be an object like a beach ball. Naming some polygons blue, some red, and some yellow will allow three different colors to be assigned to the same object.

While the beach ball is a simple example, the use of surface names is a powerful tool. Suppose some of the panels on the beach ball were to be transparent while others were to have a mylar look to them. By using surface names, one can easily assign the shaders to the appropriate surfaces without building complex composite maps for the different surface attributes. Because the beach ball in Figure 2-22 uses three different surface names for the same object, we can color apply three different textures to the same object.

FIGURE 2-22 Using many surface names on the same object can be a very powerful tool. Applying different textures or colors to each surface can give an object many different characteristics.

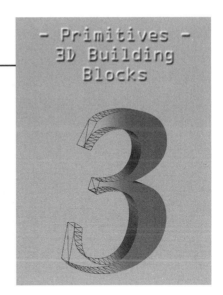

- Primitives -
3D Building
Blocks

→ Primitives—3D Building Blocks

Before we can get into building complex shapes, we need to start with the building blocks. Building a computer model is a process of creating, dissecting and rebuilding new or existing shapes. Typically, shapes are created as a series of pieces, which are then joined to form a complete object. This chapter will explain the basic building components from which all other objects can be built. The building components used in 3D modeling are called *primitives*.

Primitives come in both two and three dimensional form. Two dimensional primitives are used extensively in 3D modeling to create other three dimensional shapes through many processes such as lathing, lofting, and sweeping.

Curves are also a big part of three dimensional modeling. Curves can be created through the use of splines or by dissecting a 2d primitive for its points. Either way, the use of curves is needed to create organic objects, such as water pouring from a faucet.

Dissecting a Model

Before beginning to build a model, the entire model must be dissected. As in real-life manufacturing, computer models are built of many parts. Although we think of a pencil as a single object, a pencil consists of four parts, the lead, the wood, the eraser, and the eraser holder. All of the objects used to make a pencil are primitives. **Figure 3-1 shows a pencil taken apart to reveal the nature of its parts**.

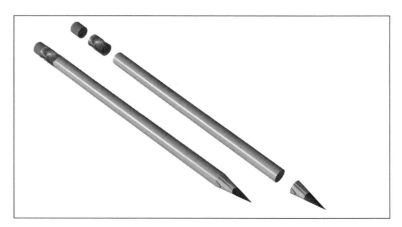

FIGURE 3-1 By dissecting an object, we can see what type of parts are needed for its construction. The difficult part of 3D modeling is dissecting an object that doesn't exist or dissecting an object in your mind.

By breaking a model down into smaller parts, we can accurately decide what type of pieces need to be modeled. The old adage "divide and conquer" really applies here. By analyzing the object to define some of the major parts, and then dissecting those parts into smaller parts, you will find that it is much easier to complete even the most complex models than it is to just start building. Planning and dissecting is the key to successful 3D modeling.

TIP: The easiest way to construct a complex model is to analyze and plan the modeling. Take apart the object in your mind or on paper. Dissecting every object before you model it helps to decide what is the most efficient way to build the entire object.

What Are Primitives?

As the name implies, primitives are the simplest or most primitive of shapes. Although they are very basic in nature, primitives are the foundation of modeling and can be used to create very complex shapes. **The four primitives standard in most modeling packages (see Figure 3-2) are the cube, the sphere, the cone, and the cylinder.**

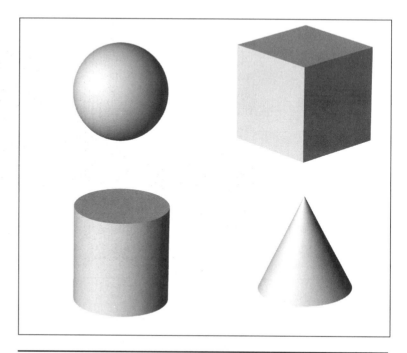

FIGURE 3-2   The four basic modeling primitives available in most modelers.

Although it may not seem possible, all other shapes can be made from the primitives. By using entire primitives or by dissecting the primitive, we can build any object. **All of the objects in Figure 3-3 were built entirely from primitives.**

FIGURE 3-3 Primitives can be used to create any object imaginable through the use of various tools.

The Cube

Of all the primitives, the cube is the most basic. A cube consists of eight planar surfaces (called faces) joined at their ends. What makes a cube unique is that every face is perpendicular to each of its adjoining faces. Although a perfect cube is made up of eight equal sides, they may be scaled to create rectangles of any proportion.

Cubes are used to create many planar objects, such as table tops, walls, floors, and ceilings. Cubes are very useful as starting objects for manufactured goods, since many times they have a typical cubic shape. **Several examples of modified cubes can be seen in Figure 3-4.**

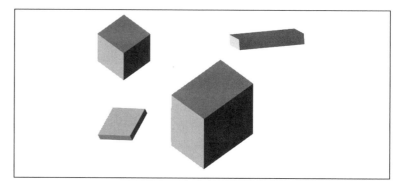

FIGURE 3-4   While all of the objects in this image were derived from cubes, only the one on the upper left is a perfect cube.

The Sphere

Second in simplicity only to the cube, the sphere is an integral part of 3D modeling. Using basic geometry, the computer creates a sphere from a user-supplied radius. The radius is the distance or length from the center point to the edge of the sphere. Spheres are essential in creating organic shapes. Many times, parts of sphere are also used to modify other objects, such as rounded edges on a cube. **Several spheres are shown in Figure 3-5.**

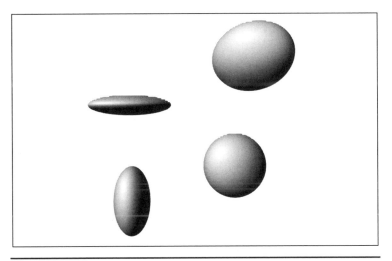

FIGURE 3-5 Spheres are an integral part of organic modeling. They are frequently used on Boolean operations, and are the basis of metaballs.

The Cylinder

Almost a derivative of the sphere, the cylinder is really just a circle that has been extruded to give it depth. Unlike the sphere, which is smooth on all sides, the cylinder has sharp edges where the end caps meet the body of the cylinder. Cylinders are used for creating such objects as pencils, coins, flag poles, and soda cans. **Like all the primitives, cylinders are used extensively for deriving other objects as seen in Figure 3-6.**

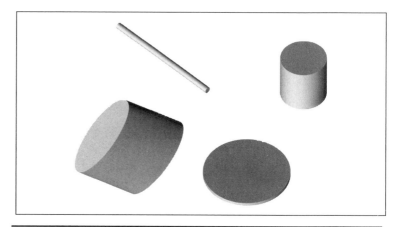

FIGURE 3-6 Using a cylinder, we can create objects as diverse as coins and pencils. All of the objects pictured were originally cylinders.

The Cone

Of all the primitives, the cone most resembles the cylinder. In a practical sense, the cone is a cylinder with one end converging to a single point. While it may not be used as often as the other primitives, the cone is still a very important primitive. A cone can be used as a beam of light, or party hat, or the lead in a pencil. There is no wrong way to use a primitive, it is just a matter of how efficiently you use them. Because of their optimized code, using a primitive will save you rendering time and create smaller object files. **Examples of cones can be seen in Figure 3-7.**

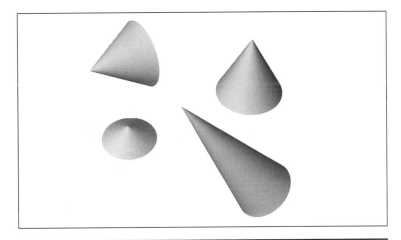

FIGURE 3-7 Like other primitives, cones can be used to create many different shapes, either by scaling the sides or through other modeling operations. All of these objects were derived from a cone.

Types of Primitives

Within the class of primitives there are two types, 2D and 3D primitives. The only difference between the two dimensional primitives and three dimensional primitives is the lack of depth on the part of the 2D primitives.

Although it would seem that the 3D primitives were derived from the 2D primitives, the opposite is true. The two dimensional primitives are not actually real objects. They are simply representations of their 3D counterparts, created so that they may be drawn on a two dimensional surface. They are for the most part a silhouette or profile of each of the 3D primitives. **Figure 3-8 shows the three dimensional primitives along with their two dimensional counterparts.**

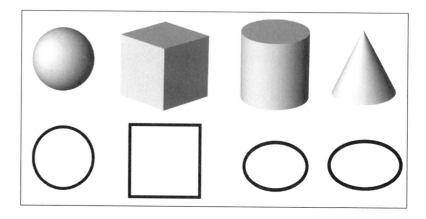

FIGURE 3-8 The 3D and 2D primitives are interrelated and each can be manipulated to create the other.

Two dimensional primitives are part of a subset of objects called *two dimensional surface objects*. Surface objects are created in only two dimensions, and therefore they lack depth. They are used primarily to create three dimensional objects through various functions. **For more information on 2D surface objects, see the section called** *2D Surface Objects* **later in this chapter.**

Primitives are also special because they are highly optimized mathematical representations. They are the very essential aspects of geometry. 3D primitives can be considered the atoms of 3D modeling. With them all other objects may be built. Once edited though, a primitive is no longer considered a primitive, because the geometry is no longer optimized.

Although primitives may seem limiting at first, one will quickly discover that primitives are the basis of modeling. Because they are the most basic objects in a 3D model, they are also the foundation from which all other objects can be built. **Figure 3-9 was created entirely with primitives.**

FIGURE 3-9 This scene was created entirely from primitives, mostly cubes, which had been stretched and flattened to create the various boards needed to make the easel.

Editing Primitives

While primitives may be edited, it is essential to understand the principle behind primitives. When it is possible to use a primitive as is, it is more efficient to do so. By editing a primitive, it is no longer optimized. Editing primitives is not prohibited or discouraged, but it is noteworthy to mention that the efficiency of the original primitive is lost when edited.

In a perfect world, a 3D modeler would not be concerned with polygons and memory limitations. We all know this is not a perfect world and therefore conserving polygons should be a concern. Not only will this keep your model clean, but you will save on rendering time as well.

Be advised that memory concerns should not impede an artist's work. A good habit to get into is to create clean models. Carelessly adding too many points when building simple objects will compound exponentially when building more complex objects. Not only does clean modeling make for better models, they are also easier to edit later and will render faster, as well.

TIP: Use the least number of points necessary to create the quality needed for an object. For example, when creating a sphere, 24 to 48 segments are normally all that are necessary to create a smooth curve. Using more than 48 segments will increase rendering time substantially but may produce only a slightly smoother curve. Size and closeness to the camera should also determine how many segments or points to use on a curved object.

Primitives are a great starting point for more complex models. A primitive may start as a cylinder, then be manipulated into a dinosaur head or a wheel on a sports car. There really is no definitive answer. The beauty of 3D modeling is that it is a visualization tool used not only to create images, but also models that can be manipulated, animated, and rendered so realistically that in some cases it is impossible to tell the real model from the imaginary one.

Dissecting Primitives

When using primitives to create other objects, the primitives may themselves no longer appear as primitives. They may be cut, dissected, stripped of segments, or subdivided into many parts. This is all part of the building process. Primitives were created as a starting point for all other shapes.

Because of simpler manufacturing methods, many of the real-world objects around us are created by simply combining primitives. Other objects may use parts of many primitives to create beveled edges or smoothly rounded corners. It is when one begins to create more organic shapes, such as people, animals, flowers, and flowing liquids, that intense primitive editing is involved.

By dissecting a primitive, you can use a portion of a sphere to create a yo-yo. Although this is a very simple model, the concept has many applications.

 TECHNIQUE: Creating the Yo-Yo Through Primitive Dissection

1. Using a sphere primitive, create a perfect two dimensional circle. Be sure the measurements are 1 unit on all axes except the Z axis. We do not need any depth. **Figure 3-10 shows the two dimensional circle**.

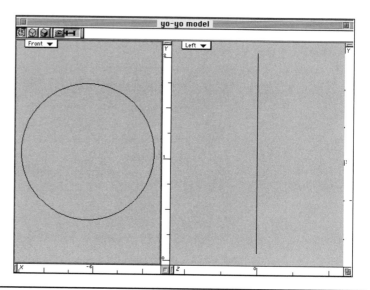

FIGURE 3-10 The 2D circle that will be used to create one side of the yo-yo body.

2. Edit the circle by removing all of the points to the left of the center point. You should now have a half circle. **Figure 3-11 illustrates the left circle.**

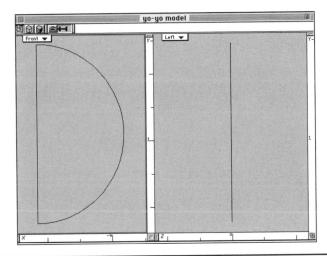

FIGURE 3-11 By dividing the circle in half, we will edit it further to create the desired shape.

3. Now remove the lower half of the points in the half circle. **You should end up with an object similar to the one in Figure 3-12.**

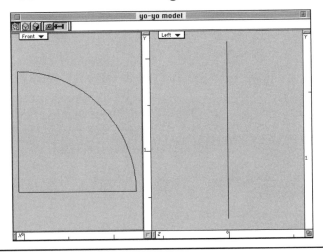

FIGURE 3-12 Dividing the circle further, we need only move the points to elongate the profile for the yo-yo body.

4. Selecting the bottom row of points, pull downward (along the *Y* axis) to form a long edge to create the image in Figure 3-13.

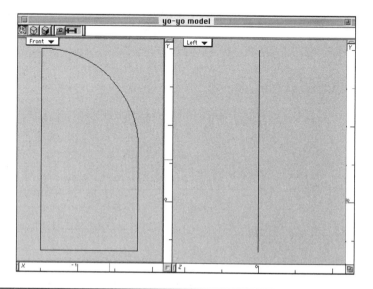

FIGURE 3-13 We now have the completed 2D profile, ready for lathing.

5. We have now dissected and edited a primitive to create the basis of the yo-yo shape. **By performing a lathe or sweep operation (lathe and sweep operations are explained in Chapter 4) on the silhouette we have created one side of the yo-yo (see Figure 3-14).**

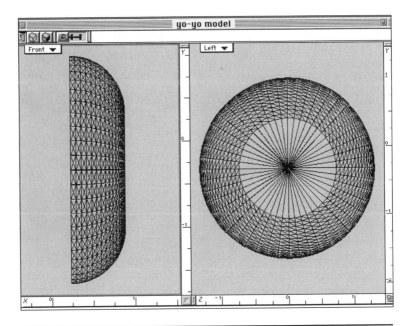

FIGURE 3-14 After the lathe operation, we now have a 3D object.

6. By mirroring the right side of the yo-yo, we can create another copy in a single step. You can mirror an object by scaling it minus 100% if you do not have a mirror function. You must also flip the polygon normals after using this method of mirroring an object. **We now have both sides of the nearly completed yo-yo (see Figure 3-15).**

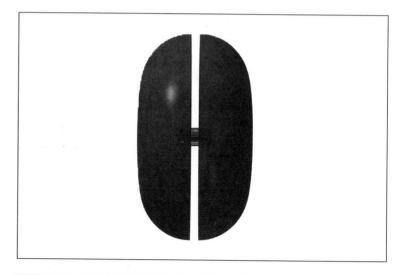

FIGURE 3-15 By mirroring the right side, we have an exact mirror of either side of the yo-yo. The mirror function is highly useful when creating symmetrical objects.

By adding a small cylinder in the center to connect the two pieces, we have created another shape from dissecting primitives. We can also use a circle primitive to create the string by extruding the primitive along the path. **Path extrusion is also explained in Chapter 4.**

TRICK: When combining primitives, or any two objects, there is a trick for saving points and polygons. Typically, due to the angle of intersection of two objects, more points will be generated if the two objects are fused using tools such as the Boolean union. For saving points and polygons, simply group the two objects. If your modeling software provides a means for counting points and polygons, check the count before and after to make sure that grouping will save points. This method will not work correctly if the objects are transparent, since the overlapping polygons will be visible.

Excessive Detail

Building a computer model may be compared to a manufacturing plant. It starts with an idea for a model or scene and is then subdivided into smaller and smaller working parts. There is a point when objects become too small to notice in a scene, yet will be rendered by the computer anyway. A good rule of thumb is that if polygons become smaller than the size of a pixel, they do not need to be there, since a pixel can only be one color.

 TIP: When creating small objects, use good judgment if the object is smaller than five pixels. Objects smaller than five pixels are hardly recognizable and may be reduced to a single colored primitive to save modeling and rendering time.

Remember, animation is more forgiving than still art. When creating a still image, polygon count should not be an issue (providing your computer can render it). For animation, objects can be a little rougher around the edges, especially if the object is moving, is far off in the background, or if the camera moves past it so fast that it is hardly recognizable.

Although this is not a license to produce loose or inaccurate models, it should be noted that every polygon which is not serving a purpose should be eliminated for a cleaner model or animation.

TIP: While detail is very important in building a realistic model, excessive detail can be prohibitive. Objects with excessive detail will bog down a system. Save rendering time by modeling only the detail that is necessary. It is important to realize also, that the level of detail for a still image is much higher than that of an animation.

The detail for the watch in Figure 3-16 is excessive for an animation, but for close-up shots like this one, the detail is appropriate. Notice that even the ridges on the bezel were modeled. For still images where the camera is not this close or for animation, a bump map may replace the modeled bezel. The bezel alone contains over 9000 points which could save considerable time if replaced by a bump map. The detail would not be accurate enough for a still image, but it would be fine for an animation.

FIGURE 3-16 While the detail for this shot is needed, the same amount of detail for an animation of this object would be considered excessive. Cutting out excessive detail will help cut down on rendering and modeling time. Know what the output is before modeling to avoid making time-consuming changes later.

2D Surface Objects

Two dimensional surface objects are objects that have been created in only two dimensions. They have height and width, but they do not have depth. The very fact that 2D surface objects are created in only two dimensions, and that they exist within the three dimensional world of modeling space, makes them very unique.

Two dimensional objects can be open or closed and are not considered solid. The surface objects are typically drawings created on a single plane and are primarily used to create object geometry through other modeling functions. **Figure 3-17 contains open and closed 2D surface objects which can be used to create three dimensional shapes.**

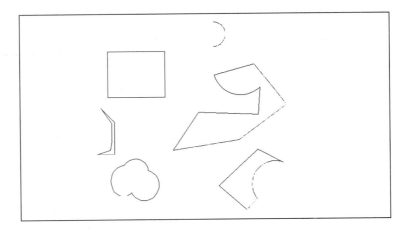

FIGURE 3-17 Open and closed 2D surface objects like these are used to generate many different kinds of 3D objects.

Nonplanar 2D Surface Objects

Since they are normally created by drawing on a two dimensional plane, the 2D surface objects are typically planar. A 2D planar surface will render in the 3D environment when rendered from any angle other than exactly 90° off of the missing dimension. From that angle, the object will appear invisible since it has no depth. To alleviate the planarity problem we need to make the two dimensional surface nonplanar. Although the surface appears solid, the object is not considered a solid object since it has no volume. **The leaf pictured in Figure 3-18 is a nonplanar 2D surface.** This object was created using the splined edges of a two dimensional rectangle. **For more information about splines, see the chapter on NURBS, splines, and meshes.**

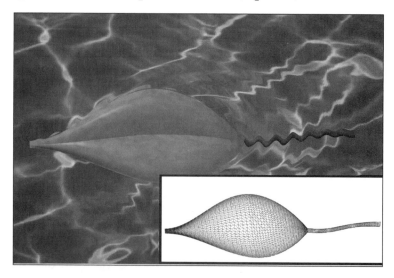

FIGURE 3-18 Because this leaf is a 2D surface object, the polygons that make up the surface must consist of triangulated mesh to keep them planar during the rendering phase. The object itself is a nonplanar 2D surface object.

2D Surface Profiles

Primarily, the two dimensional surface objects are used as profiles in lathing, sweeping, and extruding. By creating a 2D surface object of the profile of an object and applying other operators such as the sweep, many types of shapes can be created. **Figure 3-19 shows the profile (left) used to create the detail in the picture frame (right).** Using an object lathe with only four segments, a picture frame can be created with a fancy edge in a matter of seconds.

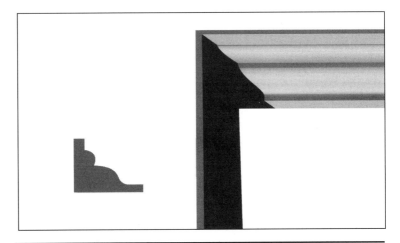

FIGURE 3-19 The profile on the left was used during a lathe operation to create the picture frame detail on the right. The lathe used four segments so that the frame would only have four sides. The object was then stretched so that it was not a perfect square.

Profiles can also be used to create objects using lofting (skinned), sweeping, or extrusion. Any time an object's profile is consistent throughout the entire object, a 2D surface object can be used to create the 3D object. **All of the objects pictured in Figure 3-20 started as 2D surface objects.**

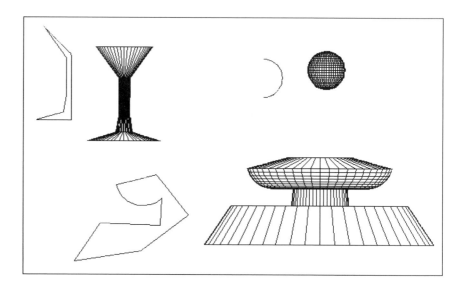

FIGURE 3-20 Through the use of lofting, lathing, sweeping, and extrusion, we can create a variety of 3D shapes from 2D surface objects.

2D Bézier Curves

To create flowing curves on 2D surface objects, many modelers make use of *Bézier curves*. A Bézier curve is a mathematical representation of a line or curve. Points along the curve are used to influence the curve by placing positive or negative tension on the curve. Each point has its own set of handles to control the amount of tension placed on the curve. Because Bézier curves are based on mathematics, they are very accurate and smooth at any scale. Bézier curves also use less memory than polygonal shapes. **Figure 3-21 is a diagram of a Bézier curve and its handles.**

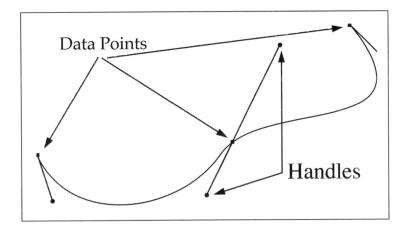

FIGURE 3-21 Using Bézier or spline curves allows for smooth, mathematically accurate curves and lines.

Changing the shape of a Bézier object involves repositioning "handles" on the Bézier points. Each point within a two dimensional Bézier object has two Bézier handles protruding from the center of the point. Moving either handle on a point will affect the tension of the entire point, unless the continuity is broken. **The illustration in Figure 3-22 shows how the curve is affected on both sides when continuity is not broken.**

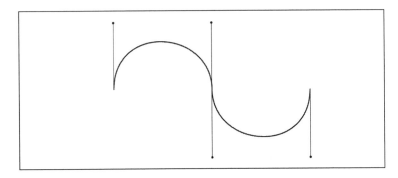

FIGURE 3-22 When the continuity is intact, the spline curve will react equally on both sides of the vertex.

Bézier Handles

A Bézier handle is an imaginary line that extends from the anchor point outward. The Bézier "handles" can be rotated around their anchor point. As one handle is rotated, its opposite handle is rotated exactly the same amount in the opposite direction. Handles may also be pulled farther away or closer to the anchor point to create a larger or smaller curve. The positioning of the Bézier handles directly affects the nature of the curve through that point. Typically, holding the option key while dragging one of the handles will break the continuity and influence between the two handles of a single point. By breaking the continuity, the tension coming into a curve could be greater than the tension leaving, or vice versa. **Breaking continuity is necessary when drawing a straight line off one side of a Bézier curve as is evidenced by the illustration in Figure 3-23.**

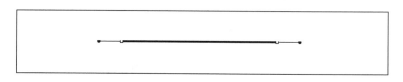

FIGURE 3-23 It is necessary to break the continuity of a spline in order to create a straight line.

Changing Curve Tension

Moving the handle toward or away from the anchor point directly affects the amplitude of the curve. Moving the Bézier handle closer to the anchor point flattens the curve, while pulling it away opens the curve. **In Figure 3-24, notice how the two curves differ.** The curve on the right is a result of pulling the **Bottom** point outward to open the curve.

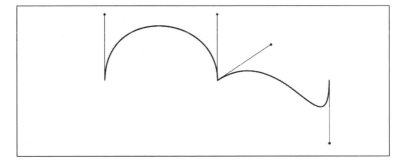

FIGURE 3-24 By breaking the continuity of a spline, we can create a curve with different amounts of tension on each side of the vertex.

The curve itself can be changed by rotating the Bézier handle around the anchor point by some degree. Since the Bézier handles control where the line enters the point, rotating the **Bottom** Bézier handle to the right side will cause the line to enter the anchor point from the right side. **In Figure 3-25 we can see that the line, which originally entered the point from the left, is now entering from the right, via a large curve.**

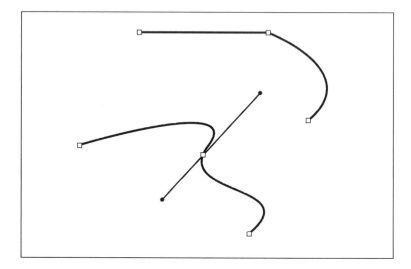

FIGURE 3-25 By changing the tension of a spline, we also affect where and how the curve enters the vertex. This works for both 2D and 3D splines.

Knowing how the Bézier curve works is essential to creating sophisticated 2D and 3D shapes. Bézier handles are also present in 3D through the use of spline objects. Naturally, in a three dimensional spline object, there are six Bézier handles at each point, since each axis must have two handles to control opposing tension.

From 2D Art to 3D Object

With more and more 3D artwork being used in presentation and visualization, there comes a need to convert old 2D artwork (such as logos) to three dimensional objects. Standard line art and text are examples of 2D art that are easily converted to three dimensional form. There are also programs available that are used exclusively for creating three dimensional artwork for two dimensional presentations. Programs such as Strata Type 3D and RayDream's addDepth are designed specifically for 2D presentation media, yet employ many of the same characteristics of three dimensional modeling, without many of the intricacies found in high-end 3D modelers. While their functionality is limited and normally doesn't include animation, these types of software programs are excellent for individuals who would like to create some dazzling text and logos for slide presentations or printed output.

As the trend toward high-impact graphics continues, many printed materials will contain aspects of 2D converted artwork. Charts and graphs that were once flat can now jump off the page by using programs such as RayDream's addDepth to give boring statistics new life. **Notice how easily 2D line is given three dimensions. The user need only add the material color**.

FIGURE 3-26 Through the use of programs such as addDepth from RayDream, we can convert 2D artwork into 3D images. Although they can't be animated, this type of artwork adds more impact to dry presentations.

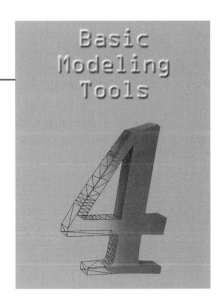

Basic Modeling Tools

Whether you are a carpenter, a pilot, a doctor, or a student, tools can make your task easier. Some tools help a little and some make extremely difficult tasks much easier. The computer and 3D modeling software are just such tools.

Tools come in many forms. An artist's paintbrushes are tools, as well as the paint and canvas. Even the painting itself is a tool, a tool of communication. To create complex 3D graphics, it is important to learn to use the tools available. Some tools are very simple to use, such as the selection tool, while other tools such as bones and inverse kinematics tend to be more difficult. In the end, even the most difficult to use tools can make the task they were designed for much easier to accomplish.

Some tools that aid in the transition from 2D to 2D. These tools are the easiest to understand and the least difficult to learn and use. Even though they may be easy to use, it is these tools which are most valuable, because they are used so frequently when modeling objects.

2D Sculpting and Drawing

Many shapes are derivatives of two dimensional objects. We create a two dimensional shape or profile, then using one or more tools we manipulate the two dimensional object into a three dimensional form. The extrude and sweep tools are examples of tools which derive a three dimensional object from a two dimensional surface object. Since 2D surface objects could be any planar shape, we need a way to edit and create 2D surface objects.

Typically, manipulation of two dimensional objects is controlled through the manipulation of points. A 2D primitive is loaded and individual or groups of points are selected and edited using the standard editing tools for that program. By moving, adding, or deleting points, the original 2D primitive can be changed to produce a profile for lathing, or a face for extruding. **In Figure 4-1, the image on the left is the original 2D primitive. After manipulating the points, a profile is formed.** The object on the right is the final object—a martini glass created from a 2D surface object primitive.

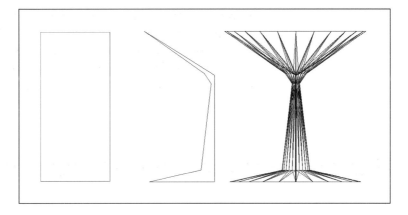

FIGURE 4-1 A 2D primitive can be used to create a profile, which in turn is used to create the final 3D object.

There is also another unique tool for creating complex two dimensional geometry. In programs such as Strata StudioPro, the tool is known as the 2D *sculptor*. The 2D sculptor is used to edit 2D surface objects. When editing an open surface, the sculptor is similar to a point editor, except that all points can be converted to a Bézier spline. The real treat is when editing closed 2D surface objects.

The 2D sculptor is used exclusively for editing two dimensional shapes. With this tool you can create smooth curves and sharp corners. It is also useful for cutting holes into the 2D geometry. The 2D sculptor is similar to a 1-bit paint program in that it allows you to add to or subtract geometry from a 2D object. Only black and white pixels are used. The black pixels represent geometry data and the white pixels represent the lack of data. With this method, you can easily add to or subtract geometry from an object. **Figure 4-2 shows two objects after using the 2D sculptor**. The object on the left started as a solid box. By subtracting all but the outer rim, we created a window. After adding a thin vertical and horizontal rectangle, we were able to create window panes. On the right, a large roof rectangle had three skylights put in by simple subtraction.

FIGURE 4-2 By using enclosed 2D surface objects, we can make 3D objects with holes in them.

The creation of objects such as windows or skylights in a ceiling is a perfect example of the 2D sculptor's abilities, although any type of object created with a 2D primitive may use the 2D sculptor to add or subtract geometry.

If your modeler of choice does not have this tool, there are alternate ways to create the same effect. The 2D sculptor tool is really just a Boolean tool for two dimensional objects. If your modeler does not have the 2D sculptor, **see the section on Boolean for more information about creating the same effect.**

TECHNIQUE: Steps for 2D Sculpting

1. Create a general outline of a 2D shape to sculpt.

2. Select the object and invoke the 2D sculptor tool.

3. Using the various drawing tools, select either the Add or Subtract option. With the correct tool selected, draw the shape desired for the Add or Subtract operation. Areas of geometry are shown in black, while areas lacking data are shown in white. Geometry may be added to the object as long it is not converted to a 3D object through another modeling operation.

4. Once the object is of the desired shape, it may be used with other operations to create a 3D object.

EXERCISE:

1. Create a 2D rectangle 4 units wide by 2 units high (see Figure 4-3).

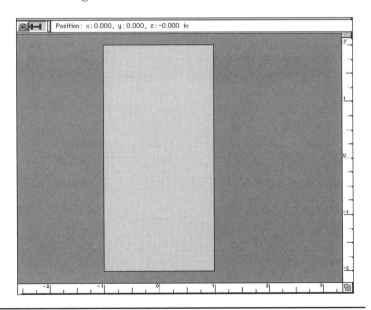

FIGURE 4-3 A two dimensional rectangle used for sculpting.

2. With the object selected, invoke the 2D sculptor. In some applications, such as Strata StudioPro you are presented with the object containing all of the points used to make up the object. This is very useful for final tweaking of the object. You may adjust any of the points or select the paint tool to "paint" on more geometry. For purposes of this example, click on the paint tool within the 2D sculptor. Figure 4-4 contains a screen shot of the 2D sculptor in Strata StudioPro.

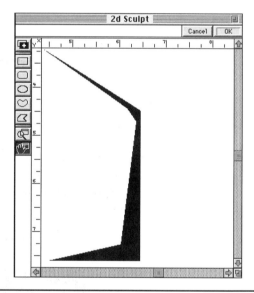

FIGURE 4-4 The 2D sculptor in Strata StudioPro allows users to change a 2D object's geometry by either moving individual points, or by "painting in" new geometry.

3. Using the rectangle tool, set the mode for subtraction. This may be either a menu item or an icon. Setting the subtraction mode will subtract geometry from the object, thereby creating holes in the object. Figure 4-5 illustrates the tools used in subtraction geometry.

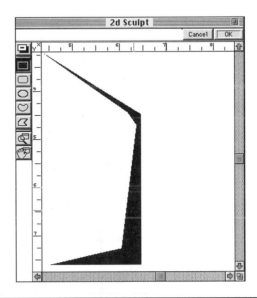

FIGURE 4-5 Setting the mode to subtraction, the user can "paint out" any unwanted geometry.

4. Windows can also be created in the rectangle by dragging the rectangle tool over a portion of the original rectangle where a skylight would be (see Figure 4-6).

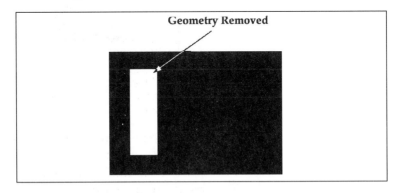

FIGURE 4-6 The hole was cut out of the 2D object's geometry through the paint Subtract mode in Strata StudioPro's 2D sculptor.

5. Create a total of three skylights evenly spaced within the rectangle to complete the skylights (see Figure 4-7).

TIP: You can even out the edges of the subtracted geometry by using the add tool and dragging over the edges of the skylights until they are all even.

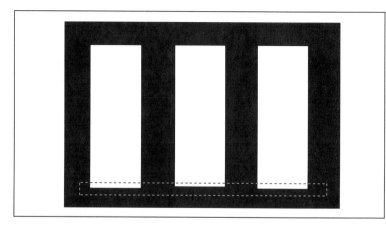

FIGURE 4-7 The 2D roof, complete with skylights. By dragging the Add rectangle tool over the edges of the newly formed holes, we can even them out.

Extrude Tool

Although probably the easiest tool to use, the extrude tool is an essential tool in the 3D modeler's toolbox. The extrusion tool works strictly on 2D surface objects. As we already know, the difference between a two dimensional object and a three dimensional object is the depth. Extruding an object will give it depth. Extrusion is very useful for creating three dimensional text, building architecture, and even for generating terrain. **The objects in Figure 4-8 were created using extrusion on a 2D surface object.**

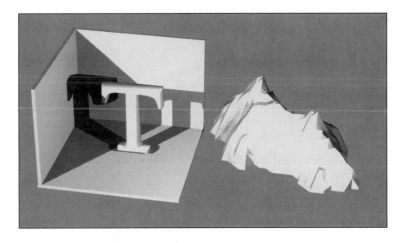

FIGURE 4-8 Although very different in their looks, all of these objects were created using extrusion.

Extrusion Depth

The depth parameter of an extrusion affects how long the extrusion will be in units. The extrusion depth of a car key would be only a few millimeters, while the extruded depth of a wall would be a few meters.

The rules for extruding an object are simple: An object is pulled through 3D space along a specified axis to the desired depth. This process is similar to making cookies.

The cookie cutter represents the 2D shape, which has no depth yet, and the dough is the extrusion process. When the dough is rolled out to the desired thickness, the cookie cutter is pressed through the dough. This is the same effect is achieved by setting an extrusion depth.

TECHNIQUE: Standard Extrusion

1. Create a 2D object of any shape.

2. With the 2D object selected, choose the extrusion menu option, icon, or tool. Typically, the extrusion tool is view dependent in that the object will be extruded along the same axis as the view port.

3. Choose the extrusion depth. Some programs will present an entry field to enter a number for the depth, while others require that you physically extend the extrusion bounding box to the desired length. Other programs will use the length of a. path which you must create prior to the extrusion process. **Figure 4-9 shows the extrusion process through Strata StudioPro.**

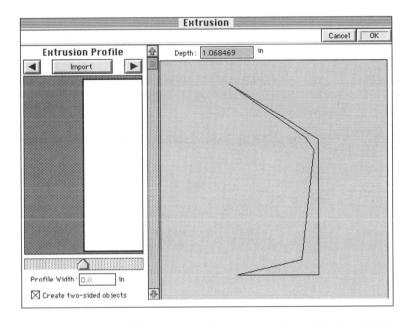

FIGURE 4-9 There are many approaches to the same result. Here we see the extrusion parameter dialogs from Strata StudioPro (left) and Lightwave 3D.

Extrusion with Bevel

In addition to adding depth to an object, some programs offer an extrusion profile as another parameter in the extrusion process. The extrusion profile can be used to add a beveled edge on top of the extrusion. Setting an extrusion profile is very useful for creating extruded objects from text to couch cushions. **Figure 4-10 compares the difference between beveled text and non-beveled.**

FIGURE 4-10 The use of a beveled edge on text gives the object a more realistic look. Some programs incorporate a beveled edge during extrusion.

Extrusion Profile

Software which offers an extrusion with bevel option typically provides an extrusion profile. The extrusion profile is the type of bevel that is applied to the extruded object. Different profiles will yield different faces on the extruded object. **Figure 4-11 shows some sample extrusion profiles and the result of the extrusion.**

FIGURE 4-11 Different extrusion profiles can be used to create different bevels on objects.

Typically, when the extrusion profile option is present, there is also a check box option which allows you to choose to have the extrusion applied to both sides of the object. If you do not activate the check box, the extrusion profile will only be applied to the front face of the extruded object. If the check box is not present, the extrusion profile will be applied to both sides. Applying the profile to both sides increases the polygon count, and is best not applied unless the back of the object will be viewed.

Profile Magnitude

The profile magnitude parameter in the extrusion profile lets the user set the severity of the beveled extrusion. This parameter is set in the current units and affects the beveled edge only. This is not used to control the overall length of the extrusion, but a very extreme profile magnitude could, in effect make the object longer than the extruded length. **Figure 4-12 shows a profile magnitude settings dialog and the results of two different profile magnitudes applied to the same object.**

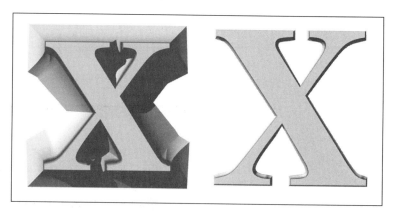

FIGURE 4-12 Setting the profile magnitude will increase or decrease the inset and depth of the extruded bevel.

TECHNIQUE: Steps to Extrusion with Bevel

1. Create a 2D object of any shape.

2. With the 2D object selected, choose the extrusion menu option, icon, or tool. Be sure your current

view of the object is along the path of the extrusion if your modeling software is view dependent.

3. Choose the extrusion depth. Some programs will present an entry field for entering a number for the depth.

4. Choose the profile and profile magnitude. The profile defines the extrusion face—flat, beveled, etc. The profile magnitude determines how pronounced or amplified the profile will be.

TIP: Although it does not control the depth of the object, the profile magnitude will affect it. Using too much profile amplification may distort the object beyond recognition.

EXERCISE: An Extruded Recliner

Extrusion can be used for many things that may not be so obvious at first. More than just a tool used to build walls and windows, the extrusion tool can be used to create many other shapes. **In this example, we will build the easy chair pictured in Figure 4-13 using 2D primitives and the extrusion tool.**

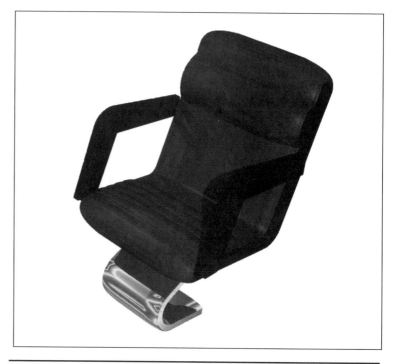

FIGURE 4-13 This chair was created entirely by using 2D surface objects with an extruded beveled edge. Different profiles were used to create different cushion types.

1. **Open the Recliner Example or build your own by creating the same 2D shapes as the ones pictured in Figure 4-14.** In this model, you will find 2D primitives used to build the chair. Be sure you are in a front view if the modeler you are using is view dependent when extruding.

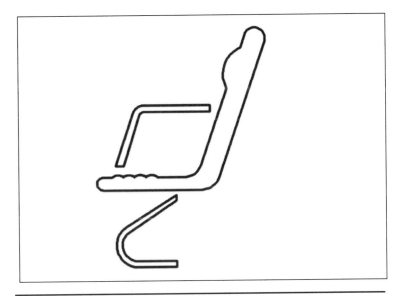

FIGURE 4-14 The 2D surface objects used to create the easy chair.

2. Select the base of the chair. **Using a flat extrusion as seen in Figure 4-15, extrude this to a depth of 3.5 feet**.

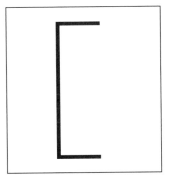

FIGURE 4-15 A flat extrusion profile used to create the base of the chair. Using a flat profile will not create a beveled edge on the extruded object.

3. Select the bottom cushion. **Choose the extrude tool and set the profile to that of rounded edges or similar as shown in Figure 4-16.** Change the profile magnitude to something very minimal (< 0.05 feet). Extrude the cushion to a depth of 2.5 feet. If the profile magnitude or extrusion depth is set too high, you will notice that the object will become distorted. If your extruded object becomes distorted, select undo immediately and reextrude with lower profile magnitude parameters.

FIGURE 4-16 The curved profile used for the cushions on the chair.

4. Select either of the arms. Using the same profile magnitude, extrude each of the arms to a depth of 3.5 feet. Extrude both of the arms, but extrude each separately.

5. Now that all of the pieces of the chair have been extruded, we need to align them. Align the arms with the sides of the cushion and center the support stand.

6. You may need to switch to different views to get a good idea of alignment. After all of the pieces have been placed in their appropriate places, you need only add some funky textures to finish your recliner and relax.

This example demonstrates that extrusion is not just for text any more; it can be used to create a variety of objects. We can also use more advanced extrusion extensions, such as extrude along a path, which is described next in this chapter.

 TIP: Extrude each object separately. Extruding a group of objects together may cause their geometry to overlap each other's. This is more common with intricate 2D surface objects with an intricate profile or high profile magnitude.

 TRICK: When extruding, if the modeling software you are using is view dependent, varying the angle of extrusion can create some very unique effects.

Extrude Along a Path

Extrusion along a path is great for creating rope, electrical cords, or any other object whose cross section is consistent along a nonlinear path. Unlike the standard extrusion, extruding along a path lets you perform the extrusion along a two or three dimensional path which you define. The cord for the mouse in **Figure 4-17 was created by extruding a 2D circle along a curved path.**

FIGURE 4-17 Using an extrusion along a path, you can create any object with a consistent profile along that path. The mouse cord was created by extruding a 2D circle along a wavy path.

Defining the Path

Defining a path for extrusion may be done one of two ways. All programs that offer an extrude along a path option, require that the path be created before the extrusion is performed. Some programs allow you to draw the path using the pen tool, while others allow you to drag the object through the scene as though animating the object to create the path.

To create the path, use the standard tools used to create a spline. Some programs require that you convert the spline to a path, while others do not. Although the path may have been drawn in two dimensions, you can typically go back and edit the points on the path so that it travels on all axes. Having a path three dimensional path, adds more realism to the extruded object.

Align to the Path

To create an extruded object which follows the true curves in the path, you must remember to align the object to the path. If the path starts out moving along the X axis, be sure the 2D surface object is perpendicular to the X axis. This ensures that as the object is extruded along the path, it will remain perpendicular to the path for the entire distance of the path. If the object is not aligned properly at the beginning, unexpected results could occur and the extruded object will have bends and kinks in it. **The image in Figure 4-18 shows the result of a properly aligned object to its path on top, and an improperly aligned object on the bottom.**

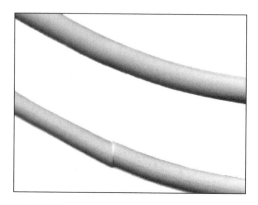

FIGURE 4-18 The object at the top was aligned to the path prior to extrusion. The object on the bottom was not properly aligned. Although the differences are slight, an improperly aligned object will create a noticeable error which takes away from the integrity of the model.

TIP: Aligning the object to the path not only ensures that the object will have a consistent shape throughout the path, but will also produce a smoother and more consistent mesh.

TECHNIQUE: To Create an Extrusion Along a Path:

1. Create a 2D shape which defines the cross section of the object.

2. Define the path of extrusion (either animated or drawn).

- Link or associate the 2D object to the path.

- Align the object to the path.

- Perform the extrude.

EXERCISE: Building a Mouse Pad, Mouse, and Cord

The mouse pad scene pictured in **Figure 4-17 is made entirely of extruded objects through the use of standard extrusion, path extrude, and extruded with a beveled edge options.** Although the objects are simple, they illustrate how many different ways an object can be extruded. We can build the mouse pad scene using the following steps:

1. **To create the mouse pad scene, we will need all of the 2D surface objects pictured in Figure 4-19.** Since all of these objects will not have the same orientation, you may want to create them as called for in the lesson.

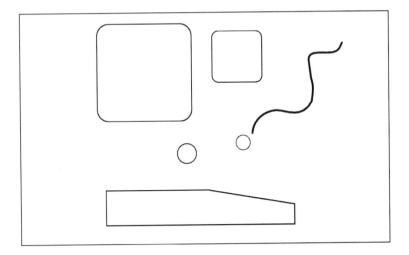

FIGURE 4-19 These 2D surface objects are all that is needed to create the entire mouse pad scene. The surface objects pictured here are not oriented as they would be in the modeling phase.

2. Using a top view, create a standard 2D surface rectangle with dimensions of 3 feet along the X axis and 2 feet along the Z axis. Using a standard extrusion and while in a top view, extrude the desktop rectangle 1 inch along the Y axis. We have now created the top of the desk. **Figure 4-20 shows the 2D surface object from the top view and the extruded rectangle desktop from an isometric angle**. Save the desktop object.

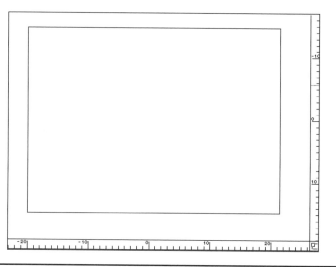

FIGURE 4-20 The 2D rectangle used to create the desktop in the mouse pad scene.

3. While in a top view, create a rounded rectangle 2D surface object with dimensions of 9 inches along the X axis and 7.5 inches along the Z axis. Extrude this object with a standard extrusion a distance of 0.25 inch along the Y axis. This will be our mouse pad. **The 2D surface object used for the mouse pad and the finished pad are pictured in Figure 4-21.** Save the mouse pad object.

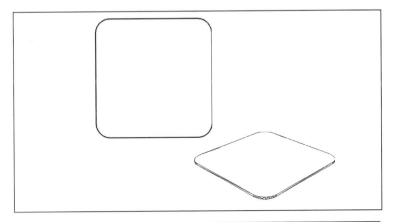

FIGURE 4-21 The 2D surface object used to create the mouse pad and the finished object.

4. Change views to a right side view. This means that we are now viewing the objects on their right sides, looking toward the left. While in this view, create the 2D surface object for the body of the mouse. The dimensions should be approximately 4 inches along the Z axis and 1.25 inches along the Y axis. The mouse body will use a beveled extrusion with a rounded profile. Set the profile extrusion to a small amount of about 0.04 inches. Extrude the mouse body 2 inches along the X axis. **Both the 2D surface object and the extruded mouse are pictured in Figure 4-22.** Save the mouse body object.

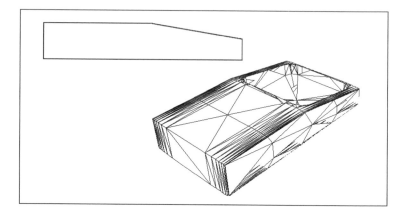

FIGURE 4-22 The mouse body 2D surface object and the finished mouse body.

5. **Moving back to the top view, create the mouse button pictured in Figure 4-23.** The mouse button should fit nicely inside the mouse bottom when completed and should start with dimensions of 2 inches along the X axis and about 1.5 inches along the Z axis. Adjust these dimensions to fit your specific mouse body. Extrude the mouse button 0.25 inch along the Y axis. Save the mouse button object.

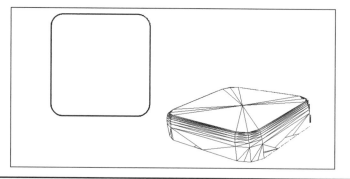

FIGURE 4-23 This 2D surface object is used to create the mouse button by extruding it along the Y axis.

6. To create the mouse cord, we need to first create the path. To create an accurate path, position the mouse parts, mouse pad, and table in the correct relation to each other. The mouse pad should rest on the table while the mouse rests on the pad. Place the button over the space for the mouse button on the mouse body. **From the right side view, the objects should look like the image in Figure 4-24.** From the top view, create a wavy line that to represents the mouse cord.

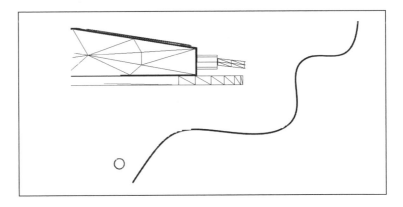

FIGURE 4-24 The extrusion path of the mouse cord as viewed from above. The 2D circle must be aligned to the path properly to produce a smooth extrusion.

7. Moving to a side view, align the path so that the starting end appears to exit from the smaller side of the mouse body. Adjust the point on the path so that there is a gentle slope until the path is slightly above the table object. The distance between the path and the table top should be the same as the radius of the 2D circle we will use to create the cord.

8. From the front view, create a 2D circle using a radius equal to the distance between the extrusion path and the table top.

9. Use a top and side view to position the 2D circle so that it is perpendicular to the path. Be sure to align the 2D circle to the path.

10. Extrude the 2D circle object through the path. This will create the cord for the mouse. You may now add textures to taste.

Lathe Tool

A standard lathe is a piece of machinery used in a wood-worker's shop that spins a piece of wood very rapidly so that sharp instruments applied to the wood create smooth indentations and curves out of the block of wood. It is the process used to create legs on wooden tables and chairs.

In the 3D world, any symmetrical object can be created in this manner, such as vases, pulleys, or table legs. **The objects in Figure 4-25 were created using the lathe tool.** The lathe tool can be used on any axis with a lathe degree from 0 to 360°. A partial lathe can be used for creating bends in pipes or rounded corners.

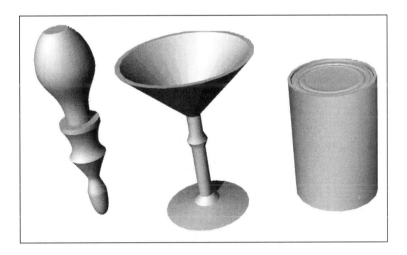

FIGURE 4-25 These objects were created using a lathe tool. Objects can be lathed from any axis to produce any shape which is symmetrical along an axis.

In the 3D modeling world, the lathe tool works by taking a 2D surface object and using it as a profile to create ribs along the desire segment angle. **Using the profiles shown in Figure 4-26, we can create the objects pictured in Figure 4-25.** As you examine the profiles, notice that they are really only one-half of a profile of the objects.

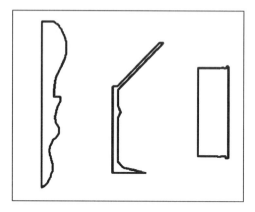

FIGURE 4-26 These profiles can be used to create the objects in Figure 4-25. Notice that the profiles are actually one-half of a complete profile. Since the profile will be lathed 360°, you need only create one-half of the profile when the lathe axis is set at one edge.

Many variations of the lathe tool are possible. You may lathe an object less than 360° or you may change the axis of the lathe. The lathe axis may also be placed off center to create other objects such as the torus (a shape which looks like a donut). More complex objects can be created by using an asymmetrical profile and performing the lathe at only 180°. **Figure 4-27 shows an example of an object which was created with off-center axes or asymmetrical shapes.** Because there are data on both sides of the lathe axis, we get 360° of geometry after the lathe. If we were to perform the lathe operation for 360°, the geometry would begin to intersect itself after 180°.

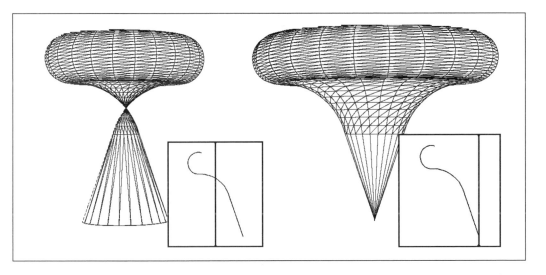

FIGURE 4-27 An object can be lathed with a centered lathe axis or an off-center axis. Changing the position of the lathe axis can dramatically change the shape of the finished object.

 TECHNIQUE: Using the Lathe

1. Create a 2D cross section of the item to be lathed. Since only one-half of the cross section will be used, you may create just the left or right half (vertical axis) or the top or bottom (horizontal axis).

2. Select the object and choose the lathe tool. Within the lathe tool, align the axis along the edge of the cross section or wherever appropriate for the particular object. **Figure 4-28 shows a typical lathe parameter box (from Strata StudioPro).**

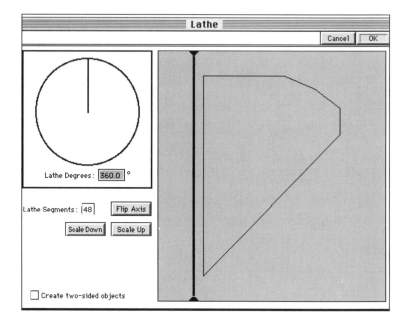

FIGURE 4-28 A lathe dialog showing the possible parameters during a lathe operation. This dialog box comes from Strata StudioPro.

3. Choose the appropriate lathe degrees. Since not all objects are completely round, you may use less than 360°.

4. Choose the number of segments to be used during the lathe process. The higher number of segments used, the smoother the object because more points are generated for the geometry. Normally, 24 segments is sufficient for background objects. If the camera closes in tight on an object, use more segments to ensure that the edges do not appear faceted.

5. Choose single or double-sided polygons for the extruded object. See the section on double-sided polygons for an explanation of both. Double-sided polygons are important on transparent objects.

6. Perform the extrusion.

EXERCISE: Creating a Soup Can

FIGURE 4-29 By creating a profile, lathing it, and adding a texture map, we get lunch in space.

To create the soup can pictured in Figure 4-29, we must first create the cross-section profile. The cross section is then rotated around an axis the specified degrees to create the 3D shape. **Figure 4-30 shows a complete cross section, and one-half of the cross section.** Typically, you need only create one side of a profile when using the lathe.

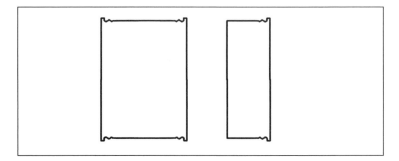

FIGURE 4-30 By creating one-half of a cross section of an object's profile, you are ready to lathe. The complete profile of the object is shown
on the left for comparison. When performing a lathe operation, you need
only create one-half of a profile of an object.

Lathes Variations

When using the lathe tool, you may also create asymmetrical objects by performing a partial lathe. Interesting shapes
can be created by using an asymmetrical profile and positioning the lathe axis in the center of the profile. When
using an asymmetrical profile, you may only lathe 180°
before the geometry begins to intersect itself.

Variations on lathing include using lower numbers of segments or partial lathes (less than 360 degrees) to create
objects such as jewels or portions of spheres. **Figure 4-31
shows a 2D object which has been lathed with 8 segments (right) to create a diamond and with 48 segments
(left)**. The use of segments plays an important role in creating the correct look of an object. If we had used more segments, we would have something similar to a vase.

TIP: The more segments you use to create a curved surface the smoother the curve. A caveat, however, is that more segments means a higher memory load in both file size and rendering time.

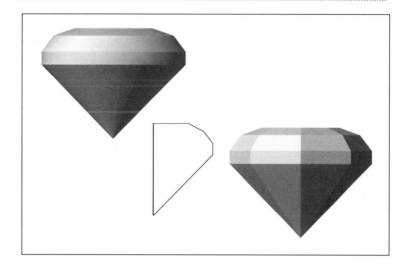

FIGURE 4-31 The number of segments used during a lathe operation can alter the shape of the finished object. Using 8 segments for the jewel on the right, we can see that the object no longer looks like the jewel we intended when we use 48 segments.

Smoothing/Faceting

We know that all objects created with polygons will have a faceted appearance due to the flat nature of polygons. Since polygons are still flat surfaces, how do we create a curved surface using flat edges? There are two possible solutions to the flat polygon problem.

To give a polygonal object a smooth surface, we rely on rendering tricks. The rendering algorithm uses a technique known as *smoothing* when rendering segmented objects. The smoothing process calculates the angle of the light in relation to the surface normal attached to a polygon. By smooth shading each polygon, the transition between polygons is hardly noticeable. The only place where the polygons are noticeable is along an object's edge. **Figure 4-32 shows an object which has smooth shading but visibly flat edges.**

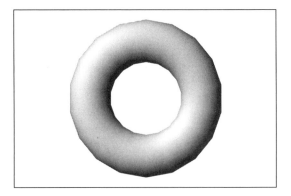

FIGURE 4-32 Although the torus pictured has been smoothed, you will notice that the edges of the object are still faceted. To remove these visual segments, we need to increase the number of edges, thereby making the size of each segment smaller.

To fix the problem of visibly segmented edges we need to add more edges. In the real world, to create a smooth curve out of straight objects, we need to use many small straight objects. The more straight edges in a smaller space, the smoother the curve. **Figure 4-33 shows how a smooth curve can be created using many straight lines.** On the left I used six lines to make the curve while on the right I used 56 lines to make the same curve. Notice that the curve on the right is many times smoother than the same curve on the left. The secret to making a smooth curve with flat polygons is to increase the number of segments used to create the object. More segments translates to more polygons and a smoother curve.

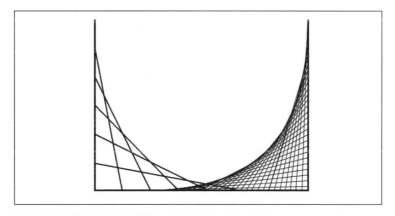

FIGURE 4-33 An old exercise in geometry. The more straight edges you use to create a curve, the smoother the curve.

TIP: Changing to a higher density of polygons requires more memory than a setting of lower density, due to the increase in the number of points and polygons associated with that object.

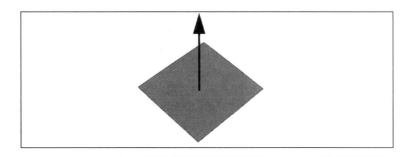

FIGURE 4-34 Surface normals are used to calculate a polygon's direction. Surface normals extend outward, perpendicular from a polygon's surface and aid in the proper shading of a polygon's surface. Surface normals are attached to every polygon but are not rendered.

Surface Normals

In rendering algorithms we use surface normals to smoothly shade flat polygons along a surface. Surface normals are mathematical perpendiculars which project outward from the surface of each polygon. The normals are invisible and do not render, but changing their relational angle to the associated polygon can drastically affect the way the surface is rendered. **Figure 4-34 illustrates what a surface normal looks like**.

By analyzing the angle between an object's surface normals and the angle of the light source on that surface, rendering algorithms can interpolate the differences between neighboring polygons to create a smoothly shaded curve. **Figure 4-35 show the difference between a flat shaded algorithm which does not use surface normals and a Phong shaded object**. Notice how the Phong shading algorithm uses surface normals to create a smoother curve.

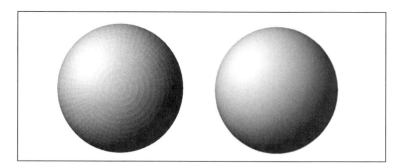

FIGURE 4-35 The difference between flat shading and smooth shading. The flat shading is quicker but does not produce any shading on a polygon. Each polygon is a single color. The smooth shading algorithm will interpolate the average color of a polygon and create a smooth surface across many polygons.

Tools such as bump maps allow the user to control the angle of the surface normals. When using a bump map, the surface normals which typically are perpendicular to the surface are bent by the levels of gray in the bump map. Bump maps are used in textures to simulate deformations in a surface when there are none. **Figure 4-36 shows a bump map and the results after it is applied to a surface. For more information about bump maps see Chapter 6.**

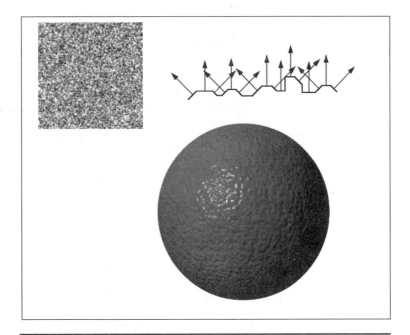

FIGURE 4-36 Bump maps are used to alter the position of the surface normals on an object's surface. Bump maps can simulate changes in an object's surface, such as waves, pits, and many types of surface attributes. The bump map only changes the surface normals and not the actual geometry. To change an object's geometry, use a displacement map.

Interpolation

Interpolation is the process of averaging the associated color changes within an image. Since a polygonal surface is not a true smooth curve, interpolating will average the pixels on the surface of a polygon to create a smooth gradient across the face of a flat surface. Interpolation across all of the polygons making up the curve gives the illusion of a smooth, curved surface. This smoothing technique is performed at rendering time automatically by certain rendering algorithms. There is no change in the number of polygons on an object when surface normals have been added.

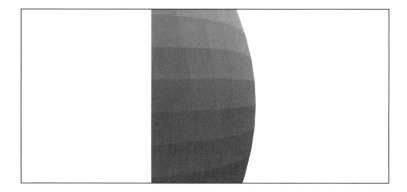

FIGURE 4-37   Without surface normals, all objects would appear faceted, such as the sphere in this illustration. This object was rendered using a flat shading algorithm, since flat shading does not consider normals when rendering.

If there were no surface normals, the rendered objects would appear similar to a flat shaded surface view. **Although the sphere in Figure 4-37 has normals attached to it, it was rendered using a flat shading algorithm which doesn't consider normals when rendering.**

Triangulated Mesh

In addition to using surface normals and a higher number of segments to create a smoother surface, a smoother curve may also be created by using triangulated mesh. As the name implies, all the polygons used in the creation of an object with triangulated mesh have only three sides. In triangulated mesh, all of the polygons within the mesh share vertices with the adjacent polygons. This creates a relationship between all the polygons which allows for three surface normals attached to each vertex point, resulting in a smoother curve. **Figure 4-38 depicts an object created with triangulated mesh**.

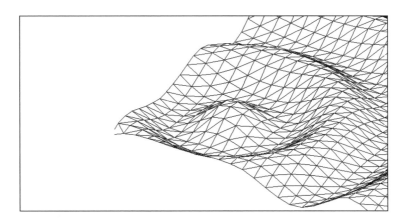

FIGURE 4-38 Triangulated mesh is used to create a smoother curve on surfaces. Triangulated mesh assures that all polygons are planar, making a better surface for animating difficult objects, such as water. Triangulated mesh also uses three surface normals for each vertex, instead of just the one for each polygon. This also makes for a smoother rendered surface.

Guaranteed Planar

Because the polygons used in triangulated mesh contain only three vertices, they are guaranteed to be planar. This is a major consideration if the surface is to be animated, as is done for water or waving flags. When using polygons with four or more sides, the points may lie on different axes due to point snapping or point editing done by either the user or the software itself. On triangulated mesh, the sides will always be planar, due to the mathematical nature of a three-sided object.

If a water object created without triangulated mesh was animated, the surface might tend to break up, because non-planar polygons will not render. Using triangulated mesh, there will be no holes in the geometry since all triangulated polygons are guaranteed to be planar, and will always render. **Notice the different in renderings in Figure 4-39**. The object on the left uses standard polygons, while the object on the right was created with triangulated mesh.

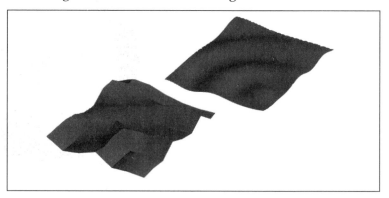

FIGURE 4-39 Using triangulated mesh ensures that all polygons are planar. When a surface is displaced, such as the water example in this illustration, dense triangulated mesh is needed to keep the surface from breaking apart as it goes through its motions.

Faceting

Faceting is the process of disconnecting the polygons that make up a 3D object. This includes text, triangulated mesh objects, and spline-based objects. When an object is faceted, all of the polygons become individual and unrelated polygons. These polygons can then be manipulated separately, although manipulating the polygons could become tedious work. **Figure 4-40 shows an object that has been faceted**. Faceting an object may become necessary when portions of the object need to be removed or used in creating special effects. In an object explosion, the object could be faceted so that all of the polygons can be animated in their own separate way to produce the effect of an exploded object.

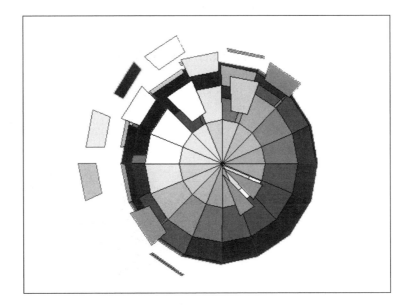

FIGURE 4-40 Faceting an object removes the bonds that organize the object as a single unit.

Why Faceting?

There are a few reasons for faceting. The main reason is to manipulate any one or group of polygons separately from the rest of the object. This may mean to apply a different texture or to remove some of the unwanted polygons. Separate polygonal groups may need to be smoothed differently than others. Whatever the reason, faceting allows you complete control over each of the individual polygons.

2 Sided Polygons

Typically, objects are created with single-sided polygons. Only the side of a polygon that contains a surface normal will be rendered. Single-sided polygons are polygons that contain surface normals on one side only. If a single-sided polygon were to be rendered from behind, the polygon would be invisible. Normals are typically only on one side of a polygon because, unless the object is transparent, the back of a polygon will not be seen. Even normals which are not seen must be considered during the rendering process. If there were normals on both sides by default, the inside of an object would be considered for rendering, making rendering times longer. Two-sided polygons are only needed when objects contain transparent surfaces or when using a 2D surface as a 3D object. **The transparent sphere and the leaf in Figure 4-41 use double-sided polygons so that both sides of the polygons are visible**—the sphere because the object has transparent surfaces which reveal the back sides of the polygons, and the leaf because it is really a nonplanar 2D surface, which actually has no depth.

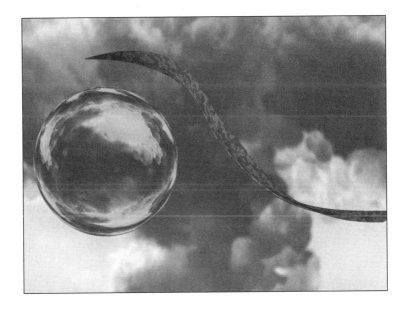

FIGURE 4-41 Double-sided polygons are a necessity when creating transparent and 2D nonplanar objects. Since an object can only be seen on the side which has the surface normals, a single-sided polygon is not visible from its back side. Creating an object with double-sided polygons creates surface normals for both sides.

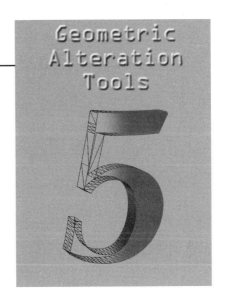

Geometric
Alteration
Tools

Geometric Alteration Tools

In the 3D modeling world, one can never have too much RAM or too fast a machine. As computers become faster and more powerful, so does the software. Fortunately many 3D modeling programs are taking advantage of the more powerful computers and faster chips by creating more powerful modeling tools. In many cases, tools are developed before they can actually be utilized efficiently on the current generation of computers.

Although not all software packages come with the most sophisticated tools, many midrange software packages are beginning to have some very advanced 3D modeling and animation tools, once present in only the most sophisticated and expensive software packages. Many of today's modeling and rendering packages are integrated so that third-party developers can create tools which are not present in the standard version of the software. These third-party extensions are also known as *plug-ins*.

Plug-ins are extensions which, when loaded on a computer system, become integrated with a specific software program. A plug-in is typically a specialized tool or filter created by a company separate from the software manufacturer. Some companies survive solely on providing plug-ins for existing software packages.

The advanced tools in this chapter add a great deal of functionality to the modeling toolbox. Some of these tools come standard in many software packages, while others are available through third-party plug-ins. Some tools are more complicated than others, but generally, once the learning curve has been achieved, these tools will save countless hours when modeling complex shapes.

First a couple of caveats about the advanced tools. More than a beginner's knowledge base is required to fully utilize these tools. They requires general modeling knowledge and being comfortable with the 3D coordinate system, spline curves, and spline mesh.

TIP: Due to the complexity of some advanced modeling tools, you should be comfortable with your knowledge of the 3D coordinate system, spline curves, meshes, and have a good understanding of 3D modeling.

Duplicate/Replicate

Very often an object is duplicated many times. Building a spiral staircase involves duplicating the same step many times. Instead of modeling each step individually, we need only create one step and duplicate it. **Figure 5-1 illustrates how a single step can be replicated to create this entire stairway with a single click of the mouse**.

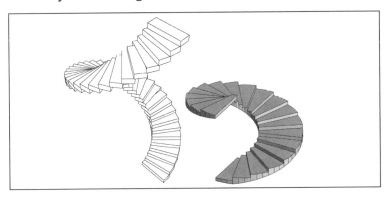

FIGURE 5-1 By using a replicate tool, repetitive objects such as the staircase can be created instantly by entering the correct parameters.

For instances where we may need only one copy of an object, we may use the clone or copy and paste methods. When creating many duplications of an object, the replicate command is quite handy.

The power of the replicate tool comes from its ability to offset objects from the previous replication. In the stairway example, a single step was created and then replicated with an offset of 6 inches along the Y axis and rotated 6° along the Y for 360°. Setting these parameters created the stairway instantly. I needed only to go in and tweak the texture angle on each object to avoid the look of a cloned object.

The pivot point of the original step was also offset so that the steps would create an area of space in the middle.

When choosing the rotational amount, use a clone of the original and place the two objects directly on top of one another. By rotating the clone on top of the original, we can easily see what rotational amount will keep the steps in line with each other. **In Figure 5-2 we can see that a rotation of 12.81° is the maximum before the two steps become separate**.

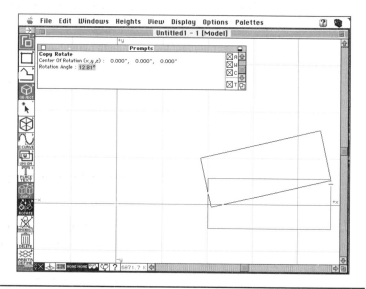

FIGURE 5-2 By using a single clone of the object to be replicated, we can find the correct rotation needed to keep the duplicate objects in line with the original.

TIP: When defining the distance and rotational offset of a duplicated object, create a single duplicate of the object, move it to the next logical position desired, and measure the distance of the change. This may also be used for choosing the rotation amount. By rotating a copy of the object over itself, we can see what the difference in rotational amount needs to be to keep the objects in the correct perspective.

TECHNIQUE: Replicating an Object

1. Create the original object to be replicated.

2. Define the rotation, distance offset, and axis offset.

3. Enter the number of repetitions needed for the task.

4. Relax and enjoy, while the computer duplicates the objects and places them in the correct position for you.

5. It is suggested that as each replicated object receives a surface texture, the center point be changed to avoid the clone look. If the shader was applied before the replication operation, simply change the application angle of the texture for each object. This will give a sense of realism to the clones.

Triangulation

Triangulation is the process of changing all or some of the polygons that make up the surfaces of three-sided polygons. The reason for creating three-sided polygons, or triangulated mesh, is to create objects with complex geometry so that they appear smoother when rendered and to ensure planar polygons. **Figure 5-3 compares the difference between standard and triangulated polygons**.

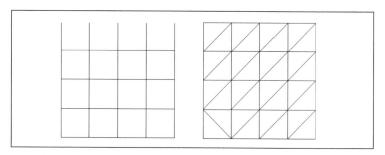

FIGURE 5-3 Triangulated mesh uses the same points as standard polygons, but every polygon has only three vertices. Because each polygon only has three points, the polygon is guaranteed to be planar, unlike four-sided polygons which can become nonplanar if one of the vertices is moved along a nonplanar axis.

Triangulation ensures planarity since all three points pivot off one another. In a four-sided polygon, points which move off of the current plane will cause the polygon to become "broken" or nonplanar, which will render incorrectly or not at all. This will make the object appear to have unwanted holes in the surface geometry when rendered. **The difference in standard polygons and triangulated polygons can be seen in the rendered water surfaces in Figure 5-4**.

FIGURE 5-4 Notice how the triangulated mesh on the left appears smooth, while the standard polygons on the right become nonplanar and break apart, causing holes in the object's geometry.

Triangulated mesh can be used on simple objects, such as planes, cubes, or spheres or very complex objects which contain many curves. When morphing or animating the surface of an object, such as through displacement maps, triangulated mesh will ensure that the polygons remain planar throughout the animation.

TECHNIQUE: Creating Triangulated Mesh

1. Select the object to be triangulated.

2. Check the density of the polygons. If the polygon size is too large, the mesh will not be very dense. A note for those of you who are keeping track of points and polygons: when using triangulated mesh the polygon count will be higher, but the point count may not necessarily change. This is due to the fact that the triangulated mesh will share the same points that the four-sided polygons used, although the triangulated mesh will contain an extra edge dividing the polygon in half.

3. If the polygons are not very dense (less than 48 points for 360°) you may need to increase the polygon count. To increase the number of polygons which make up the object, edit the object's polygon parameters. Some software will allow you to edit the polygon count directly (through a dialog box), or by recreating the object through the derivation tool used to create it, such as a relathe or reextrude. Lightwave 3D even has a button which, when clicked, will double the number of polygons in the object by dividing all polygons to half their size.

4. After the desired density of polygons has been achieved, triangulate the polygons by selecting the triangulate option. Objects which are created using Bézier curves will have to be converted to polygonal before they may be triangulated. In Lightwave 3D, there is a button called Triple, which will create triangulated mesh.

5. Once the object's polygons have been triangulated, any type of surface deformation will produce a much cleaner rendered surface than if the object's geometry had not been triangulated.

Displacement Maps

One of the easiest to use of the advanced tools is the displacement map. A displacement map does just what its name implies—it displaces a surface. This means that an image or procedural texture is used to change the surface geometry of an object. Unlike a bump map, which merely affects the way light reacts to an object, the displacement map actually changes the object's surface geometry. This is an important consideration when texturing objects. **Figure 5-5 shows how the edges appear differently on a bump-mapped object and the same map applied as a displacement map**.

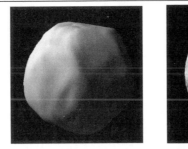

FIGURE 5-5 The major disadvantage of a bump map is the fact that the edges of the object remain unchanged by the bump. Notice how the edges of the sphere on the right remain perfectly round, while the object with the displacement map (left) is no longer a perfect sphere.

 TRICK: When rendering an object whose edges are not visible or unaffected, use a bump map instead of a displacement map. The bump map can be as convincing as the displacement map without the overhead in rendering time. Beware: The edges of a bump-mapped object will not be affected by the bump map.

A displacement map is very useful for creating a surface which may be too difficult or time consuming to model. Consider the difficulty of modeling a flag waving in the wind. **Using a displacement map on the flag pictured in Figure 5-6 allows the flag to be animated relatively easily by applying a ripple texture across the surface**. Since the texture can have velocity and falloff, the flag can appear to wave in the wind with a randomness like that of the changes in wind speed.

165

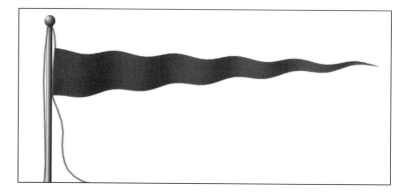

FIGURE 5-6 For objects which need to change dynamically in shape, such as a flag floating in the breeze, there is no better answer than to use a displacement map.

The flag example is a relatively simple explanation to a very powerful tool. Imagine creating a flowing liquid such as a bubbling brook. Although modeling the shape of the water as it curves through the forest is easy, creating enough randomness in the surface to make it appear as though it runs over small rocks could prove very difficult. Using a displacement map makes the entire task infinitely easier. Let it be known that animating liquid is about as organic as modeling can get, and the task can prove extremely difficult and time consuming.

TIP: When to choose between a bump map and a displacement map:

- *Displacement:* When an object is the focus and its edges are visible—edges are smooth on a bump map.

- *Displacement:* When object geometry needs to be animated—flags, flowing water, etc.

- *Bump:* Object in background, accessory object, edges of object are not in scene.

- *Bump:* Polygon count in scene is very high—to the point of impeding rendering.

 TECHNIQUE: Applying a Displacement Map

1. Create a gray-scale image of the displacement pattern you want to use.

2. Load the image into the rendering software.

3. Apply the gray-scale image through the displacement parameters via the object's surface control dialog box. Be sure the displacement map is applied along the correct axis. If the axis is incorrect, the object may not be displaced or the displacement may appear skewed.

4. Check the displacement amplitude. If the amplitude is too low, the displacement will not affect the geometry. If the amplitude is too high, the object will be displaced into obscurity and may be unrecognizable.

5. Check that the texture is sized properly. If the texture is too small, the displacement may be ineffective, while a map that is too large, will displace the object such that it cannot be recognized.

Object Deformation

Object deformation is the process of changing an object's shape through "deformities." The deformities can be created from pulling points on a model, or through object deformation and deformation areas. Object deformation works best with spline objects because they tend to produce more realistic models which have softer curves, instead of sharp corners and spikes like polygonal objects. **Compare the objects in Figure 5-7 to see the difference between pulling points on a polygonal object verses a spline object.**

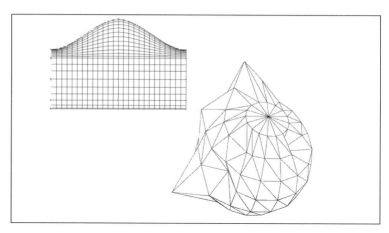

FIGURE 5-7   When using displacement or any other form of object deformation, use triangulated mesh or spline objects. When deformation is applied to a polygonal object (even triangulated mesh), strong spikes may occur where the point had been pulled.

Point Deformation

As a deformation tool, point deformation can become tedious when creating complex models this way. Each point must be pulled and pushed until the desired shape is created, all the while avoiding unnecessary creases in the geometry. As with all types of surface or solid deformation, the denser the polygon mesh, the smoother the surface along bends and curves. When deforming an object through point or vertex movement, be sure to use triangulated mesh. If working with spline objects, you may need only to subdivide the mesh to produce a smoother surface.

To avoid spikes and sharp edges normally associated with point editing, you should use any available gravity or flex controls. Changing the weight setting can produce sharp spikes, or smooth flowing curves, when points are pulled. **Figure 5-7 displays the difference in gravity applied to an object's points.**

Deformation Areas

Object deformation makes use of deformation objects. Electric Image Animation System and Caligari trueSpace 2.0 make use of deformation areas. If deformation sounds similar to displacement, it is. Both functions change the shape of an object dynamically, but the displacement works with gray-scale maps while the object deformation is accomplished through spline objects. Deformation of an object could be as subtle as a small ripple on a pond or as radical as pushing a piano through a keyhole.

Imagine if you needed to push a piano through a keyhole for a character animation. Modeling the piano as it squeezed through the keyhole would be very difficult. By using a deformation object in the area of the keyhole, however, the completed piano model would be adjusted as it went through the keyhole. The deformation area would be area of the key in which the piano was to pass through. **Figure 5-8 shows what a deformation area may look like**.

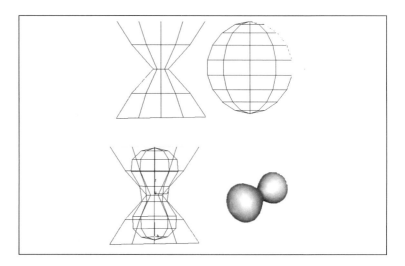

FIGURE 5-8 Using a deformation area such as the one above, can make an object retain its properties as it enters and exits the deformation area. While within the deformation area, the object will conform to the shape of the deformation object's geometry.

TIP: In order for a deform tool to give the proper effect, the object should consist of triangulated mesh so that the newly distorted object will deform smoothly. If the polygons are too large, or the mesh is not dense enough, the deformation will appear blocky and obvious. While increased density on the mesh will increase memory requirements, this type of effect is not intended for gutless computers.

Typically, deformation works best with spline objects. Due to the ability of the splines to retain clean lines because of their mathematical accuracy, the deformation will appear cleaner when a spline object is used. In fact, some software, only spline objects may be used during a deformation.

Because they are advanced molding tool, modeling and deformation tools may not be found in some of the lower end modelers. Molding and deformation also have higher memory requirements than some of the more basic tools.

Sweep

The sweep tool is used to create a variety of shapes by extruding the cross section along a path or axis. The sweep function is a cross between the lathe function and the extrude function. In many programs, the sweep function replaces the lathe function by extruding a shape along a single axis with no change in position. The sweep function allows for a change in object position and size as it is extruded along the axis.

The sweep tool simplifies some of the tedious processes used to create objects that contain a lot of repetition, such as a coiled spring or the railing on a spiral stairway. Some common objects created using the sweep tool are springs, telephone cords, or seashells. **Figure 5-9 contains some common objects created using the sweep tool**.

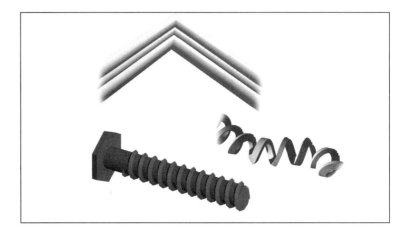

FIGURE 5-9 The sweep tool is a cross between the lathe tool and the extrude tool. 2D surface objects are extruded through space as they rotate along an axis.

 TECHNIQUE: Sweeping an Object

1. Define the 2D object to be swept. In many programs sweeping only works on 2D objects.

2. Choose the axis the 2D object is to be swept around or choose a path object to sweep along.

3. Define the level of movement for the sweep. This involves segment rotation, progressive size of each segment (larger or smaller), and number of segments used to define the entire shape.

The sweep tool produces objects that typically contain a high number of polygons. Using a large number of swept objects will slow rendering time considerably. For background objects, or objects which are very small, you may be able to use a bump or transparency map to create the same illusion. **Figure 5-10 shows an object which appears to be a sweep object**. In fact, the object contains a bump map to create the illusion.

FIGURE 5-10 While the sweep tool can create some very complex geometry, it does not come without the price of a heavy polygon count. Using a very clever bump map, you can create a very similar effect on some types of objects. This twisted column was created using a bump map instead of a sweep tool.

TIP: Using the sweep tool may produce a very high polygon count. There are times when a bump map may suffice in creating the same illusion as the swept object, while the memory savings will be astronomical. When image quality won't suffer, use a bump map in place of a swept object.

Boolean Operations

Boolean operations are mathematical operations performed on two 3D objects whose geometries intersect in 3D space. More specifically, these operations are binary operations involving two objects and altering both shapes depending on the type of operation performed and their intersecting geometry.

Typically, Boolean operations involve the subtraction, union, and intersection of two objects. Boolean operations allow the modeler to create perfectly matching pieces that fit together by using a Boolean function on either object. Imagine trying to model two objects independently which must fit snugly. The task would be very difficult. **The ball and socket pieces created in Figure 5-11 fit snugly because the shapes were used in a Boolean operation to guarantee a perfect fit**.

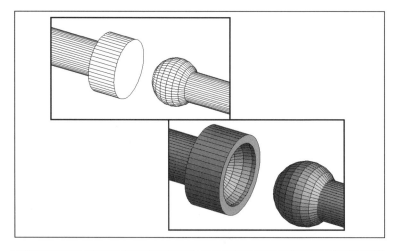

FIGURE 5-11 Since the ball was used to create the socket using a Boolean subtract, the ball will fit perfectly in the socket.

While the Boolean tool works best with solid modeled objects, it can also be simulated with surface modelers. Since the surface modeler creates objects which are just a collection of faces, Booleans may sometimes not be as cleans as with solid modelers. For all practical purposes and general Boolean operations, there is little difference in the output.

Software with Boolean Features

Boolean operations are becoming more popular and prevalent in modeling software. Many packages have added this tool in the latest release with others promising to do so. Of the modeling software I evaluated, nearly all contained Boolean functions including Strata StudioPro 1.5 (Macintosh), Pixel Putty Solo (Macintosh), form•Z (Macintosh, Windows), 3D Studio 4.0 (DOS), Lightwave 3D (Amiga, Windows, SGI), and Caligari trueSpace 2.0 (Windows).

Boolean Add

The Boolean Add function (also called joining) joins two objects. This is very similar to a grouping of the two objects, because all of the geometry remains intact, yet the two objects become one. The major difference, however, is that once objects have been joined using a Boolean Add function, they cannot be unjoined at will like a group classification allows. The objects can be undone if the Undo is performed immediately following the operation, or your software package has multiple Undos.

The Boolean Add function is similar to the Boolean Union operation, except that all of the geometry remains. This is a very important fact when deciding between the Add and Union operations. Everyone has his or her own reasons for modeling a particular way. But deciding if the Add operation is the best choice for any particular object depends on how the object will be used, such as in a still image or animation, or if the object has any moving parts, which become exposed during the animation. One reason that you may want to keep all of the geometry using the Add operation may be that the surface on an outer portion of an object may be semitransparent, which would reveal the geometry of another object inside.

TIP: When performing any of the Boolean operations, it is important to check the integrity of the data after the operation. Due to the nature of points and polygons, it is wise to check for extra or missing polygons or points in your object after the operation. You may end up with points that are scattered or multiple points occupying the same location in space. You may also want to merge points that coexist at the same location in 3D space.

Boolean Union

The Boolean Union function is very similar to the Boolean Add function except that any intersecting geometry between the two objects is deleted. The two objects are joined at their intersection point.

Using the Union function is useful for creating complex shapes by incorporating the geometry from other shapes. Objects which are asymmetrical or organic can be dissected and modeled separately then joined using the Boolean Union function.

The key to the Union function is that any geometry which is overlapped by the two objects will be deleted. Removing the excess geometry is the key behind the union function. This works especially well when piecing together complex objects that have transparent surfaces. **Figure 5-12 shows two transparent objects that used the Boolean union operation**.

FIGURE 5-12 The difference in a Union operation (right) and an Add operation is that any geometry which is common to both objects is removed during the Union operation. The two objects are then joined to create a single object.

TRICK: When performing Boolean functions on objects there may be more polygons created than there were before, even if geometry is eliminated. This is due to the angle of intersection of the two parts. If the object appears the same but has more points and polygons after the Boolean operation, simply group the two objects together instead of performing the Boolean. This of course will not work correctly if either of the objects is transparent or if the intersecting geometry must be removed.

Boolean Subtract

The Boolean Subtract operation will subtract the geometry of one object from that of another. The two objects must have some intersecting geometry for the Boolean Subtract to work properly. If a cylinder was subtracted from a cube, the cube would have a hole where the cylinder was. This function is used extensively for carving out intricate sections of objects or for showing cutaway views of complex composite objects.

To perform the Boolean Subtract, you must have two objects. One object, the affected object, will receive the results of the Boolean subtraction operation. The other object is the subtraction object. Depending on the program you are using, the subtraction object is either left intact or removed from the scene as a result of the Boolean Subtract operation. In either case, the affected object will lose any intersecting geometry between itself and the subtraction object. **Figure 5-13 illustrates how the affected object and the subtraction object interact, and the results of a Boolean Subtract operation.**

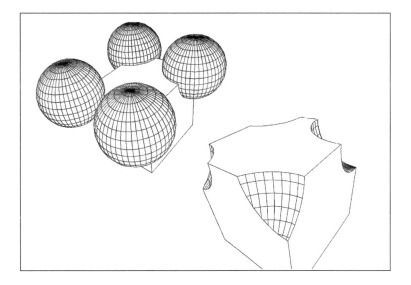

FIGURE 5-13 During a subtraction operation, the affected geometry will retain all of its geometry except that which intersects with the subtraction object. The subtraction object is used solely for the use of the Boolean and in some programs is actually deleted after the operation. When the Subtract operation is used to make two pieces fit snugly, be sure to save a copy of the subtraction object before applying the Boolean.

 TECHNIQUE: Boolean Subtract

1. Select the object which is to have a portion of its geometry removed. This is called the affected object.

2. Determine which object is to be used for the subtraction process. This object is called the subtraction object. In programs such as Lightwave 3D, you must place the subtraction object in a background layer. In other programs, such as StudioPro, the selection of affected object and subtraction object is made through a dialog box.

179

3. Check that the two objects intersect as desired then apply the Boolean subtraction operation. Once the operation has been completed, a new object will replace the old one. In many programs, the original objects are lost. Because Lightwave 3D works in layers, the subtraction object is still available after the Boolean operation.

4. Check the geometry of the new object created as a result of the Boolean. At times, due to sophisticated geometry, there may be some extra or missing polygons. Check the geometry for holes by inspecting the wireframe model or by rendering a simple shaded view

Boolean Intersection

The Boolean Intersection operation is created in very much the same manner as the other Boolean operations. The Boolean Intersection operation retains only the geometry where the two objects share common 3D space. If two cubes were intersecting slightly at the corners, only the data where the two cubes overlap would remain after the Boolean Intersection operation. All nonintersecting geometry would be removed.

The Boolean intersect operation can be used to create complex pieces which must fit snugly into other geometry. After performing the Intersection operation, the resultant object will fit perfectly into a copy of the geometry that created it. **As seen in Figure 5-14, by performing an intersection on a 3D cork and a virtual bottle, we can create a cork that fits perfectly into the bottle opening.**

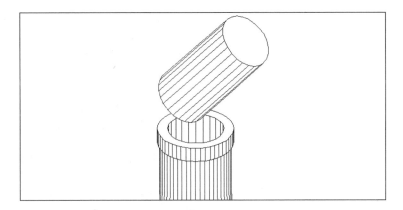

FIGURE 5-14 By using a copy of the bottle, we can create a cork which will fit snugly inside the bottle through the use of the Boolean Intersection operation.

2D Transformation Tools

While the Boolean operations are used to create new shapes through the interaction of two 3D objects, other tools are available that use 2D objects to create or modify 3D objects. These tools are unique in that they are really adaptations or conglomerations of other tools and techniques that can be applied fairly easily to a single object or polygon.

Skinning/Lofting

A transformation tool which creates 3D objects entirely of 2D surface objects is the skinning or lofting tool. *Skinning*, also known as *lofting*, is a process which will cover two or more two dimensional "ribs" with a virtual skin, so as to create a three dimensional solid object. Very similar to the way old airplane wings were constructed, a series of ribs is used to define the profile. The ribs are then "skinned" or "lofted" so the ribs become the skeleton of the object itself. **The illustration in Figure 5-15 contains three ribs which will be skinned to form a 3D object.** Although only three ribs are used originally in this illustration, the computer will automatically generate in-between ribs to create smooth geometry. The number of ribs placed between the originals is dependent on the geometry density setting selected prior to the skinning operation.

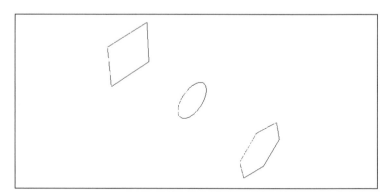

FIGURE 5-15 Using the three ribs shown above, we can use lofting to create a solid shape. Lofting or skinning is a process which applies a surface over associated ribs.

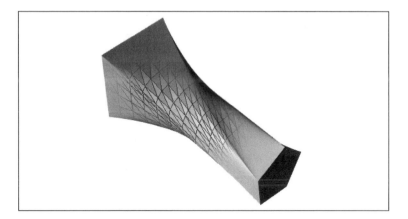

FIGURE 5-16 Once the ribs have been skinned, the resulting object would appear as it does in this image. This image was composited with the unrendered object to show how the ribs are generated and the skin applied. The ribs are not visible when the object is rendered.

Skinning is ideal for objects which are asymmetrical. **Notice that the example used for Figures 5-15 and 5-16 has a square base which gradually changes to a pentagon at the other end**. Objects which do not have a consistent profile are perfect candidates for skinning or lofting. **Because of the pour spout on the water pitcher in Figure 5-17, it cannot be lathed, yet it is a perfect candidate for skinning**. Using a number of ribs, we can easily create the pitcher and the spout. The handle was created using an extrusion along a path.

FIGURE 5-17 The teapot does not have a profile which can be lathed due to the pour spout. Using a series of ribs, each with less of a spout, makes it easy to create a realistic pitcher. The handle was created by extruding along a path.

Skinning is also very useful as a low-end substitute for creating organic objects which are more difficult or impossible to model using other modeling techniques. Objects such as animals, skeletons, and statues can be created using skinning and lofting procedures. Although the process is a very basic one, implementation can become very tedious as the complexity and number of ribs increase.

TIP: Rib placement and orientation are crucial when building a lofted object. Lofters use the rib's original orientation as a reference point when creating the "skin." Ribs that are rotated or twisting will produce incorrect geometry. When creating the ribs of an object, start with a base rib, then clone and modify it as needed for each successive rib. Continuing this process through all ribs will ensure that they are correctly oriented.

TECHNIQUE: Skinning and Lofting

1. Create a base rib using a 2D surface object. Edit the object to create the desired cross-sectional shape.

2. Continue creating ribs at all the areas where the object has the most severe shape changes. It is normally a good idea to have a sketch of the object you are trying to create to make rib identification easier.

3. Since the lofting tool is really a variation of the sweep tool, it is typical that you must identify the order in which the ribs are to be lofted. Some programs require that you link the object while others simply require that you select them in order.

4. Invoke the skin command. If the ribs have been linked in the correct order, you should get the desired shape.

FIGURE 5-18 Does not look natural, due to the missing ribs. By adding more ribs through the curves, the object has a more defined shape.

Figure 5-18 shows an object which needs more reference ribs. The solution is to undo the lofting and add more ribs to smooth out the object profile. The object in Figure 5-18 has ribs which were rotated or flipped 180°. The solution is to undo the lofting and rotate the rib which is twisting the geometry. The twisted rib is the latter rib in the linked chain of ribs where the twist occurs.

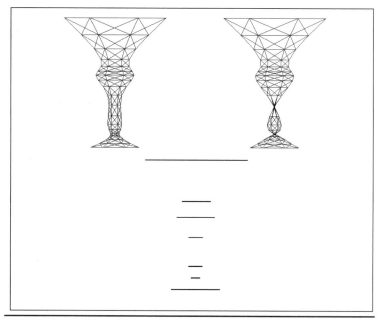

FIGURE 5-19 When ribs are flipped 180°, the resulting object becomes twisted. This is due to the path of the skinning operation which enters the ribs from the same side. Flipping the rib 180° will correct this problem.

 TIP: If the shape is too blocky, especially around curves, you may need to add more ribs to the object. When too few reference ribs are added, there are not enough in-between ribs to smooth the angle.

Bevel

Like the lofting tool, the bevel tool will create geometry from a 2D surface. The bevel command will create an additional beveled edge to a selected polygon, giving the object depth and a more 3D appearance. The entire operation will duplicate the selected polygon, shift and inset it by the values requested, and reconnect the new edges with additional polygons. **Beveling is used not only for text, but to create some interesting effects as seen in Figure 5-20.**

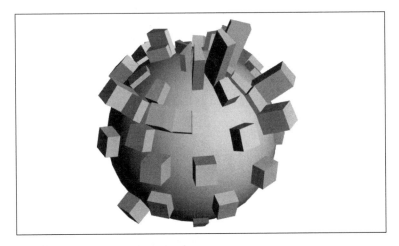

FIGURE 5-20 Beveling can be used for many types of objects, although most commonly for text. A bevel is really just an extrusion with a degree of inset.

The bevel shift amount is equivalent to the length of the extrusion. This value may be either positive or negative on any of the axes. The inset amount is the distance from the edges of the originally selected polygon and the newly created polygons. A bevel with an inset value of zero will have the same effect as an extrusion.

187

The bevel command works well on text, although some intricate fonts may result in intersecting polygons if the inset value is set too high. Be sure the inset values are not larger than one-half the width of the thinnest part of the font, to avoid overlapping and an incorrectly beveled edge.

TECHNIQUE: Beveling an Object

1. Select the polygon or group of polygons to be beveled. Choose the bevel command (provided your software has this feature).

2. Provide the inset value and the shift value for the bevel procedure. The inset value determines the distance between the new and original polygon. This value may be positive (inward) or negative (outward). The shift value determines the extrusion amount of the newly created face. This value may be positive (outward) or negative (inward).

Not all modeling software provides an explicit bevel feature. This does not mean that the feature doesn't exist, it is just a matter of using other tools. Some software provides this feature as part of the extrusion tool. By selecting different profiles, you can create beveled edges of many types.

Rounding

Like the bevel tool, rounding incorporates 2D surface objects into existing 3D geometry. Rounding is the process used to create smooth edges where two or more polygons produce a sharp edge. There are many cases in which objects have a combination of smooth and rounded edges. Typically furniture and manufactured goods have smooth edges, as opposed to sharp 90° edges which come naturally in modeling. **The cube in Figure 5-21 has been rounded along all of its edges**.

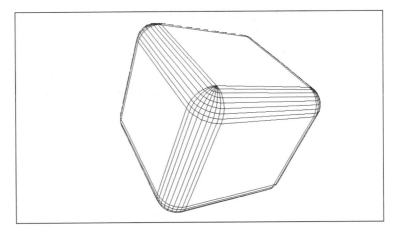

FIGURE 5-21 A rounded cube. Notice how all of the edges and corners are not sharp, but smoothly rounded. Rounding is used in many applications, since most manufactured objects do not have razor sharp edges.

Some of the higher end modelers supply rounding functions. With software which provides a rounding function, you simply select the edge to be rounded and the radius of the round. The software will then recreate the edge with as many vertices as necessary to create the smoothness of the angle requested.

Although there is a built-in feature that will do the rounding for you, there are alternate ways of creating a rounded edge on an object. Using a sphere as a template, we will recreate the object from a partial sphere. This method works well on any object which needs rounded edges.

TECHNIQUE: Rounding an Edge

1. Using the original edge as a guide, create a sphere whose edges meet, but do not exceed the edges of the corner to be rounded. Create the sphere with mesh that is dense enough to create a smooth edge (8 to 16 segments should be sufficient). **Figure 5-22 show the sphere placed in the corner**. It is best to lock the original object or work in layers when replacing geometry to avoid unwanted editing of the original.

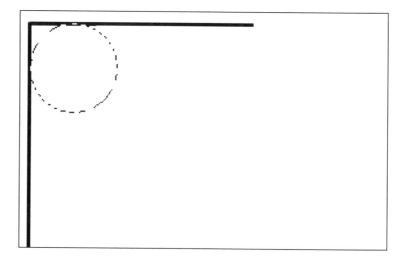

FIGURE 5-22 Using the corner as a guide in a background layer or locked down, we create a new corner by using a 2D circle which will be lathed 90° to form a rounded corner.

2. After the sphere has been completed, use a series of Boolean operations to reduce the sphere to one-quarter of the shape. This involves cutting the cube in half along the X, Y, and Z axes. Perform the Boolean along each axis separately. **When**

completed, the sphere should look like the shape in Figure 5-23.

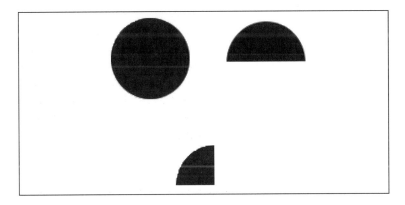

FIGURE 5-23 Divide the sphere in half until it is only one-quarter its size. Be sure to remove the back half of the sphere also.

3. What we have created so far is the rounded corner of the object. We still need to create the other corner and the rounded edge. Use a mirroring function to create the other corner. If you do not have a mirror function, remember you can create a mirror of an object by scaling a duplicate object minus 100%. Remember to check for flipped polygons on the mirrored object. Move the new corner object so that it coincides with the original corner.

4. Here's the tricky part. We now have both corners and need only to create the edge. Duplicate the curve by using a duplicate corner object or by recreating a 2D surface object curve with the same radius and same number of segments. Once created, extrude the 2D surface object to fit between the two corners.

5. Now that we have the two corners and the edge created, use the Boolean Union function to weld a corner to the edge, then the other corner to the new composite edge.

6. We are now ready to replace the old edge with the new edge. You must remove the old edge before inserting the new rounded edge. In some cases, this can be done by faceting that edge and rearranging the points so that they line up with the new rounded edge. Perform a Boolean Union to join the new rounded edge with the original sides. Merge any redundant points.

Note: As with any 3D object, it is easier to build correctly the first time than to try to edit the shape later. With preplanning, building the rounded edge into the object (instead of replacing it) would alleviate the need to remove and replace the old edge.

 TIP: If your modeling software does not provide a rounding function edit the points on a circle and recreate the rounded edge by performing a partial lathe. Once the edge has been rounded, you may replace with the old edge by performing a Boolean Subtract with the old edge on itself, then a Boolean Union to insert the new edge.

Twist and Warp

The twist function allows you to take an object and twist it (see Figure 5-24), very much like a rubber band. A simple tool to use, the twist function can be very effective for many purposes. Animating objects and including a slight twist for torso movement can be a very convincing subtlety. It is the subtleties of modeling that make the most dramatic impact on an image or animation.

FIGURE 5-24 The use of a twist function allows you to twist an object along any axis. To ensure planarity, use triangulated mesh before twisting an object.

The twist function takes as parameters the degree of twist, the axis to twist around, and the center of the twist. You may also perform this manually by clicking and dragging the mouse for a selected object. When twisting an object, be sure that the polygons have been triangulated so that the mesh will remain planar. Nonplanar polygons will cause errors and will produce holes in the object during the rendering process.

TIP: When twisting a 3D object, be sure the polygons are made of triangulated mesh. Because of the twisting of the points, nontriangulated mesh will quickly become nonplanar and will render incorrectly.

TECHNIQUE: Twisting an Object

1. Create an object to be twisted. Select the object.

2. Create a medium-sized mesh on the object's surface. Be sure to triangulate the polygons to ensure their planarity. Polygons that are not planar will result in rendering errors and leave holes in the final image.

3. Using either numeric input or by clicking and holding the mouse, select the axis in which to twist the object around. When using the mouse clicking method (Lightwave 3D), the axis which is not showing in that view is the axis the twist will revolve around. For example, if the X and Y axes are visible, the twist will occur around the Z axis.

4. Using the mouse input method, the object will continue to twist as long as the mouse button is held while the mouse is dragged.

5. If using a twist tool which requires parameters to be set in a dialog box, such as the one in Strata StudioPro or the numeric input option in Lightwave 3D, you must input the twist degree and angle. StudioPro allows you to animate the twisting sequence automatically by clicking the animate check box. Animating the twist will create keyframes at a specified number of degrees of twist. In programs which do not have the animate feature built in, you can achieve the same effect through the use of morph targets.

Bend

The bend feature is similar to the twist object, but with its focus around the object and not through it. Using the bend function, you can bend an object as though it were pliable. The bend feature may also be used in animation, by using smaller degrees of bend over time. **Animating a bend over time can give the object the illusion of being very flexible as demonstrated by the objects in Figure 5-25.**

FIGURE 5-25 Bending objects can make them appear real or as though they were made of flexible material. Bending an object may take place over time, as in animation, by creating morph targets which bend more with each successive morph.

 TECHNIQUE: Bending an Object

1. Before bending an object, be sure the polygons have been converted to triangulated mesh. As with any operation which requires geometry to create smooth curves, triangulated mesh should be used. Triangulated mesh will ensure that all polygons

remain planar and alleviates any nonplanar polygon rendering errors. After triangulating the geometry, select the object to bend.

2. Choose the bend angle through numeric input or through one of the standard axis views. Some programs control bend angle through mouse movement. If your software accepts mouse input for bend angle, click and hold the mouse as you drag it to the desired angle. The screen should redraw the object to show the amount of bend being applied. If your software uses numeric input for bend angle you may enter any amount up to 360°. **Figure 5-26 illustrates objects that have different degrees of bend.**

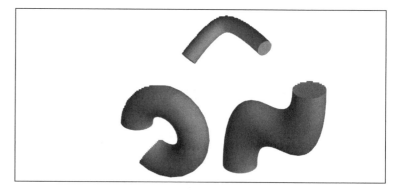

FIGURE 5-26   Objects can be bent any percentage of 360°, including higher. Using an angle of direction, objects such as springs can be created.

3. A third parameter controls the bend direction. The bend direction is in relation to the view in which the bend is being applied. A typical bend direction is 90°. This keeps the bend from being skewed in any other direction. **Figure 5-27 shows a cylinder**

with the same bend angle but different bend direction amounts applied.

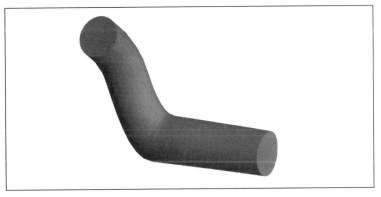

FIGURE 5-27 In this image the object was bent 90°, but also had a direction angle of 45° applied.

Stretch or Nonuniform Scale

The stretch feature, also called a nonuniform scale, enables the user to scale an object or group of polygons independently. Using the stretch feature, objects can be made longer, thinner, thicker, or shorter on selected sides. Since these are nonuniform scale tools, they do not affect all sides equally. **The objects in Figure 5-28 were stretched by using a nonuniform scale tool**.

FIGURE 5-28 Using a nonuniform scale tool, objects can be stretched and squashed along a single axis.

TECHNIQUE: Nonuniform Scale and Stretching

1. The nonuniform scale and stretch tools work by selecting an axis to be scaled or stretched. The axis can be chosen through a numeric input dialog box or by clicking the mouse on an object from one of the standard axis views.

2. After selecting the axis to scale or stretch, simply move the mouse to coordinate the degree of the scale. Typically, the nonuniform scale and the stretch tools act on one axis only, but some programs offer modifier keys to allow two axes to be affected by the operation. Check your local listings for details.

Mirror Object

To create a set of identical bookends, each of the bookends must mirror the other. Instead of remodeling the entire object again in an opposite design, the mirror tool will create an exact mirror of the object geometry. Many modeling packages include a mirror function as part of the tool set. Some programs do not supply an explicit mirror tool, but there are ways to overcome this.

The mirror tool will mirror objects, polygons, or points after they have been created. This tool can be used to create identical points as part of an extrusion object or mirror entire objects, as in the bookends example.

The mirror tool provides the capability to create complex asymmetrical shapes which involve mirrored geometry. Many manufactured objects have mirrored geometry. Chairs, desks, phones, and cars are all complex objects which contain mirrored geometry. By creating just one-half of the object and using the mirror tool, the task becomes half as difficult. The mirror tool will also ensure that objects contain exactly the same dimensions on both sides.

If the modeling software you currently use does not have a mirror function, simply create a duplicate of the object you would like to mirror and scale it negative 100%. This will create an exact duplicate of the original object. When using this method for mirroring and object, be sure to check that the surface normals are not facing the inside of the object. This will cause the front side of the object to be invisible.

TRICK: If your favorite modeling package does not include a mirror function, don't despair. In many software packages, if you scale an object to negative 100% you will have created an object that is a mirror of itself. When using this method to mirror an object, be sure to check that the normals are facing outward. If they are not, flip the normals by using a smoothing command or a flip polygon command (whichever your software provides).

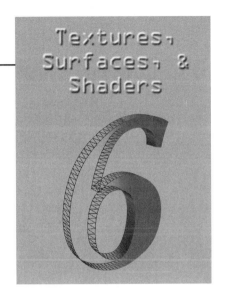

Textures, Surfaces, and Shaders

Texture is everything! For realistic 3D computer graphics, textures can make or break the image. The only single more influential element in a scene would be the lighting. Sure, modeling the object takes a lot of work, but put a bad texture on a great model and you still have a bad scene. On the other hand, if the object was not modeled perfectly, or corners were cut to save time, a good texture map can cover it up in the final render.

Since computer-generated graphics are merely mathematical and do not have any realistic characteristics of their own, surface attributes need to be applied to each object. These attributes control everything which affects the way the surface of the object looks (such as a wood grain or shiny metal), as well as how it reacts to light (transparent, smooth, rough, etc.). There are many surface attributes and all allow the 3D artist to control even the most subtle of changes in surface conditions. The surface attribute controllers are collectively known as *shaders, textures*, or *surfaces* depending on the type of software you use. For purposes of clarity, I will refer to them as shaders in this chapter, unless referring to a specific software's implementation. Figure 6-1 depicts an example of a texture dialog from Strata StudioPro Blitz 1.75.

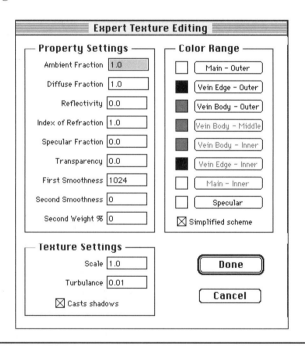

FIGURE 6-1 Texture setup dialogs such as the one in Strata StudioPro make applying textures very easy. Some surface texture editors are very numeric and offer little feedback until the scene is rendered.

Regardless of whether they are called textures, shaders, or surfaces, they all serve the same purpose—to give the object color and substance. Textures are used to turn ordinary (or sometimes extraordinary) geometry into surfaces which look like real wood, stone, or any other type of material. This is all done by setting attributes which control a variety of conditions, such as the color, smoothness, or reflectivity of a surface.

Models of a beach ball and an orange are very similar. Both are spherical, yet the beach ball is quite a bit larger than the orange. If you were to view the two objects side by side in a wireframe mode, they would be virtually indistinguishable. In fact, the same model can be used for both objects. **In Figure 6-2, I used the same model for both the beach ball and the orange, but I applied different shaders to each. This shows how a shader can really change the way a shape is perceived**. Learning how to create realistic shaders can really increase the realism of a model or scene.

FIGURE 6-2 Although the two objects look very different, the model used to create each is exactly the same. The only difference is in the texture attributes applied to each.

Shaders

As you may have noticed in Figure 6-2, the models were exactly the same, but because of the shader applied to each, they were perceived as different objects. While this is a simple example, the lesson is clear; shaders control how an object is perceived. To learn how and why a shader has this much control over objects, we need to know what a shader is.

A shader is the collection of all object attributes which control the way a surface reacts to light. Within a shader, an infinite number of possible textures and surfaces can be created. Shaders use a variety of maps (procedural, planar, and rotoscopic), colors, noise, and a host of other variables which allow for the creation of some very realistic surfaces.

Some elements are common to all shaders. These elements are the basic properties of all things in existence. They are color, shininess, bump, reflectivity, glow, transparency, and refraction. Some materials may not appear to have these attributes, in which case their attribute setting for that attribute would be set to zero or one.

Shaders also make use of surface maps. Surface maps are color or gray-scale images which are applied to an attribute. An example of a good use of surface maps is in the reflectivity field. Since there is no real environment in the computer model, we must add our own. **Figure 6-3 shows two spheres, each of which has different reflection maps applied to them**. Although they are in the same environment, their reflection maps are used to reflect different environments

FIGURE 6-3 By using different reflection maps in the same environment we can create some nice effects. The use of appropriate reflection maps as inappropriate reflections will distract the viewer and take away from the realism in the scene.

TIP: Save all shaders. When you create a shader that you feel portrays an excellent replica of a material, save the shader to an external file. Once saved, the shader can be imported into another model to be used again. Creating and saving a library of shaders means not having to repeat work.

Shader Attributes

Associated with every shader are certain attributes which influence the way an object is rendered. Essentially, the attributes of a shader control the way light is reflected when it hits the object. In rendering algorithms such as radiosity, where the attributes of neighboring objects directly influence an object, having the correct settings for each object is an important role.

Shader Color—Diffuse

Every shader must have a color. There are two color attributes which control the color of an object, the diffuse color and the specular color. The diffuse color is the color of the object in moderate light, or the actual color of the object. The specular color is the color of the highlights of the object.

Setting the diffuse color is not always as simple as choosing the color from a color wheel. Because of the other attributes set for the shader, as well as lighting, the diffuse color may have to be adjusted to a different color than the desired color so that you do actually get the desired color in the final render. Setting this color correctly may be a matter of trial and error at first to get the correct settings.

Instead of choosing a color for the shader, one may choose to use a color maps. A color map can be used to give an object many colors or a specific color pattern, such as plaid or polka dots. The color map is basically an image that is projected onto the object's surface. Color maps are used when complex color patterns need to be applied to a single surface. Since only one shader can be applied to an object in most cases, applying a color map allows a single surface to have more than one color. Color maps are used for creating backdrops, patterns on objects, or for simplifying geometry. **Figure 6-4 shows an object with a single color and one with a color map.**

FIGURE 6-4 Using a color map, many colors can be attached to a surface. Photographs, or drawings may also be applied to the object to create more realistic features through the use of color maps.

Shader Color—Specular

As objects receive light, the majority of it is reflected off the object in all directions. On places where the angle of the object reflects light directly into the camera, a highlight appears. The highlight color is called the specular color. Typically, the specular color is the same as that of the light being reflected. In metal surfaces, the specular highlight is more of a derivative of the diffuse color.

To control the specular highlight color of an object, we set the specular color attribute. The default specular color is white, producing specular highlights which are the same color as the lights being used in the scene. Using colors other than white will produce a specular highlight of that color. Color maps may also be used instead of a single color for the specular color. Using different types of color maps for a specular color can produce some interesting effects for glass and other shiny surfaces. **The pieces of glass in Figure 6-5 show how the use of a specular map affects the surface of the glass.** The glass on the left has a singular specular color, whereas the glass on the right uses a color map.

FIGURE 6-5 Through the use of specular maps, objects can be made to reflect a rainbow of colors which are not actually present in the scene.

Shininess/Gloss

The shininess or glossiness of an object give the illusion of a very smooth surface material. Since everything is not glossy, setting the correct gloss of an object's surface helps portray a material more realistically. A mug of porcelain would have less gloss than a mug made of steel, but more gloss than a mug made of plastic.

Knowing how much gloss to use takes experience and trial and error. Many times trial and error is the best way of seeing what the final output will be due to other aspects of lighting within the scene. There are a few guidelines to narrow the chances.

TECHNIQUE: Applying Gloss

1. *Low gloss:* By setting the gloss low, the object has more of a matte appearance, making the surface look rougher. Specular highlights will be more diffused giving the surface a matte appearance.

2. *High gloss:* Choosing a higher gloss setting will give an increased number of sharper specular highlights.

TIP: When increasing the gloss in a shader, be sure to lower the diffuse settings and ambient attribute values to somewhere between 60% and 70%. Having the ambient and diffuse setting too high will take away from the realism of the material.

Bump Maps

Rendering software can take advantage of its ability to simulate lighting effects to create artificial bumps and irregularities on an object's surface by using bump maps. Bump maps are used to change the angle of the surface normals of a surface. Surface normals are invisible lines perpendicular to a polygon's face. **Figure 6-6 shows how surface normals are affected by bump maps.**

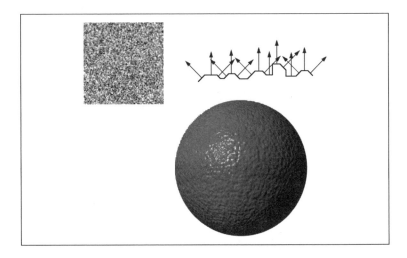

FIGURE 6-6 Applying a bump map to a surface affects its surface normals. This illustration shows how surface normals are bent to simulate changes in an object's surface where there are none.

The surface normal is used to tell the rendering algorithm which way the polygon is facing, so that the correct lighting will be applied to that polygon. A bump map is used to alter the angles of the surface normals without changing the surface geometry. During rendering, the altered normals will now reflect light according to the bump map and not according to the actual geometry.

To create a bump map, use an 8-bit gray-scale image map. The white areas in the map are used to represent areas which are raised, while black is used for areas which are sunken. The gradient area between the black and white is the transitional area which affects the lighting. Bump maps are used extensively to create surface imperfections which would be too difficult or tedious to model. **The orange in Figure 6-7 uses a simple bump map created by adding blur to a standard noise filter**. The bump map used is pictured on the right.

FIGURE 6-7 The surface of the orange on the left was created using a bump map (right) to simulate the small imperfections and pits in the orange's surface.

Bump maps can save a lot of modeling time. There are times when a bump map will work perfectly instead of actual geometry and there are times when a bump map will not be good enough. A prime example of when a bump is not going to be good enough is when the object's surface edges are shown close-up. Because the bump map does not change the surface geometry, the surface edges will appear unaffected. **As can be seen in a close-up of the orange in Figure 6-8, the edges are still perfectly smooth, unaffected by the bump map**. For close-up shots like this, a bump cannot present the illusion as well as a displacement map or other deformation tool can.

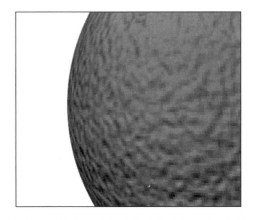

FIGURE 6-8 When using a bump map, the edges of the object's geometry are unaffected. Notice how the orange, although bumpy in surface, has a smooth curve along its edges.

TIP: When creating bump maps, add a minimum blur of 1 to 2 pixels to the map. For sharp bumps, this should not affect the sharpness of the bump, yet it will produce a better map. To make the bump softer, add a higher degree of blur to the map.

TECHNIQUE: Creating a Bump Map

- Using a paint program or image processing software such as Adobe Photoshop 3.0, create a grayscale image where white represents areas where the geometry will be high, and black represents areas where the geometry will be low. Any areas of gray will create bumps relative to the level of gray. Darker grays will appear lower than lighter grays.

Bump Amplitude

The bump amplitude attribute controls how severely the bump map is going to affect the surface to which it is applied. The roughness of an orange peel would work with a bump amplitude of 2, while the surface of the moon may require a more severe bump amplitude of 8 to 10. Changing the bump amplitude changes the influence the difference in color has on the height scale.

TIP: When using maps to affect a surface, whether it be bump, transparency, reflectivity, or any other attribute, areas of the map that are white will be affected the most, while areas which are darker will be affected the least. Varying the shader transparency level will cause the shader to use that level as its highest value. For example, if the shader transparency level is only 50%, the object at its most transparent level will only be 50% transparent. All other values are scaled according to the map applied.

Generally, a bump amplitude of 1 will have no effect on the surface. The upper limit of a bump amplitude is somewhat unlimited; for most cases, however, the most practical range may be from 2 to 10. **Figure 6-9 shows the same object with a bump amplitude of 2 on the left and an amplitude of 10 on the right**.

FIGURE 6-9 Using different bump amplitudes changes the height of the bumps created by the bump map.

Although the bump map will save a lot of rendering time, it is not always the answer to modeling geometry. At the same time, there are many times when the use of a bump map to simulate geometry is the best answer.

TIP: Use a bump map to simulate geometry when the object is in the background or the edges of the object will not be under close scrutiny. Use explicit geometry when a close up of the area in question is inevitable and the object is not animated. Animation is very forgiving, but still images are not.

Reflectivity

Whereas the bump amplitude attribute controls the roughness of a surface, the reflectivity attribute of an object's surface shader controls how reflective an object's surface is.

Reflection is the ability of a surface to act like a mirror. A mirror has a reflection value of 100%, while a material like cement has a very low reflectivity and a very matte appearance. Using the correct amount of reflectivity is extremely important. In many beginning 3D modeler's scenes, reflectivity is overused primarily because it is exciting to see the virtual environment of the scene reflected on the objects within.

 TRICK: Use a gray-scale reflection map to break up the reflectivity of an object. This can make a scene look more realistic because it makes the surface appear less perfect. Adding small variances in a surface lends to a more realistic looking object. Figure 6-10 shows the type of map that is good for breaking up the reflections on a surface.

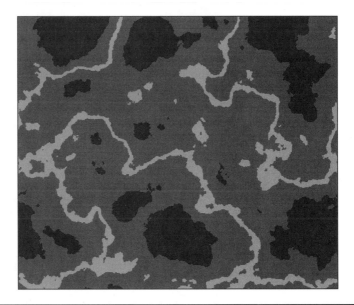

FIGURE 6-10 A reflection map can break up the perfect reflection associated with computer rendering. The whiter areas of the reflection map will have a higher percentage of reflection than the darker areas.

TECHNIQUE: For Higher Reflectivity

- Increase the reflectivity factor and specular level.

- Lower the diffuse and ambient influence.

Be assured that subtle uses of reflectivity can be more aesthetically pleasing than a scene full of highly reflective surfaces, under normal conditions. When an image or animation comes under the close scrutiny of the discerning critic, surfaces which show realistic levels of reflectivity (and the lack thereof) will be well received. **Notice how the slight reflection used in the right image in Figure 6-11 appears more realistic than on the left where a high level of reflection was used**.

FIGURE 6-11 Using the right amount of surface reflection can greatly enhance a scene. While a piece of polished marble may be reflective, very rarely will it reflect in the way that a mirror does. Adding only a slight reflection is normally more convincing than a higher reflection rate.

TIP: Let the type of material dictate what type of reflectivity is needed for the objects within the scene. Beginning 3D artists tend to add a lot of reflectivity to their scenes because it looks cool but, realistically, all objects are not that reflective. There is a time and a place for it (like the lens flare thing), but when used in subtle ways, it becomes more effective than just making everything a superreflective alloy.

Transparency

Most smooth surfaces have some amount of reflectivity, even transparent surfaces. Transparency is the ability of an object to allow light to pass through its surface. Levels of transparency range from opaque (solid) to 100% transparent (invisible). Lighting, surface glow, specularity, and other factors can alter the effect of the transparency. Objects which are very reflective, yet very transparent such as glass, are very difficult to create for the beginning modeler. Objects such as glass need very fine adjusting and often require specular and reflection maps to create a realistic effect. **Figure 6-12 shows two objects with different levels of transparency**.

FIGURE 6-12 Objects can have varying degrees of transparency. Objects which are intended to be invisible will have a transparency of 100%, while more opaque objects may have no transparency. When using transparency, you may also want to add a degree of refraction to distort objects viewed through the transparent material.

 TECHNIQUE: For Higher Transparency

- Increase transparency level.

- Lower diffuse, ambient, and specular levels and reduce reflectivity.

- Refractive values will still cause the objects seen through an object with 100% transparency to appear skewed.

Transparency Maps

Sometimes, objects are not transparent across the entire surface. To aid in creating variations in surfaces, transparency maps are used. Transparency maps can be used to create windows in a cube used to create a house. Just like the bump map, a transparency map can simulate geometry, or the lack thereof. As with all surface maps, areas of white are affected the most, while black areas are least affected. Gray shades in between white and black represent different levels of transparency. **The image of Africa in Figure 6-13 was rendered with a transparency may to produce the continent's shape from a single polygon plane.**

FIGURE 6-13 This image was created using a transparency map instead of actual geometry. By creating a transparency map out of the silhouette of the continent, I was able to mask out all of the ocean. The continent circling the globe was created with a one polygon 2D surface rectangle.

TIP: Transparency maps may be used to hide portions of geometry, to cloud glass, or to give objects "windows" where there are none (such as in an airplane fuselage).

Glow

In addition to transparency, objects may also have a glow attribute applied, like the soft light coming from a Christmas bulb. Glow is the amount of emitted light from an object's surface. Since the light in a computer environment is simulated, this attribute simulates light emitted from a surface. Since rendering algorithms cannot render actual backlighting effects, use the glow attribute to create the illusion of backlighting.

Glow values start at zero with no limit, but most objects will be fully glowing with a value of one. Although the surface may appear to be glowing when rendered, it must be understood that the glow actually produces no light in a scene, unless an algorithm which can calculate interobject diffuse illumination, such as radiosity, is used.

Glow effects are used to make an object's surface appear to glow, and will not produce light. To create the effect of the object actually emitting light, add a point light (the same color as the glowing object) in the area. Use a heavy falloff or decay, so that the entire scene is not by the glow. **For example, a candle will not only appear to glow, but it will also throw light. For the flame to throw light, you must also place a small light around the flame, as seen in Figure 6-14.**

FIGURE 6-14 Adding glow to an object makes it appear to be self-illuminated.

TECHNIQUE: Adding Glow

- Glow simulates a surface emitting light by increasing the level of reflected diffuse light.

- While there is no set limit, most objects will be fully glowing at a level of one and appear to emit light. Fully glowing objects will not light a scene, unless an algorithm using interobject diffuse illumination is used.

TIP: To simulate the illusion of an object emitting light, set its glow level close to one and place a small light at the same location as the object. Be sure to turn off shadow casting for the object which is glowing so that light may pass through it unobstructed.

Refraction

To experience refraction, place your finger in a glass filled with water. Your finger will appear to bend as it enters the water. The bending effect on your finger is known as refraction. By definition, refraction is the degree to which light is bent as it passes through a surface. Since all images we see are a result of the light they reflect, images which are viewed through a refractive material will appear distorted to some degree. Air is said to have a refractive value of one and does not refract. **In Figure 6-15 we can see refraction occurring in the bubbles, by the way the cloud texture is warped**.

FIGURE 6-15 Using refraction gives transparent objects additional realism by distorting objects seen through them.

The science behind refraction is somewhat simple. Light enters a transparent surface at some angle. As the light enters the material, it is bent to some degree, depending on the material it is entering. As the light leaves the material, the light is returned to the entering angle and sent on a path parallel to that at which it entered. **Figure 6-16 shows a diagram of how light is refracted**.

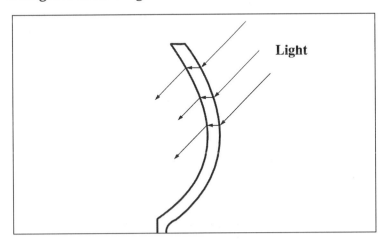

FIGURE 6-16 Light which enters a transparent surface is bent according to the density of the material from which it is made. The light will then exit parallel to the path in which it entered the material.

In computer simulation, the laws of refraction similarly apply when a surface has been set with refraction. Since objects viewed through still air at sea level have no refraction, the minimum refractive value is one. While there is no upper limit (unless set by the software), there is a practical limit. In the real world, there are no known transparent substances which have a refraction index much higher than 2.0.

TIP: When rendering a scene which contains many transparent objects with refraction, it may be necessary to increase the number of layers the raytracer will pass through before giving up. Normally, the transparency recursion is set to a modest number (around 6) which forces the light ray to pass through that number of surfaces before stopping. Using a higher number will force the renderer to pass through more surfaces. If the number of the transparency recursion is too low, transparent surfaces which exceed that number will be rendered as black. A higher recursion value also increases rendering time.

Procedural Textures

Where shaders use maps to create various patterns on an object's surface, procedural textures use mathematical equations. Procedural textures are mathematical shaders which have no beginning and no end. In fact, procedural textures are volumetric textures, meaning they are mapped *through* the object as opposed to *on* the object. **Procedural textures give the object the appearance that it was cut from a block of the material as opposed to being built with it (see Figure 6-17).**

FIGURE 6-17 Using a procedural texture guarantees that the texture will be mapped mathematically through the object, not applied to its surface. This creates patterns which follow correctly along grooves and gouges in an object's surface geometry.

Procedural textures are not maps, instead they are mathematical formulas which have colors attached to different variables within the formula. The idea behind a procedural texture is that it will look more natural because the shader is applied through the object geometry, not around it. This allows rings on wood and marble to be consistent through the object.

Procedural textures are normally associated with wood, stone, and marble and nearly every rendering program will come with at least one of each. Typically, procedural textures found with most programs will suffice as they are for some surfaces, but the real power behind the procedural textures is the ability to edit them. Tweaking the variables and colors will allow you to create an infinite amount of your own personal shaders that you may find handy for other uses. A shader which started out as marble can be edited to look like many other unrelated surfaces such as dinosaur skin or the surface of a leaf.

TIP: Use a procedural texture on asymmetrical objects which do not receive a planar texture well. A procedural texture allows the pattern to flow smoothly over the sides and around curves, as though the object was cut out of a single block of stone (or wood, marble, etc.), whereas a planar texture may stretch as it is mapped on curves.

Using Maps

Many shaders use existing 2D images as part of the surface shader. The existing images are loaded into the shader library and applied to the surface of the object for the attribute to which it has been linked. Using maps in a shader gives the modeler the ability to simulate environments and conditions which do not really exist in the scene. Maps can be used to simulate geometry, reflections, shadows, or any other attribute of lighting. Maps may also be used as artwork for floor design, labels on cans, or wooden floorboards. **All of the objects in Figure 6-18 have an image map applied to them.**

FIGURE 6-18 The use of image maps allows photographs or other rendered images to be applied to an object's surface.

 TECHNIQUE: Using Maps

1. *Create a shader:* Start with a default shader. Set the attributes to the desired values.

2. *Select the attribute:* Select an attribute to apply an image map to. The image map can be any existing

2D image. The format varies for software, but most Macintosh-based products prefer PICT, while the PC can accommodate many different types, including .TGA, IPAS .BXP, and .IFF. Some programs, such as Lightwave 3D, require that you preload the images before requesting their use in a shader.

3. *Use a map:* Use the smallest map possible to create the effect. Large maps require large amounts of memory because they must be loaded into memory at render time.

4. *Choose the tiling style:* Some software provides the ability to choose a normal or mirrored tiling style. A mirror style will place a mirror image of the shader, if the shader must be tiled. The default is a standard end-to-end tiling format.

Rotoscoping/Sequence Maps

A rotoscoping texture, or sequence map as it is also known, is used to play a movie on a surface. It is like playing an animation within an animation. An example of a good place for rotoscoping would be an animation containing a television set. As the animation brings the television set into view, the television can play an animation on the screen to make it appear as though the television set actually works.

Using a sequence map, or rotoscoping shader, the television screen surface would contain a shader which would contain a movie clip. Instead of the shader supplying the surface of the television screen with a single color map, the color map would change each frame in the animation to correspond to the frame in the movie clip. The frame rate of the film clip and the animation should be synchronized to ensure proper playback of the rotoscoped shader.

TECHNIQUE: Rotoscoping/Sequence Textures

1. *Create the rotoscoping shader:* Some software has specific shader types which handle the creation of a rotoscope shader. Others use a standard shader.

2. *Choose the movie:* If your software has a rotoscope-specific shader, you need to load the movie to use as the image map.

3. *Choose the image:* If your software uses the sequencer method, you need to select an image in the sequence. While some software such as Lightwave 3D use the format [namenumber.format] (dave001.iff), others may require you to enter the sequence identification name. This assumes that all images have the same prefix (i.e., dave001, dave002,...). Images for a sequence map must also reside in the same directory space.

4. *Set the start time:* Regardless of whether your software is a rotoscoper or sequencer, you must set the start time. Some software requires a start time, while others require a frame number in which to start the sequence running.

5. Typically, rotoscoping software which allows you to link a movie to the texture, also requires that you specify a frame rate in which to play the

movie. For video playback, animation requires 30 frames per second, but an animation can be created at any playback rate.

TRICK: Using a rotoscoping texture or sequencer can create some interesting special effects. To create an animated cloud sequence, you could film some clouds using time lapse photography, then play the film loop back on a flat plane hanging over the scene. For animation, this adds a more realistic effect than a stationary background. The use of an animation within an animation presents some powerful opportunities.

Mapping

Mapping is used to describe the angle and scale in which a shader is applied to a surface. Also included in mapping style are options that determine whether the shader will be applied in a cylindrical, cubic, spherical, or planar fashion. A shader which has been applied using the incorrect style or from the wrong angle will appear unnatural.

TECHNIQUE: Mapping

1. *Select an object:* Select the object in which the shader is to be applied. If the texture has been applied already, you can still change the mapping.

2. *Mapping angle/seam angle:* The mapping angle, also called the seam angle, is the angle at which the shader has been applied. The mapping angle is in

relation to the object's original orientation. If a wall object is oriented so that its face is along the Z axis, the shader should be applied along the Z axis. In this example, if the shader was applied on any other axis, the shader would appear stretched over the surface of the wall.

3. *Texture size:* This will scale the shader in size. Increasing the size will make the images and attributes contained in the shader larger. It is often necessary to scale shaders to fit properly, especially when using procedural shaders and image maps. When scaling a shader, start with a scale of 100%, then scale up or down by 50% each time until the desired size has been reached. Using the law of halves, this is the quickest way to find the appropriate size.

4. *Tile style:* The shader could be tiled in the standard end-to-end fashion or in a mirrored style, where the shader is mirrored along its edges. There is also an option for no tiling in which the shader will be used one tile only.

5. *Mapping style:* The mapping style is used to correlate an object's primitive geometry. A shader applied to a sphere is mapped differently than that of a cube. While most programs will provide the style which best describes the object automatically, you may want to change this for some interesting effects. See the section on Mapping Style for more information.

TRICK: When scaling a shader, use the law of halves. The quickest way to a correct number, such as shader scale, is to divide the range in half with each guess. For example, assume that the correct scale of a shader is 13%. First guess is 50. If that is too large, guess 25. The shader still looks too big, so we guess 12.5, half of 25. We now see that the shader is very close to the appropriate size and adjust slightly.

Mapping Styles

Using the primitives as a guide, most modeling software allows several types of mapping. Although a shader or texture can be applied from any angle, it is important for the rendering software to understand how the texture is to be mapped to its respective surface. By choosing a mapping shape which best describes the type of shader application you are looking for, you can be assured that the shader or texture will render appropriately.

Planar Mapping

The most basic of mapping types is the planar mapping type. Shaders and texture maps are applied to the object as though it were a flat surface. In a planar application the map is projected onto the object's surface the same way a slide projector projects an image on a screen. **A problem with a planar projection is that the texture becomes distorted around curves, as is evident in Figure 6-19.**

FIGURE 6-19 How a texture is mapped on an object will greatly influence the way the texture appears on its surface. Applying a planar surface to a curved object results in a stretched texture. Although this may be what you intend, this is not the standard choice for texture application.

TIP: Be careful when using a planar projection on an object whose surface contains curves. Even curves of the smallest degrees will distort the texture map as it is applied to the surface. At times this may be desirable and can even create some interesting effects, but at other times, unwanted distortion may occur.

Cubic Mapping

Somewhat similar to the planar projection is the cubic projection. Using cubic mapping, the shader is applied to the object equally on all six sides (top, bottom, front, back, left, and right) in a planar fashion. If the object were a cube, the surface would look identical on all sides. **Figure 6-20 shows the effects of a shader applied in a cubic mapping style**.

FIGURE 6-20 A cubic mapping style applies the surface on six sides of the object, using both sides of each axis.

Spherical Mapping

The spherical mapping style is used for objects which most closely resemble a sphere in appearance. When applied to a surface, the shader is applied along the specified axis and gathered at the poles. This produces good results on an object which is spherical but its very noticeable on cubic objects. **Figure 6-21 shows the effects of a shader applied in a spherical mapping style**.

FIGURE 6-21 A spherical mapping technique will map the texture to the object from one axis and gather the texture at the poles along the opposite axis.

Cylindrical Mapping

The cylindrical mapping style is used for objects which most closely resemble a cylinder. Objects which are long and symmetrical fall into this category. Using the cylindrical mapping style will project the texture onto the surface and allow for the natural roundness of the shape. Similar to the spherical wrapping style, the cylinder's texture is gathered at the poles. **Figure 6-22 shows the effects of a shader applied in a cylindrical mapping style**.

FIGURE 6-22 A cylindrical mapping style is very similar to spherical mapping in that it is also gathered at the poles of the opposite axis.

 TIP: When choosing a mapping style, choose the style which best represents the object. Although an egg is not completely spherical or cylindrical, either mapping style may be appropriate for that shape. Experiment with different mapping styles and mapping angles to produce interesting results.

Cylindrical with Caps

The cylindrical with caps mapping style works like a cross between the cylindrical and cubic mapping styles. In this mapping style the face gets the same mapping as the cylindrical style, while the end caps get a planar mapping style.

Figure 6-23 shows the effects of a shader applied in a cylinder with caps mapping style.

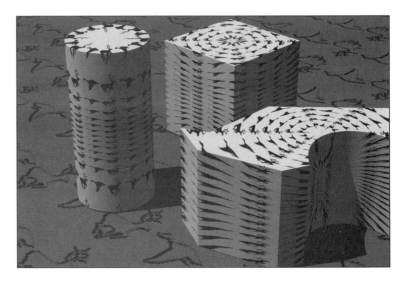

FIGURE 6-23 If we use the cylindrical with caps mapping style, the axis in which the mapping was applied will receive the traditional cylindrical mapping style, while the opposite axis will be mapped in a planar fashion.

TIP: If after many attempts, the texture or shader does not appear correctly on the object, regardless of the angle of application, try changing the type of application. Depending on how the shader or texture map was created, it may be necessary to use something other than the obvious mapping type to apply the texture correctly. Remember that when you use a mapping type other than what is recommended for that object, it may be necessary to change the application angle to suite the new mapping.

Image Map Scale and Resolution

Using the correct scale and resolution for an image map can earn big savings in the memory department and also produce a quality rendering. Using an image map that is too large wastes memory, while an image that is too small will appear pixelated when rendered from close-in or may produce too many tiles and look repetitive.

To keep the scale of an image map in perspective, use a map that will not appear pixelated when the object is closest to the camera. Scaling a map down will not affect its resolution because the data are there. When scaling an image up, data must be supplied to the pixels where there was none, so the object will appear blocky because of the duplication of pixels.

TRICK: To create an image map with the correct resolution and scale, advance to the frame where the object in question is closest to the camera. Render the frame in the quickest mode—it is for estimation only and shaders need not be present. Bring the rendered frame into an image processing program like Photoshop and use the crop tool, to crop the rendered frame down to a rectangle the size of the object in question. You can now use the cropped rendering as a starting point for the size of the image map in it shader.

TECHNIQUE: Image Scale and Resolution

- *Scale:* The scale of an image map should never be enlarged. To avoid pixelization, scale smaller, never larger.

- *Resolution:* To keep the image from getting too large, use a resolution that looks clean when the surface using the image map is at its largest.

Image Map Color Depth

When producing color images (or gray scale, for that matter), color depth should be a consideration. Color depth determines how much memory is to be used by each pixel. The higher the color depth, the more colors allowable, but the larger the file size.

An image with a 1-bit color depth will be displayed in black and white because the pixel is either turned on or off. To determine the number of colors available at a certain color depth, multiply 2 to the power of the color depth. A color depth of 8 bits equals 2x2x2x2x2x2x2x2=256. Therefore, 256 colors can be displayed at a color depth of 8 bits. Currently the range of color depth is from 1 bit per pixel to 32 bits per pixel. This gives an effective color range of black and white (1 bit per pixel) to over 16 million colors (24 bits per pixel).

Textures on Lights

Many rendering packages allow textures to be applied to lights. Light textures are also known as *gels*. Gels open up a whole world of lighting effects. Gels placed on lights can be used to create unique shadows, stained glass effects, and implied effects, such as window panes or leaves from a tree outside.

Applying a gel to a light works the same way as applying a shader to a surface. Of course, on lights there is no bump, reflection, or transparency. Using a gel on lights gives them less of a clinical look by breaking up the light. Since computer-generated light is simulated, adding a gel to lighting gives the scene a look of some randomness, similar to the real world. **The lights in Figure 6-24 have a variety of gels applied to create different lighting effects**.

FIGURE 6-24 Gels allow you to simulate simulate objects which do not exist. This is the same type of effect as creating shadow bunnies during movies by holding you hands in front of the light source.

TRICK: If your rendering software does not allow for textures or image maps to be applied to lights, there is an alternative method. Using a flat plane, create an object with the desired cut-out and place it directly in front of a spot light. Close the cone angle of the light so that it does not overlap the plane. The light will take the shape of the cut-out in the plane. Add another plane with 95% transparency and a color map attached to give the light color. Although not as elegant as a gel, this trick accomplishes the same feat.

Surface and Shader Properties

There are several surface properties which are common to most shaders. Some of the more higher end renderers offer more controls. This is a comprehensive list of the most common options in all shaders. The names may vary slightly, although every attempt was made to make the name as generic as possible.

Ambient Control

The ambient level is the degree of darkness in areas of indirect light. On a surface, ambient controls will dictate how dark an object can get when not directly illuminated. The ambient control is a percentage control meaning that an ambient level of 100% means that the objects will receive 100% of the ambient light and its surfaces will be no darker than the ambient light level set for the environment. A level of 50% means that the object will only receive 50% of the ambient light existing in an environment, making any shadows on that object appear darker.

Diffuse Level

The diffuse level of an object's surface sets the amount of light that is scattered in all directions as opposed to reflecting it directly. Objects with a high diffuse level will appear to be more of a rough surface such as the plastic of a computer case, while objects with a low diffuse level will reflect light very much like shiny metal does. The higher the diffuse setting, the brighter the surface will be when it renders.

Luminosity/Glow

Surfaces which appear to glow are said to be luminescent. The amount of the glow is controlled by the luminosity or glow level. By giving an object the ability to glow, the object's surface will appear as though it were giving off light when rendered. Luminosity and glow controls only make the object appear to glow. Unless using radiosity or another algorithm which uses interobject diffuse illumination, the glow effect will not appear on other objects. In short, the luminosity or glow from an object will not light up the scene or illuminate any other objects. To increase the apparent glow of an object, increase the luminosity factor.

Specular Level

As an object reflects light, specular highlights are created where the object reflects light back toward the light source. Specular highlights appear as spots of intense light (usually white) due to a shiny or glossy surface. The specular highlight is typically the color of the light, unless set otherwise. Materials such as metal will have lower specular levels than surfaces made of glass or plastic.

Specular Color/Color Highlights

When an object has specular highlights, they are normally created in the colors of the light sources which created them. Since the specular characteristics of a surface help the human eye decipher what an object's material is made of, adding color highlights can create a more realistic surface.

Materials such as metal will have specular highlights closer to the diffuse color than the light source color. To create more realistic metallic surface materials, set the specular highlights and glossiness to a low value, while making the specular highlights a washed out version of the diffuse color.

Glossiness

In conjunction with specular color and highlights, as well as the diffuse color, there is also the glossiness of an object which gives the human eye clues about what a surface is made of. The glossiness of an object's surface is also related to the way it spreads light. The glossiness affects the way that a surface's specular light is reflected. Since all specular highlights do not look the same for all objects, this control allows the user to control the spread of the highlight on a surface. Values set low will generate a softer highlight than a value set very high, which will create highlights as tight and bright pinpoints of light on the surface of an object.

Reflectivity

The reflectivity of an object dictates how well it reflects the surrounding objects and environment. Reflectivity levels set low will create a surface that is slightly reflective, such as a store window, while setting a value of 100% will cause the surface to act like a mirror.

Transparency

Transparency controls will make an object either more or less opaque. Setting a lower value in transparency will make the object less transparent or opaque. By setting the transparency very high, objects can be made translucent, such as frosted glass, or completely transparent or invisible. An object which is 100% transparent can still receive specular highlights which may be very visible, depending on the specular levels set.

Refraction

As light enters an object it is refracted. Refracted light is distorted as it enters and leaves a transparent surface. As the human eye sees the refracted light, an illusion of a distorted object is created. By setting the refraction level of a transparent object very high, objects seen through the transparent surface can be distorted beyond recognition. Air has a refractive value of 1.0 in a perfect vacuum. Most surfaces will never get above a level of 2.0 in refraction. Adding a slight refraction to a glass object gives a more realistic texture.

Creating Realistic Textures

Creating realistic looking textures and shaders takes a lot of effort and a good deal of practice. Because of the intricacies with each of the different rendering packages, do not get discouraged because your textures do not look the way you would like on the first render. In many cases, it is trial and error until you really understand how the rendering package that you are using handles the different attributes of the shader.

When you first start out creating textures, save all of them no matter how bad or good you think they may be. Each one you create will give you a little more experience in dealing with a virtual environment and the quirks of creating digital art.

There are a few basic keys to creating realistic textures. As always, you will find your own tricks to creating certain effects, but keep these in mind and the basics will come easier.

- Use quality maps: When creating a shader or texture map, be sure to use a quality map. This includes maps with the correct resolution, good color, and correct size. If the shader is to be tiled, be sure that any maps (bump, color, transparency, etc.) are seamless. Maps that are not seamless will leave a visible seam across the surface of the object.

- Hide seams: If using a shader or texture which uses an image map that is not seamless, be sure the seam is not visible. The most obvious trick is to place the seam where it is not visible. This requires specific mapping techniques to ensure that the image map seam will be out of view of the camera. If the object or camera is animated, be sure to keep the seam out of the view of the camera by avoiding direct line of sight with the camera or by post-production cleanup.

- Reduce reflectivity: Keep reflectivity on surfaces down. Look at the world around you. Not everything you see reflects like a mirror. It is a common mistake of novice 3D modelers to put a high reflective setting on most textures. Not only does this not look realistic, but it increases rendering time. Normally, objects which have a high gloss such as polished stone, glass, metal, or plastic will not reflect like a perfect mirror. To make a surface look more realistic, do not make it look new (unless that is the purpose). Add a gray-scale map to adjust the ambient, specular, diffuse, or reflectivity attributes. Using a gray-scale map with random swirls and splotches will help keep the surface from looking "too perfect" and will give a more natural appearance to the texture of the object.

Creating Seamless Textures

Part of creating a realistic texture is being sure that the texture is seamless. A seamless texture is one in which the left, right, top, and bottom sides will blend unnoticeably. If the texture is not seamless, a dark line may show up on the object where the shader's image maps end when rendered.

The process of creating seamless image maps ranges from very simple to very complex. It is important to be sure that, when making a seamless image, the image is not too small or the pattern too repetitious. **Seams may render as a raised ridge, as seen in Figure 6-25**.

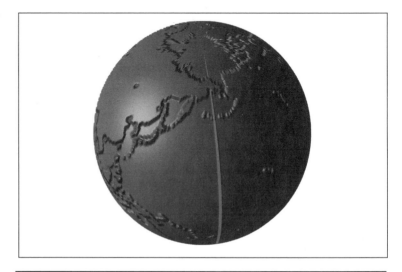

FIGURE 6-25 When using maps on any attribute in a surface, it is very important to make the map seamless if at all possible. Seams that show up in a rendered image must be cleaned up using image processing software such as Adobe Photoshop. If seams cannot be avoided for a certain texture map, place the seam in a location where it is not visible to the camera.

TECHNIQUE: Creating a Seamless Image

1. Using your favorite image processing tool (mine happens to be Adobe Photoshop 3.0), load an image to be made seamless.

2. Using an offset tool (in Photoshop it is Filter->Other->Offset), offset the image by 25 pixels in both the horizontal and vertical directions. Be sure that the wrap-around option is selected.

3. With a very small brush, use a combination of the clone tool and the blur tool to clean the seams right out of the image. Be very careful near the edges of the image to avoid making another seam.

4. When completed, offset the image back to its original position by using negative values of the same amount as the first offset operation.

5. With the image in its original position, check for any new seams that may have been inadvertently created.

TIP: Use of a texture creation program, such as Specular's TextureScape, allows you to create seamless textures automatically. Simply define the pattern and colors, and TextureScape does the rest. TextureScape can also be used to create animated textures.

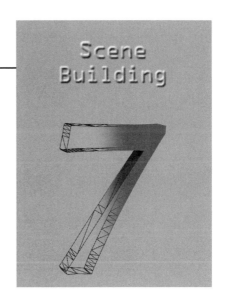

Scene
Building

7

→ Building the Scene

To create a rendered image or animation, there must be objects contained in the scene. Some software packages are designed to model objects right in the scene. Others require you to model the object in a modeler, then load the individual objects into a scene layout program. It is also not unusual to use a combination of modeling software programs to create your object and another program still to render the image or animation. There are a wide variety of tools to use, and a well-balanced tool set makes for a smoother project life cycle. A feature to look for in modeling or rendering software is the type of file formats which each can import or export. Having a wide variety of formats from which to choose will make the software more versatile.

Adding Shapes and Objects

Objects or shapes take on an important role in 3D modeling. In fact, they are not only the actors, but every prop on the stage, including the stage. No matter how you build an object, whether from a single primitive, or a combination of splines and patches, the object will eventually be placed in a scene for rendering.

To render a collection of objects, we need to build a scene of the objects we have created. You will find that some programs, such as Lightwave 3D have separate programs to model and render in, while other programs such as StudioPro allow you to model and render in the same application. Both types of programs have their advantages, but for now we are concerned with building the scene.

 TECHNIQUE: Building a Scene

- *Center pivot points:* Be sure pivot points are centered on objects or offset correctly. If the pivot point is set incorrectly, the object may not animate as intended. Setting the pivot point to the center of the object is a good starting rule of thumb. There are many times when the center point must be offset, but generally, the pivot point will be in the center of the object.

- *Name all objects:* Be sure all surfaces or objects are named or accessible. For some animation systems, such as Lightwave 3D Layout (Amiga, PC, SGI), surfaces which are not named use the default name "default." To apply shaders to surfaces in Lightwave 3D, the surfaces must be named. For complex objects made into a composite object, trying to name the surface after it has been added to other surfaces can be a real pain.

- *Avoid excessive detail:* Although computers are getting faster every year, it is important to remember that a polygon saved is rendering time earned. The most interesting scenes do not always have the most detail. Still images require more detail than does animation, generally speaking. Objects in proximity to the camera require more detail than objects farther away. Regardless of whether the detail can be seen with the human eye, the computer knows the detail is there and must calculate it even if it is too small to be seen.

- *Use lots of detail:* Contrary to the preceding point, there are times when minute detail is necessary. There is no substitute for quality. To make an image or animation the best it can be, you must supply all of the detail. There is still the law of diminishing returns, and detail should be cut only until quality suffers.

- *Use correct lighting:* Lighting within a scene is extremely important. The two most important aspects of 3D modeling and animation are lighting and textures (shaders). Lighting should be conscientiously applied and not just added until objects are visible. The lighting will set the mood of the scene or animation, and incorrect lighting will be obvious to the critic. Use multiple lights and shadow maps to create effects of softer shadows. **For lighting tips, see Chapter 8**.

- *Keep objects in line:* Check that objects do not inadvertently pass through one another's geometry. A common problem with animation is that objects may clip other objects as they move through the scene. Two common causes of object collision are incorrect motion paths and incorrect tension applied to a keyframe. Tension controls how an object accelerates and decelerates through a keyframe, as well as how it is affected through curves. Without tension, objects may stop short, move in a jerky motion, or make very wide curves which can cause them to pass through other objects unintentionally.

Null Objects

Another type of object that can be added to a scene is the null object. Although not really an object, the Null is used as a parent object as a means of controlling objects and groups of objects during animation. The Null is only visible in the layout of a scene and does not get rendered.

Null objects are also very useful when objects are related in their movement. A Null object may be used to keep the objects in sync with each other. The Null object works similar to a grouping, but objects which are child objects of the Null are not restricted in their movement as are objects of a group. Objects which are parented to a Null will retain all of their own movement but will also inherit the movement of the Null.

Null objects may also be used for models which contain many pieces or objects which are related only in the fact that they are part of the same device. Creating a stream of soap bubbles which rises out of a bubble blower and wafts across the room would require the use of a Null. The bubbles will flow in the same general direction, due to the wind or flowing air, but will also have their own free floating animation paths. In this situation, several Nulls may be used to control the flowing bubbles. Regardless of how many Null objects are used to control the individual bubbles, a main Null object would be used to move the seemingly random group of bubbles through the air along a similar, yet not exact path.

 TECHNIQUE: Adding a Null object

1. Before adding a Null object to your scene, be sure the object in which you into to parent to the Null is centered at (0,0,0). This ensures that all motion and rotation of the object will be true. There are times when an offset is desired, but it is easier to change the offset from a centered object than to change the noncentered object into a centered one after the object has been animated.

2. Create the Null object. In Lightwave 3D, you simply click on the "Add Null Object" button in the Object Options requester. You may give the Null object a name by selecting the "Save Object" button.

3. Once the Null object is created, select an object which you would like to have parented to the object. With the child object selected, press the Parent button and select the Null object from the

list. The object is now parented to the Null object and is considered a child object of the Null.

TIP: To make scene building and modification easier, name all objects, surfaces, and shaders. When creating complex scenes with many objects, it is a lot easier to find a named object than trying to remember that one particular object was called "Unnamed #25."

Delete Excess Objects and Shaders

It is a good modeling practice to keep your scene clean and free of unused objects. Objects which are loaded into a scene but not used are stealing valuable memory from your system, even if they are not within camera view. If you are not sure whether you will be using the object in the scene at a later date, save the scene under a different name and delete the object from the working copy until you decide. It is always a good idea to keep a daily backup of the working scene so that any major scene changes made one day can be undone another day.

When deleting objects, check to see if their shaders are being used by other objects. Removing excess shaders will also save memory. Image maps normally take up more memory than any individual object in a scene. Large image maps may require well over a megabyte of memory, regardless of whether they are used in the rendering process and deleting unused shaders and loaded images can save lots of memory.

TIP: Delete any unused images, shaders, and shapes from the scene. Not only will you save incredible amounts of memory, but it is a good practice to not leave stray models and images lying around your modeling space. Save the new scene under a different name if you are unsure about deleting the object.

Start an Organized Library

In animation systems that also contain a modeler, artists sometimes have the tendency to build all objects in the scene. Although this practice seems convenient at first, building objects separately can offer big savings in the long run. By creating an organized library of shapes and textures, you will always have them at your disposal for quick retrieval.

TIP: When creating libraries, organize objects and shaders into different categories such as animal, mineral, and vegetable. You may also want to make a local library for objects which are changed for a specific scene so that the original is left intact.

Since you will be creating a library of completed objects, you may want to also get in the habit of building objects to the correct scale. Building an object to the correct scale makes it easier to incorporate the object into the scene with only minor adjustments.

Consider this example: You are constructing an animation for the grand opening of a car dealership. You need to model the building, surroundings, and a lot full of cars. If you were to build each car separately, you would probably get done by the time the dealership celebrated their one-year anniversary. The logical choice is to create one car model and modify its shape or color to create different looking cars in the lot. Taking it a step further, you can build a small library of car parts and build many different cars from just a few different accessories, such as tires and bumpers.

TIP: Build all models to an accurate scale. This avoids the problem of pencils the size of houses and flowers bigger than trees. Before the first object is built, either scale the object (1 inch = 1 foot) or work in real-life measurements. Unless working on objects such as planets and solar systems, working in real scale is the least confusing and most reliable method of model construction.

Object Hierarchy

When creating a model, object hierarchy is used to create interrelated parts of objects. The same principle can be applied during scene layout and building. Using an object hierarchy, parent-child relationships are established between objects.

Object hierarchy establishes which objects are parents and which are children. Children can be parents and parents can be children, but children cannot be parents to their parents nor children to their children. What the parent-child relationship does is allow for child objects to move freely about while maintaining a relationship to their parent. As the parent object moves around the scene, the child object will follow. If a rowboat was animated, the oars would be parented to the boat. As child objects for the boat, the oars would remain in correct relationship with the boat, regardless of where the boat was moved. By creating the parent-child relationship between the boat and the oars, we need only move the boat and the oars will follow.

The reason for having this type of relationship is to keep related objects connected while allowing each the freedom of animation. While the oars move in a circular rowing pattern, the entire boat can move as a single unit. Without the parent-child link, keeping the oars in the oar locks while the boat moved and the oars rowed would be very difficult, tedious, and time consuming.

Object Center Point (Pivot Point)

When working with an object hierarchy, it is important to realize where an object's reference or pivot point lies. An object is positioned in a scene via its reference point, also known as a *pivot* or *center point*. Typically, the center point of an object is created in the center of the object's bounding box. The pivot point however, is typically created at (0,0,0) regardless of where the object itself is modeled in space. Since the pivot point and the object may not be in the same location, the visible position of the object is not necessarily the same as its given location. In other words, if a sphere's pivot point is located at the center of the sphere and placed at location (0,0,0), the object will be placed at (0,0,0) in the scene. If the center is at (1,1,0), the object will be offset by 1 unit on the X and Y axes. Having a pivot point which is not centered on an object could lead to potential problems when trying to align or animate the object. **The objects in Figure 7-1 are both located at (0,0,0) according to the pivot point**. Notice how the object on the right's physical location is different from the image in the left, due to its offset pivot point.

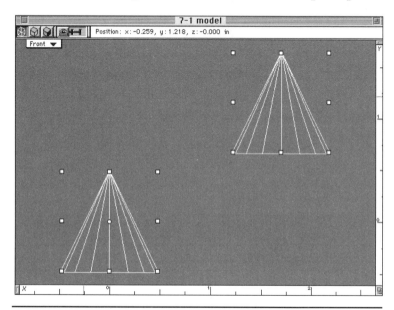

FIGURE 7-1 The position of the object's pivot point determines the location of the object. Although that sounds simple enough, the two are not always at the same location. Be sure you are aware of the position of an object's pivot point before moving, rotating, or animating an object.

The problem with a pivot point that is not centered on the object comes when animating or moving the object. When the offset object is moved, the coordinates given as feedback are those of the pivot point, not the object. When rotating or animating the offset object, the problem is compounded since the axis of the object does not reside at the center of the object. Rotations become skewed and objects that were intended to roll along may spin wildly out into space.

TIP: Before loading an object into a scene, be sure the object's pivot point has been centered on the object. There are times when the pivot point should not be centered, but at those times it is done purposely and is a conscientious effort.

TRICK: As a scene becomes more complex, the screen redraw tends to slow down. To speed screen redraws, simply replace established objects with boxes. While most software allows you to view all objects as boxes, being able to view only specific objects as boxes is not a feature I have found in any software. To replace selected objects with boxes, simply replace the shape or object with a box in the scene layout. All motion paths will remain. Be sure to attach the object's texture to the object before replacing it.

Environment Maps and Backgrounds

Since objects do not just float around in a black void, environment and background maps are added to the scene to simulate a more realistic environment in which the scene takes place. The maps range from the natural, to the mechanical, and the unnatural. You may use clouds, stars, reflective metal, oozing slime, or any other appropriate image to create an environment map. The maps are made of images which have been applied to the scene.

An environment map is an image which has been applied to an imaginary sphere surrounding the entire scene. Typically, when an image has been deemed an environment map, the software will take care of handling the way other objects in the scene handle the environment. **Figure 7-2 shows the effects of an environment map in a scene.**

FIGURE 7-2 Environment maps can more than make up for a lack of geometry. In many instances, environments are better created through the use of rotoscoping or quality images to create a realistic-looking background or environment.

Backgrounds are very much like environment maps except that they are not applied to the entire scene. Typically, the background image is used on a large flat plane, behind all other objects in the scene. A background may be used to simulate distant objects, such as a city skyline or a mountain range. Backgrounds are used in very much the same way a movie set uses a background to simulate a distant city on a sound stage. Still objects in the background are also candidates for background imaging. By rendering a single frame of the background images and applying that as a background, you can significantly cut down on rendering time.

This is very useful in complex scenes where the animated objects do not interact with those in the background image. **Figure 7-3 shows a scene where a background image was used to reduce the rendering time**.

FIGURE 7-3 Instead of modeling each and every book on the bookshelf, the entire back wall of this image is an image map. The bookshelf itself was modeled and rendered separately and the books are a Photoshop trick. While this may not be the most practical use for this trick, it is very useful for background objects which do not interact with other objects in the scene.

 TRICK: If a scene contains many objects in the background that do not interact with any animated objects, you may use a single rendered image of the background objects to cut down on rendering time. Although the image may be very large, it will still be faster than rendering many complex objects.

TIP: Let the environment map suit the environment. Since clouds do not exist inside a computer, you would not use clouds as an environment map. However, for creating reflections or a different look, there are times when you may actually use clouds inside a computer. The beauty is that you should not let conventional or even logical thinking dictate what type of environment must exist. Interesting effects can be had by using an ordinary object in an environment map.

Fog

One of the most organic substances to model is fog. With an atmospheric shader, you can add fog or haze to a scene. Adding a subtle amount of fog or haze can help create depth in a scene. Objects which are closer will be clear, while objects which are farther away may be totally engulfed in the fog. Simulated fog is strictly linear in that it does not provide areas of swirling or patchy fog. Simulated fog will appear to get denser according to the visibility distance value it is given, as discussed later. **Figure 7-4 shows the effect of fog on objects**.

FIGURE 7-4 Fog can create a sense of distance in a scene because objects farther away are engulfed in the fog.

Unlike real fog, lights which are shown through it will not produce a solid beam of light like the real world. For that effect, use a cylinder or cone with transparent edges and a glow effect to simulate the beam of light.

 TECHNIQUE: Setting Fog Parameters

- *Color*: Fog may be given any color available in the color palette. A gray fog may be used for rainy days, or pinkish hue for sunsets. The color should typically be subtle, although interesting effects can be had by experimenting with many colors. Only one color can be assigned to the fog in a scene.

- *Start Distance:* This is the distance from the camera at which the fog will start. In a foggy outdoor scene, you might set this to zero to make the fog appear to start right away. If you were to simulate a fog bank over a body of water, you may set the start distance farther, so that objects in the foreground will be unaffected by the fog effect.

- *Visibility Distance:* This is the distance at which the fog will become so thick that no objects will be visible. The smaller the visibility distance, the denser the fog.

TIP: When using fog, environment maps will not be visible. To create the same effect, use a background image on a plane just inside the visibility distance.

Fog Color

The color of the fog can be any color available to the rendering software. You would set the color by setting the red, blue, and green values, or by choosing the color from a color picker. There is no recommended setting for fog color, since the scene describes what type of fog may be in the area. Some suggestions are gray for haze and brownish orange for smog. **The image in Figure 7-5 uses the blue-green color of fog to create an underwater effect**.

FIGURE 7-5 Not only can the fog feature be used to generate fog, it can also be used to create the loss of visibility under water.

 TIP: Choose a fog color which best describes the atmospheric conditions for the scene. If the scene is a mid-summer afternoon in Los Angeles, you might want to use a fog with a heavy gray color to accentuate the smog present in the air. If using the fog to depict depth of water, you might want to use a bluish green fog. There is no definitive color to use, but you can be sure that most fog is not pure white.

Start Distance

The start distance parameter in the fog settings refers to how far from the rendering camera's viewport the fog begins. Regardless of where the camera is in the scene, a start distance of 0 will start the fog from where the camera is located. Start distance on fog is in relative coordinates, not absolute or world coordinates.

Deciding where to start the fog depends on the scene. This does not affect where the fog will become too thick to see objects. That is controlled by the visibility setting. Normally, you might start the fog at zero distance from the rendering camera. This could be perfectly acceptable unless you were going to show fog appearing on a mountain top or hovering above shimmering lake. There is no recommended setting, other than starting the fog at zero, which will affect the entire scene progressively. **Figure 7-6 displays the difference in fog start distance**.

FIGURE 7-6 Using the fog starting distance, we can create the illusion of a fog bank approaching.

Visibility Distance

The visibility setting of fog dictates how far will objects be visible before the fog becomes too thick to see any objects. The visibility is used to determine the density of the fog. With a very light fog (high visibility value), objects will be visible for a greater distance from the camera. A very heavy fog requires a low visibility value to be sure that objects which are farther away from the camera will not be visible through the fog. **Figure 7-7 shows how the visibility distance affects the objects in a scene when fog is used**.

FIGURE 7-7 The visibility distance of fog can create the illusion of a light fog or pea-soup-thick, traffic-stopping fog you can cut with a knife. The visibility distance is a measurement in units from the camera at which point objects are no longer visible through the fog.

So how do you determine the distance of the object from the camera? Knowing the distance is very important in order to correctly determine what type of settings should be set for the fog start position and the visibility. If you know that you do not want a certain object to be fully visible through the fog in a scene, you must be able to calculate its distance from the camera.

Since objects can be placed in any possible position within the scene, determining the distance from the camera is not as simple as looking at any one axis. Calculating the exact distance is fairly straightforward, provided you have a calculator that does square roots, or you are a math whiz.

The formula used to calculate an object's distance from a camera is as follows:

Distance of Object from Camera

$$=\sqrt{[(\text{Xcamera}-\text{Xobject})^2]+[(\text{Ycamera Yobject})^2]+[(\text{Xcamera}-\text{Zobject})^2]}$$

---

1 RayDream Designer 3.0 User Guide, RayDream Inc.

The object's *X*, *Y*, and *Z* coordinates are subtracted from the camera's *X*, *Y*, and *Z* coordinates and squared. The results of each pair are added and then the square root of the result is found. The final answer is the distance of the object from the camera.

To use the preceding formula, retrieve the numeric data for the camera object and the reference object. Use the coordinate data to plug into the formula.

TRICK: When using fog in a scene, the environment map will not be visible regardless of the density of the fog. This is due to the fact that most rendering software attaches the environment map to an imaginary globe surrounding the entire scene. If you have an environment map which you would like to be somewhat visible in your scene through the fog, build a sphere or cube which can engulf the entire scene and apply the environment map to the inside. Be sure the normals on the newly created environment object are facing inward (toward the camera). If the fog is too thick so that the edges of a scene are not visible, set the visibility of the fog to a higher distance.

Importing Shapes

Because the different modeling packages all offer strengths in their own areas, it is not uncommon for models in the same scene to be created using different modeling software. This is not a problem, provided the layout program and the modeling software have compatible data formats.

Currently, there is a format known as DXF (developed by Autodesk) which is common to most layout programs and modelers for import and export. The DXF format does not have the ability to retain lights, shader, or camera data. While the DXF format is not as optimized as most native formats, nearly every modeling package can read a DXF file.

Lights, Camera, Action

Building a scene is very much like creating a Hollywood film. Objects need to be loaded and choreographed, location needs to be decided, lights added, and cameras positioned. Typically, most commercial scene layout and rendering software provides an initial distant light and camera when a new scene is created. The camera is typically facing the center of the scene's universe, and the light is offset 45° overhead and 45° to the left of the camera.

While an initial light and camera are provided, these are only the bare minimum. It is rare and improbable that the default settings are exactly what the new scene requires. They are provided as a means of reference and are intended to be adjusted.

For a more realistic look to your scene, you will need to add additional light sources. The type of scene and mood you are trying to portray also influence the type and number of lights that you will need to add to your scene. In the real world, light is reflected off of everything around us, creating soft shadows. In a virtual 3D world light is simulated and does not act exactly the way its real-life counterpart does. To create a softer shadow, additional light sources need to be added to the scene. Lighting is discussed in detail in the next chapter.

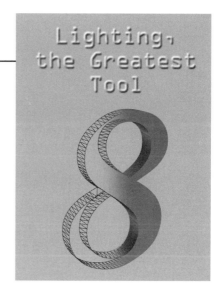

Lighting,
the Greatest
Tool

8

How Lighting Affects a Scene

Lighting is the most influential aspect of three dimensional modeling and animation. Lighting can be used to create a mood or atmosphere. Lighting can be used to imply objects which are not visible, such as the shadow created from the leaves on a tree overhead. We can also use lighting for visual impact as in explosions, lens flares, and distant stars.

In every visual experience, lighting is very important. Just like a photographer or a movie director, lighting can be used to convey many messages. By changing the color, position, or texture of a light source, many things can be implied. We could animate lights, changing their position and color over time so as to simulate the passing of time, such as from midday to sunset. Or we can show a dark, moonlit trail in which the light has a blue hue, and only silhouettes and a few shapes are discernible.

Having all this capability makes lighting a very powerful tool. Learning to use lighting correctly will benefit every 3D artist from the most basic to the most advanced special effects artist. **The image in Figure 8-1 contains many lighting techniques used to create the mood of the image**.

FIGURE 8-1 Many different lighting techniques were used to create the light in this scene, including gels and multiple lights.

TIP: Objects which do not receive light will not be visible or may appear black when the scene is rendered. When an object appears black or is not visible, check the value of the main light source and ambient light and increase slightly. You may also check to see that the object polygon normals have not been flipped. Flipped normals on a polygon render the polygon invisible since the polygon is being viewed from the back and there are no normals on the back side of a polygon unless they were created as double-sided polygons.

Light Properties

Lights, just like objects, have many properties. They may have textures applied to them and they may be animated. Some programs offer conventions which allow the light to change its properties over time. This can be used to create stunning effects, such as the pulsating light of a beacon or spaceship exhaust. **In Figure 8-2, three spotlights with textures applied to them were used to create the different shadow effects**.

FIGURE 8-2 The use of textures on spotlights, called gels, helps create funky shadow patterns, including simulated geometry such as people and trees.

Position

Lights can be positioned anywhere within a scene. Through the positioning of the lights in a scene, softer shadows, correct highlights, and special effects can be created. **Figure 8-3 shows the position of three lights used in a studio setup**.

FIGURE 8-3 A typical studio light setup.

Placing lights within a scene is not a random process. The minimum number of light sources should be used to create the desired effect, since each light source added to the model will significantly add to the rendering time. Incorrect lighting will also make the scene look unnatural. Special attention must be given to each light to avoid a scene which has incorrect shadows or conflicting light sources causing mirrored shadows when that effect is not desired.

Direction

The direction of the light is the direction in which the light will travel. Light can come from any direction, or can be animated to move about the scene, changing its direction as it travels. The direction of the light, together with the position of the light, can be used to imply a variety of moods and time settings for the scene.

Between the distant, spot, and point lights, direction has a slightly different meaning. For an omnidirectional light source, such as the point light, light will spread outwardly in all directions from the center point of the light source, while the spot light and distant light will only shine in one direction at any given time. **Figure 8-4 illustrates the use of light from different directions**.

FIGURE 8-4 Lights can be aimed in any direction. The use of multiple lights in different directions helps soften harsh shadows.

Color

Another lighting parameter that can have a strong influence on the scene is the color of the light. The color of the light can be used to imply indoors or out, as well as clinical lighting or nightclub atmosphere. Using soft orange and red lights can give the impression of a sunset, while using white and light yellow lights positioned overhead can give the same scene the impression of midday.

Because all objects reflect light, the color of the light can greatly change the color of the objects within a scene. When adding color to a light, typically only of hint of color will go along way. Colored lights should also have a higher falloff rate so as to not discolor the entire scene while providing highlights only on certain objects.

Typically colored lights are used in a local area, such as in a street light, while a white light is used to illuminate the scene. This allows the color of the light to be utilized, while maintaining proper color balance for the rest of the scene. **The streetlight in Figure 8-5 uses four different light sources**. The falloff of the lights within the streetlight is set very low and the decay is set high, so that they will only illuminate the fixture itself and not the entire scene.

FIGURE 8-5 For the lights in a streetlight, the decay or attenuation is set very high, so that the signal light does not illuminate the scene except in the immediate area.

Light Size

In the real world, lights come in a variety of sizes and shapes. In simulated lighting, the shape of the light does not matter unless your animation system supports visible lights. However, the size of the light does make a difference when rendering. The size of the light is changed to fit inside of small areas. While the size of the light does not affect its intensity, if the light is larger than the object which contains it, the light will also be used to illuminate a scene (See Figure 8-6). Although the size of the light may be changed, this does not affect the brightness or the distance in which the light shines. To set those parameters, use the light intensity and attenuation parameters respectively.

FIGURE 8-6 Changing the size of a light does not increase its intensity, but it could cause light to shine in places it was not intended. Be sure a light source which is contained within an object does not go beyond the object's geometry.

Intensity

The intensity of the light is an artificially set value which dictates the strength of the light. Lights with a high intensity value will produce the effects of a very bright light, while a lower intensity will produce a light that seems to glow more than illuminate. Typically the intensity value is a percentage factor and not an absolute value such as candle power, for which to compare settings.

The intensity of the light is a property which may be different for every light source in a scene. Since some lights may shine brighter than others, you should set this property accordingly. For example, if a candle and a lamp were both in a dark room, the intensity of the candle light source would be much less than that of the lamp. For each software program, the values of the light source differ. Typically though, the maximum value for a light source is 100%, although some programs allow you to set this number higher. For programs which do not allow the light to be set higher than 100%, simply add another light to the scene if you need more light. **Figure 8-7 demonstrates the difference light intensity can have on the scene**. The image on the left uses an intensity of 80% while the image on the right uses an intensity of 15%.

FIGURE 8-7 A candle can have different light intensities.

Falloff and Attenuation

The falloff of a light source is the amount of decay across the beam of light. The attenuation is the distance at which objects are no longer illuminated by that light source. Using the candle and lamp example, the falloff and decay of the candle may be set at 24 inches, while the lamp may be set to 15 feet. Remember that objects are only visible when they are illuminated by some light source. Unless a light source is set to infinite falloff, the light will be brightest at the location of the light, and will begin to deteriorate and become less intense as the distance from the light source increases.

Although the falloff of a light source may be set to a particular distance, objects which are located just inside the outer limit of a light source's falloff may not be illuminated. **For example, in Figure 8-8 the candlestick's falloff is set to 24 inches, yet the matchbook, located 23 inches from the lit candle, is barely visible.** Because the matchbook is near the limit of the falloff, there is very little light reaching it.

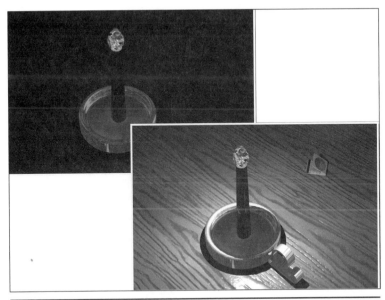

FIGURE 8-8 Though the light is very bright near the candlestick, the room quickly gets dark as you move away from the candle. Due to attenuation and falloff, the matchbook is barely visible in the scene.

Spread

The spread of a light source determines the angle from which the light moves outward from the center of the light source itself. In an omnidirectional or point light, the spread is equal in all directions. The term *spread* is primarily used when referring to spotlights. The spread angle of a spotlight directly affects the cone of light which it produces.

The spread of a spotlight is twice the angle setting. Spotlights can have any angle setting from 0 to 90°. A spot light with a setting of 90° will have a spread of 180°, while a setting of 45° will have a spread of 90°. The spread angle can be used to create different sized circles of lights in which to illuminate surfaces. **Figure 8-9 shows the use of various spotlight sizes on a scene.**

FIGURE 8-9 By changing the spread of the spotlight, we can create different sized circles of light.

Textures and Gels

Just like objects contained within the scene, some programs also allow lights to have textures and shaders applied to them, called *gels*. Using a shader on a light source allows the user to change an ordinary light into an impressive stained glass window display or a simple silhouette of a window sill. Adding a shader to a light source is a popular practice that helps simulate many different settings and special effects. **The image in Figure 8-10 has a light source with a gel to create the window sill effect on the scene.**

FIGURE 8-10 A gel was used to create the impression of light coming through a window and casting a shadow on the far floor and wall.

Types of Light

As in the real world, there are different types of lights. In 3D modeling, lights are classified by their characteristics, and not so much by their shape. In any one scene, there may be any combination of light types. In almost every scene, there is both ambient and distant light to give the entire scene illumination. Point and spotlights are added to illuminate specific areas of the model, without affecting the entire scene.

Ambient Light

Ambient light is described as indirect light, such as the light under a shady tree or in an unlit room. Ambient light comes from being reflected off of nearby objects. In the real world, ambient light comes from everywhere, since all things reflect light, including the atmosphere. Because there is no atmosphere on the moon, the shadows are very harsh. Ambient light makes the shadows softer.

In the simulated 3D environment there is no atmosphere, so light is not automatically reflected. Through the use of an ambient light setting, you can artificially set what the reflected light is going to be in the scene. By setting the ambient light, shadows can be lighter or darker, depending on the ambient light setting used. **In Figure 8-11, we notice lighter shadows due to the high ambient light setting**.

FIGURE 8-11 Using a high ambient light setting can create the loss of shadows, making the scene look flat.

Ambient light, unlike other lights, is not a physical entity. There is no ambient light object which needs to be inserted into a scene. The ambient light will exist throughout the scene in the same degree. Changing the color of the ambient light can be used to the same effect as changing other lights. It can control the scene mood and time of day. Typically, ambient light may be set in the midlevel gray to blue setting, although it can and should be changed to fit the needs of the scene.

TIP: Setting the ambient light too high will cause the scene to lack contrast, causing a scene to look flat. Use subtle color changes in the ambient light to make a more dramatic impact in shadows. Evening skies usually call for ambient light to be more blue, while daylight skies call for more of a midgray color.

Global or Distant Light

Used in conjunction with the ambient light, the global light or distant light is very much like our real-world sun. The sun is very far away, and everything on earth receives the same amount of light (excluding weather conditions). Because it is so far away, it appears that the rays of light from the sun are parallel.

In the virtual space of a 3D model, we can simulate the sun by creating a light which has the same characteristics. All objects receive the same amount of light from the global light regardless of their distance in the scene. In most modeling software, when a new scene is created, this default light is provided. Although it is normally located overhead and to the left of the camera, its position can be changed. Regardless of where the global light is placed in a scene, the only thing that actually changes is the direction in which its light affects the scene. **We can see by the image in Figure 8-12 that regardless of the objects' positions in the scene, they still receive the same amount of light from the global light source**.

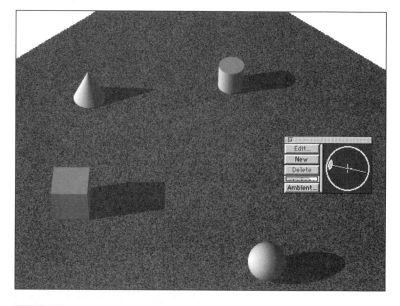

FIGURE 8-12 Objects receiving light from a global light source are equally illuminated.

Point Light

Unlike the global or distant light, the point light shines light in all directions. The point light is like a general-purpose light used for illuminating portions of the scene. In many programs, it is symbolized by a lightbulb because that is how it reacts. It will shine in all directions from it position in space. Unlike the global light, the point light can have a value of attenuation or decay. The decay of light, also known as attenuation, is the distance at which the light will no longer illuminate objects.

Point lights are very useful for increasing the light within a scene, adding lights to objects that seem to glow, or for casting shadows of implied objects, as well as other general-purpose lighting needs. The point light may also use colors, textures, falloff, and intensity to create the visual effects of color and geometry.

Point lights are placed inside such objects as lamps to make the object appear to be producing light. While the light itself is not visible, its effect on other objects is very apparent. **In the candle example in Figure 8-13, we use a point light because the characteristics of a candle dictate that light is spread in all directions**.

FIGURE 8-13 A point light, such as the candle, will spread light in all directions.

Spotlight

Since a point light shines light in all directions, the spotlight is used to illuminate specific objects or areas of a scene. The spotlight is a simulated version of its real-life namesake. The spotlight is used to create a cone of light which can be directed to a specific area within the scene. The edges of the light can be hard or soft. The spotlight may be positioned anywhere in 3D space and be pointed in any direction. Spotlights may also be made to follow an object similar to the way an actor on stage is positioned in a spotlight.

Light from the spotlight can be directed in a specific direction and with a limited amount of spread. The spread allows the circle of light created by the spotlight to become larger or smaller. Light will not be cast on objects which are behind the spotlight or outside its spread.

The spread of the spotlight controls how thin or how wide the light source spreads from the illumination point at the center of the spotlight. The spread or cone angle of the spotlight is from 0 to 90°. The cone angle will produce a spread of twice the value of the cone angle. Thus, a cone angle of 45° will produce a spread of 90°, while a cone angle of 90° will produce a spread of 180°. As the simulated light moves farther away from the light source, the spread increases, as does the area of illumination. **Figure 8-14 shows the effects of a spotlight on objects within the path of its light.**

FIGURE 8-14 Unlike the point light, the spot light can shine light in one direction only. The spread angle of the spotlight is used to create larger areas of illumination.

TIP: Be careful when setting the angle of spread on a spotlight. Because the circle of light changes with the distance between the object and the spotlight, the angle and distance of the light should be set before the angle of the spread. This holds especially true for spotlights which have been attached to objects, such as a model of a spotlight, flashlight, or car headlights.

Overexposure

Adding the various lights to a scene can lead to overexposure, if not carefully monitored. Overexposure occurs when the lighting in a scene becomes too intense. Overexposure can be avoided by using a light's decay or falloff feature. **We can easily see that the image in Figure 8-15 is overexposed because the lights' intensities are too high**.

FIGURE 8-15 Too many lights or too high of an intensity setting can create a washed-out image.

While it is necessary to add multiple lights to create a more realistic scene, more lights mean there is a greater chance of overexposure. To lessen the potential of an overexposed image, be sure that only necessary lights are used. Each light added to a scene increases the rendering time exponentially because the light has the potential to affect every object in the scene.

TECHNIQUE: Avoiding Overexposure

- *Check light intensity:* Every light does not have to be at 100% intensity. In fact, the more lights within a scene, the lower the intensity of each light may be set. Start with an intensity of 50% on all lights and adjust each light according to the desired effect. Not every light should be set at the same intensity level.

- *Use falloff and attenuation:* Some scene layout programs give lights a default setting of infinite falloff. While an infinite setting may be appropriate for some scenes, it is not practical to have all lights set with an infinite falloff. Setting the appropriate falloff will decrease the chance of a hot scene.

- *Light setup:* When using multiple lights, be sure that they are illuminating at the correct angle. In a standard studio light setup, there is a main light source, a secondary light source (placed 45° overhead and to the side and set at half the intensity of the main) and a backlight (behind the subject and with the same intensity as the main light). If the angle and intensity are incorrectly set, the scene may appear washed out due to too much direct light.

- *Check ambient settings:* Be sure that the ambient settings are not abnormally high. A high amount of ambient light will not only wash out the scene, but the entire scene will become flat with the lack of contrast between light and shadows.

- *Check surfaces:* Often, when many objects are hot, it gives the appearance of the entire scene being hot. To be sure that the object surfaces are not the cause of the hot points in the scene, check the surface reflectivity and luminosity. These two attributes can cause the object's surface to reflect too much light.

Checking Overexposure Using a Light Meter

To keep a handle on lighting within a scene, programs such as Strata's StudioPro and Vision 3D provide a light meter. This light meter is useful for avoiding casual overexposure when additional lighting is added to a scene. **The light meter used in Strata StudioPro is pictured in Figure 8-16**. The light meter consists a green bar which grows toward a red zone as the light in a scene increases. When a combination of global, spot, directional, and ambient light reaches a hot point, the light meter will show red. The red indicator in the light meter indicates that there is possibly too much light and that the scene may be washed out. In the end, it is the human eye that will decide if the image has the correct lighting, so use your own judgment for making the final decision on lighting.

FIGURE 8-16 A light meter from Strata StudioPro

Multiple-Light Studio Setup

Once all of the objects have been added to the scene, the lighting needs to be adjusted to produce the desired effect. There are so many possible combinations of lights that it is impossible to discuss them all. In fact, every scene can have its own special lighting needs and must be dealt with on an individual basis. **Figure 8-17 is a setup used to create a triple spotlight effect on a stage**. Each of the spotlights is one of the primary light colors, red, green, and blue.

FIGURE 8-17 Using three different colored spotlights, you can break up the shadows around the subject or mix colors for lighting effects.

Typically, a multiple-light setup is used in studio photography. The reason for this is to soften the shadows and bring out more highlights on the subject. By using a multiple-light setup in 3D modeling, we can create a similar effect. Using this as a basis for lighting objects, we can apply the same technique to many objects and to the scene in general.

The main light source works the same as the global light source in a 3D scene: It lights the scene. Normally, the main light is placed 45° off center and toward the front of the scene, either on the left or the right side of the camera. A second light, known as the fill light is used to soften the shadows. Since there is no atmosphere in a virtual model, the fill light is used to diffuse the shadows. Using a fill light on the opposite side of the camera (with an intensity of 50% of that of the main light) will help soften shadows.

The third light is placed at the back of the scene, overhead. This will also help soften the shadows and add highlights to the scene. Since light itself is not rendered, only its effects, place the backlight high enough to create highlights aimed directly at the top of the subject. Lights that are placed behind an object will add light to the scene and highlights on objects within the scene, but will not produce a glow of light behind the object as in real backlighting.

TECHNIQUE: Multiple-Light Studio Setup

- *Main light:* This light should be placed 45° on either side of the camera and overhead. Depending on the type of lighting desired, the intensity should be set to illuminate the entire subject.

- *Secondary light:* This light should be about half the strength of the main light source and should be on the opposite side of the camera as the main, and overhead as well. This light is used to soften the shadows.

- *Backlight:* The backlight should be as strong as the main light and directly behind the subject. The backlight is used to give the subject highlights and will also help soften the shadows.

Backlighting

Backlighting can help add depth to a scene by providing highlights which would not be present with the use of only a main light. The backlight will also make the silhouette of the subject more pronounced, an effect which is sometimes desired for its visual effectiveness. **The jewelry piece in**

Figure 8-18 uses backlight to give the gold pieces more highlights.

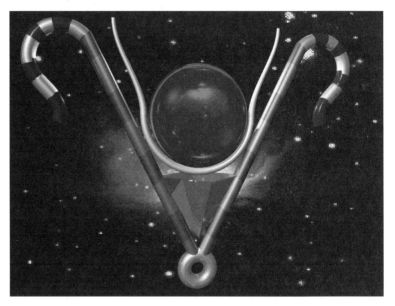

FIGURE 8-18 Backlighting can be used to give the subject more highlights.

TECHNIQUE: Backlighting

- *Position:* Either a spotlight or directional light may be used when creating backlight. The backlight must be placed behind the subject and to either side or above the subject. The direction of the light should be aimed at the back of the subject, toward the top edge.

- *Intensity:* The intensity of the backlight should be about the same as the main light. For different effects, you may want to increase the backlight and decrease or remove the main light. As a supplementary light, the backlight should not be so intense as to cast heavy shadows on the front of the subject.

Outdoor Daylight

Producing realistic outdoor lighting can be somewhat tricky. The sun produces light which is reflected from all objects. In a virtual environment, there is no atmosphere so the ambient light must be simulated. Having the correct color and intensity of the global light source and the ambient light source are key for creating realistic outdoor lighting.

To create more realistic outdoor lighting you must first decide what time of day the scene takes place. Depending on the time of day, the colors used in lighting a scene can vary dramatically. Choosing a time such as morning or evening will afford the scene many colors and longer shadows, making for a more dramatic scene.

TECHNIQUE: Outdoor Lighting

- *Type of light:* For outdoor lighting when you are trying to duplicate the effects of the sun or moon, use a distant light with the appropriate color for the time of day.

- *Color:* Scenes which take place at dusk or dawn have the most colorful lighting of the day and can be used to make a more interesting scene. When setting the color, use a hot color (such as orange or yellow) for the global light and a cooler color (blues) for the ambient light.

- *Position:* To portray an accurate mood for a particular time of day, set the light in a position which coordinates with the time of day. While overhead would signify midday, this setting is not desirable from a lighting standpoint. If you must use midday lighting, increase the ambient light dramatically.

Nighttime Lighting (Moon Effects)

Creating light for a nighttime scene requires different parameters than those for the same scene during daylight hours. During the day, light is bright and everywhere. At night, light is somewhat dimmer and decays faster. Since light at night comes from the light reflected from the moon, the light tends to be of the blue hues. Shadows are longer, darker, and many will run together, creating larger areas of shadows.

 TECHNIQUE: Night Lighting

- *Heavy decay:* Other than moonlight, any light which shines during the night is artificial. Artificial lights (flashlights, floodlights, streetlights, etc.) tend to have a heavy decay or attenuation rate. This means that the light will be brightest closest to the source but will quickly become dimmer as the light moves farther away. Setting the decay rate very high or the falloff very short, gives the effect of man-made light, typical in a nighttime scene.

- *Low intensity:* Typically, most of the light will have a low intensity. Unless using heavy spotlights, most lights at night are somewhat dim. Compared to the light of the sun and during midday, street lights and the like are very dim. To make the scene believable, use low intensity on all lights. If the scene is too dark, add more lights or increase the ambient light.

- *Low ambient light:* When creating a night scene, take note of what the world around you is like during the night. The shadows are very dark, and you may notice that most of the area is in shadow, unless directly in the path of light. The ambient light, or light reflected from other objects is very low. In fact, ambient light should be set very low with a bluish hue for convincing night-time ambient light.

- *Bright environment map:* To create nice highlights on objects during a night scene, use a reflected environment map with lots of color and light. This effect gives reflective objects very nice highlights which stand out against the dark environment.

Indoor Lighting

Indoor lighting comes in a variety of flavors. Almost no two situations are alike. "Indoors" can mean anything from a hospital, to a cozy cabin with a big fireplace, to a catacomb, deep below an evil castle. Whatever the scene, the lighting will convey the mood of the scene. The difference with indoor scenes is that the time of day does not have the same influence that it has on outdoor scenes.

When creating indoor scenes, use a variety of the studio lighting technique described earlier in this chapter. While the studio setup is not the cure-all for lighting, it will give you a basis for starting the scene. For each scene, you must really experiment with your own lighting techniques to create the exact effect you desire.

TIP: When adding lighting to a scene, let the source of the light control the way a scene is lit. The midday sun does not light the scene the same way that a row of torches will light a castle dungeon. Different light sources all have different characteristics, and it is these characteristics which add the subtleties that bring life to the scene.

Gels (Gobos)

Many rendering packages provide for images to be applied to light sources. The image placed on light sources is called a *gel*. In theater and stage productions, they are slightly different, but have a similar effect and are called *gobos*. Gels are a very powerful tool in that they can create very special lighting effects. Any image may be used as a gel, whether it is a color or gray-scale image. Images which are 1 bit (black and white with no shades in between) will act as a mask.

Gels are very powerful in that they can imply geometry which does not actually exist. Gels can be used to cast a shadow of a tree outside a bedroom window where no tree actually exists. Color gels can be used to flood a room with brilliant color, such as in a stained glass window or a night-club's dance floor lights.

Creating a gel is as simple as applying an existing image to a light source. Images used as gels do not have to be very high resolution, since they will be distorted as the light lands on different objects within the scene. **Figure 8-19 shows the effects of a gel**.

FIGURE 8-19 Gels are an important part of lighting a scene because they can cast multiple colors or shadows, as needed.

TIP: Use gels anywhere any type of special lighting is needed. If a light is intended to shine through a stained glass window, make the stained glass window object only slightly transparent and add a light with a gel containing the same image used on the stained glass object on the viewing side of the glass. Adjust the light source so that it is subtle enough to throw color highlights and color on objects without filling the entire scene (unless that is what is desired).

For programs which do not allow textures to be applied to a light source, we can use the old theatrical trick known as a gobo. A gobo is a cutout used to shine a light through to create visual lighting effects. Gobos can be created using a 3D plane with any type of shape or text cut out of it. **Figure 8-20 contains a simple gobo and shows the effect it has on the scene**. You may also apply a color map to the gobo and set the transparency level high enough so that colored light is spread over the scene. When using a gobo, you must render the scene with a ray-tracing algorithm so that the object can cast a shadow over the scene.

FIGURE 8-20 The use of gobos is an old theatrical trick.

Creating Visible Light

Although they are an important part of lighting, most software does not allow for visible lights in a rendered scene. While the effect of a light is apparent, the light itself is not visible. Visible light is used for many effects such as light from a lighthouse on a foggy night or lasers from a spaceship. The use of visible light can create very realistic subtleties which really add to the overall composition of a scene. **The light in Figure 8-21 was created by modeling the light and inserting a light object inside it to give it light**.

FIGURE 8-21 Visible light can be used wherever a beam of light is visible, such as headlights through the fog, or when using fluorescent tube lights.

Two properties make visible light unique. There is a certain amount of glow on the object and the object actually emits light. In some cases, the light may also have a bit of transparency applied to it.

TECHNIQUE: Visible Light

- *Model the light:* Create an object which is going to be the shape of the visible light. This object could be in the form of a lightbulb, fluorescent tube light, or any other shape of light you can design.

- *Set the glow:* The shader for the modeled light should contain a percentage of glow. Set the glow attribute to a value in the 25% to 40% range as a starting point and adjust as necessary.

- *Transparency:* Depending on the type of light, you may want to set the transparency of the object to a very high amount. *Note:* Setting a high glow rate will make the object opaque regardless of the transparency value used.

- *Transparent edges:* If your rending software has this option, now is the time to use it. By setting the edge transparency to transparent, you can create light beams which do not look as hard as nontransparent edges.

- *Don't cast shadows:* In the surface or texture settings, turn off any shadow casting abilities for the modeled light. This includes self-shadows, receiving shadows, and casting shadows on others. Since this is supposed to be a light source, it will be emitting light, not blocking it.

- *Add a light inside:* To give the modeled light its ability to cast light, we must add a real light source inside the model. You may have to scale the light so that it fits inside the object or you may have to use multiple lights for objects such as the tube light.

- *Attenuation and falloff:* Be sure to set the attenuation and falloff rate for the light inside the modeled light to reflect the proper type of light. For cases like the tube light where multiple lights are added to the model, you should set the attenuation and falloff so that the lights will blend together as they leave the modeled light object.

Glowing Lights

When creating visible light, we often want them to glow. A neon sign is a glowing light which emits low amounts of light. A glowing light emits only a small amount of light compared to a real light source. Glowing lights are not intended to create enough light to light an entire scene, but the light which is emitted from their surface is sometimes enough to illuminate a nearby object. **The object in Figure 8-22 has enough glow set that it actually appears to glow**.

FIGURE 8-22 Glowing lights appear to be emitting light. A neon light is an example of a light which tends to glow.

Since only a few rendering packages can create visible light (Electric Image Animation System being the best), there are many times when a glow light must be modeled. To create a glowing light, the shape of the light must be modeled, with a low level light surrounding the object.

TECHNIQUE: Creating Glowing Lights

- *Build the light:* Create a model of the shape of the desired light. The light can be any shape, such as a lightbulb or a neon sign.

- *Color and add glow to the light object:* Add a desired color to the light object and desired glow intensity to the surface shader.

- *Turn off shadows:* In the modeled light object's texture shader, be sure to turn off all shadow attributes, such as shadow casting, receiving, and self-shadow.

- *Color light source:* Color the light source the same color as the modeled light object.

- *Light intensity:* Set the intensity of the glow light source to about 75% to 90%, depending on the type of object it is to represent.

- *Set decay:* Allow the glowing light source to decay very rapidly. Glowing objects have a tendency to be bright, yet the light they produce decays very fast. A falloff of only a few inches or less can be very effective.

- *Position light source:* Position the glow light source in the same position as the glow object. You may need to add duplicate light sources along longer light objects to simulate light coming from the entire object. Because the object is set to not cast any shadows, the light will pass right through its geometry when positioned in the same space.

Lens Flares

A variation of a glowing light is the lens flare. The ever-popular lens flare makes it way into many space animations and corporate logo treatments. A lens flare is an option attached to a light which replicates the effect a light has as it is directed into the lens of a camera. Because of the

reflections of the light inside the lens, there are color arti-
facts which appear as colored circles on the opposite side of
the frame as the light source. This effect is used to give the
animation or still image the illusion that it is a real photograph or footage of a real object. **The image in Figure 8-23
incorporates a lens flare into the scene**. Notice the light
reflected opposite the light source in the frame.

FIGURE 8-23 A lens flare is used to simulate the light reflecting off of a
camera's lens.

While some programs such as Lightwave 3D and Electric
Image Animation System have an option for creating lens
flares, most other rendering software does not. This effect
can, however, be recreated using filters in Adobe Photoshop.
While this is great for still images, it can become very time
consuming when producing animation to recreate the flare
in every frame.

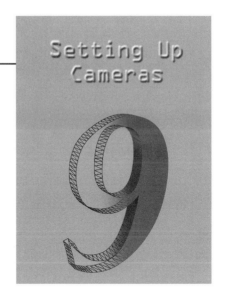

Setting Up
Cameras

9

➤ Setting Up the Cameras

To render a scene, you must first have at least one camera. A default camera is normally provided when a new scene is opened. Some programs, such as Strata StudioPro, do not provide a default camera position and require that you insert a camera from the toolbar, although a scene can be rendered from any of the default windows. Though each package has a slightly different way of creating and rendering a scene, all rendering packages make use of cameras. By using a camera, we can adjust the lens size for a specific look or move the camera about the scene.

Because cameras can have a wide range of lens sizes, the use of a camera is a very important tool when creating different types of images. Using a different sized camera lens offers a new perspective on an old scene.

The camera is the viewer's eyes and should be used as a tool of destination and enlightenment. People like to take the long way home through exciting and beautiful scenery. Cameras can take the eyes to places the feet will never know.

Adding the Camera

To be able to see your animation or images, there must be a camera to record the action. In many software packages you are provided a default camera placed at some default position. While the default camera position may vary, the default camera will typically point to either the origin (0,0,0) or at the first object loaded into the scene.

If a camera is not provided when a new scene is created, you must add your own camera from the toolbar. **For software in which the camera must be added, there is typically a toolbar or a menu selection which allows you to enter a new camera (see Figure 9-1)**.

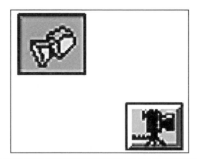

FIGURE 9-1 Adding a camera is as simple as clicking on an icon or using a menu command. Clicking either of these icons from Strata StudioPro (right) and Infini-D (left) will add a camera to the scene.

Once a camera is added to the scene, it may be used for rendering, adjusted to point to a particular object, or animated to move about the scene. You can use many of the default settings on the camera right out of the box, or you may want to adjust the lens size, f-stop, or any of the other parameters.

TIP: The camera is your vehicle of expression. Regardless of how well your objects are modeled or animated, the camera is the viewer's eyes. The camera is a tool and you must know how to use this tool well to create a great image.

Moving the Camera

Now that we've added a camera, we must be able to move it. Camera movement should be a smooth transition through frames and not like the footage provided by say, David Letterman's Monkey Cam.

Typically, the camera is handled like any other object in the scene. Most software packages even use a camera object to show the location of the camera in the scene. Although visible as an icon in the scene, the camera itself will not be rendered. It is used for visual reference and placement only.

Moving the camera typically employs the same method used when moving other objects. Whether your software uses handles or object selection, a camera can be moved to any desired position.

Once the camera has been moved, a keyframe must be added to the scene to record the movement. A series of keyframes will produce a motion path for the camera, allowing it to move around the scene. Animating a camera is not as liberal as animating an object, because camera movement is so much more noticeable to the viewer. See the section on Animating Cameras later in this chapter to learn more about camera motion.

Camera Angles

The angle of the camera is also important to achieve the correct perspective. In most cases the scene is rarely rendered head on. By moving the camera slightly off center, more perspective is achieved, giving the scene more of a three dimensional look. Perspective is what gives 3d graphics an edge over traditional 2d graphics. Use perspective to your advantage when creating still images and animation. **In Figure 9-2 you will notice that the subject has more depth on the right because the camera was placed at a slight angle**. When the subject is viewed straight on, depth perception becomes inhibited because there are fewer points of reference on the object.

FIGURE 9-2 The text on the left was rendered with the subject in the center of the frame and from straight on. The same subject is shown on the right with little perspective added. All camera attributes are the same, the camera was just moved slightly below and to the left of the subject.

Although adding a little perspective to the camera angle can bring out more of the 3d element in a scene, the camera can also be used to create extreme perspective and give the subject a sense of scale. **The angle of the boat in Figure 9-3 gives the viewer a sense of the size of the boat in comparison with the rest of the environment**. By not shooting the boat from a straight-on perspective, we can capture other objects in the background which add detail and depth to the image.

FIGURE 9-3 Because the angle of the boat is from a lower angle, we can see many other aspects of the boat and its surroundings.

Different and unusual perspective shots can create a more interesting image of even common articles. **The image in Figure 9-4 is a common pool table, yet the camera angle used gives us a different perspective of the game.** If the animation were following the eight ball around during the entire game, this type of perspective would be more interesting to watch than if it were taken from a standard above-the-table view.

FIGURE 9-4 This shot of a pool table makes a more interesting image than the same scene if viewed from a normal person's eye view.

Multiple Cameras

While some programs allow you to add and modify a single camera, others allow multiple cameras. The use of multiple cameras makes it much easier to create the final image or animation. Using multiple cameras in the same scene affords you many camera angles in a single scene. With multiple cameras, you can also keep the motion for each path from getting too complex, which aids when editing the motion paths.

An animator can set up multiple cameras, each with its own, different motion path. After rendering wireframe

317

animations from each camera, the final can be decided upon without disrupting any of the other cameras. With a single camera setup, creating multiple motion paths requires either saving multiple scenes, or saving the motion paths to a file and reloading each motion path, as you decide to use it.

TIP: When adding multiple cameras to the scene, name them for easy reference. Using names which describe where they go or what they do, such as "linear roof view" is better than a name like "Camera 3".

Lens Setting Options

Once a camera has been added to a scene, its lens must be set. While default lens settings are provided, many times they must be changed to create certain visual effects. There are a number of lens factors which affect the way an image is produced. Options such as focal length, f-stop, camera size, and depth of field will affect the way a final image is rendered.

Focal Length

Changing the perspective on a scene can be accomplished in a number of ways. Besides moving the camera to another position, you can also change the focal length of the camera lens. Most rendering software has adopted many of the same terms and procedures to make virtual cameras as close to real life as possible. Since there really is no lens used in the rendering process, we must enter the lens characteristics numerically. By changing the camera attributes, we can create any size camera lens that we need, within reason.

In real-world cameras, the focal length works in conjunction with the film size and the size of the lens. To obtain a natural perspective, you must match the correct lens with the proper film size. A 35mm camera would typically use a 50mm lens to create a normal focal length, for example. To understand more about lenses, you may want to read photography books. Most rendering software will allow you to apply that knowledge to the 3d cameras of the virtual world. **The images in Figures 9-5, 9-6, and 9-7 are shots of the same scene using various focal lengths**.

FIGURE 9-5 Using various focal lengths, different amounts of perspective can be achieved for the same scene, without moving the camera. This image was created using a standard 50mm lens.

FIGURE 9-6 This image uses a focal length of 9.29, resulting in a lens size of 626mm. Notice how the image has less perspective than a normal lens, yet the object is closer. By using a larger focal length, the camera takes on a telephoto effect, which has a tendency to create flat images.

FIGURE 9-7 This is the same scene using a focal length of .16905, resulting in a lens size of 11mm. Notice the large amount of perspective distortion that accompanies a smaller focal length.

The focal length affects the distance at which the camera is focused. Since rendering through a virtual camera renders all objects in focus, the focal length is really used to determine the amount of perspective observed through the camera window. A focal length with a high value produces a telephoto effect with low perspective, while a low value will produce a wide-angle lens with extreme perspective.

TIP: For a standard camera setting, use a camera lens setting of about 50mm (because it most closely resembles normal human vision). Experiment with different lens sizes to produce interesting results. When rendering an image or animation, try using various focal length settings and lens sizes. Adding different perspectives makes for a more exciting and interesting image.

F-Stop

While the focal length changes the perspective of the image by changing the distance between the film and the lens, the f-stop setting changes the image by changing the amount of light which enters the camera when the shutter is opened. Because the f-stop affects the amount of light entering the camera, it too affects the camera's depth of field. The depth of field is the range at which objects viewed through the camera are in focus. As the f-stop value increases, the aperture becomes smaller. A smaller aperture means less light entering the camera. The less light entering the camera, the wider the depth of field and the more objects which will be in focus.

Typically, only programs which offer depth of field rendering provide the user with an f-stop setting. By setting the correct f-stop, a more believable image can be created due to the natural limitations of a real camera. It is the virtual camera's ability to take perfectly focused images that gives it away as a model and not the real thing. Adding subtleties such as depth of field can go a long way toward creating a more realistic image.

Camera Size

Along with the focal length and f-stop settings, changing the camera's virtual size will affect the rendered image. Typically, since the camera is a representation, and not a real camera, the size does not affect the rendering. In fact, some packages do not even provide a means of sizing the camera. While this may seem inconvenient, there is a method to their madness. Changing the size of the camera will drastically change the type of image that is produced.

Similar to the way a real camera works, a bigger virtual camera uses bigger virtual film. When bigger film is used, a bigger lens must also be used to achieve a normal field of view. In addition, the focal length and f-stop must also be adjusted for normal viewing. As you can see, if the camera size were easily changeable, many other attributes would also have to be adjusted. To change the size of the camera, you must specifically enter the appropriate parameters; you cannot change it by inadvertently changing the size of an icon.

In addition, many rendering packages do not care what size the camera icon is. When flying through a keyhole, only the focal point on the camera needs to pass through the keyhole, while the rest of the camera can pass through the door. When squeezing through tight areas, it is the lens size and focal length that can make the difference between achieving a clean pass or clipped geometry.

TIP: When navigating areas with many objects in proximity, such as an asteroid field, adding more perspective to the camera will really accentuate the size and closeness of the objects, giving the impression that the camera is of diminutive size.

Depth of Field

The camera size, f-stop and focal length affect the depth of field in a real camera. In virtual cameras these same parameters must be adjusted numerically. Depth of field is the distance in which objects begin to become unfocused when viewed through a camera lens. This phenomenon is due to factors such as focal length, film size, lens size, and f-stop settings of the camera lens. The f-stop determines the amount of light allowed into the camera lens by changing the size of the aperture. Allowing more light into the camera causes the focal range to be smaller. Objects not within the focal range will become unfocused in the rendered image. As the camera renders objects which are further away, they will become increasingly blurry or unfocused. **Figure 9-8 shows the effects of depth of field.**

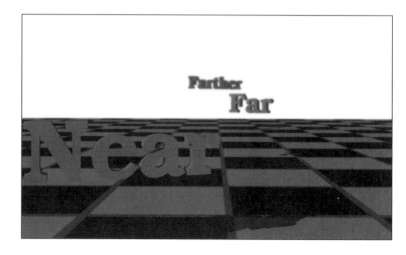

FIGURE 9-8 Depth of field creates a sense of realism because it simulates the inability of a real camera to focus every object within camera shot. Depending on the size of the aperture, objects can be made out of focus in either the background or the foreground.

Since the artificial cameras provided in rendering software are normally perfect cameras (meaning that everything is in focus), when we want a scene to have more depth, we must simulate this depth of field. Some rendering cameras have a depth of field setting which will automatically simulate the process of depth of field. In other cases, we can simulate the depth of field as a postprocess using software such as Adobe Photoshop by applying a gradient blur in the direction of the vanishing point.

Animating Cameras

Once the camera settings have been chosen, many times the camera is animated, or moved through a scene. Animating a camera may be as simple as turning to follow an object as it crosses the screen, or as complex as a fly-through of a virtual city. At either end of the spectrum, animating a camera produces more interesting and exciting animation than a stationary camera.

One of the key problems to be aware of when animating a camera is the clipping region. Objects that intersect the camera lens become clipped. This clipping region (the affective area of the camera lens) may move through polygons of objects as either the camera or the objects move through the scene. **A clipped polygon appears as a polygon which fills a portion of the screen (see Figure 9-9) and is not normally present in the object being clipped**.

FIGURE 9-9 Clipped polygons occur when the camera passes through an object's geometry. During complex animation, this is one of the most difficult tasks to avoid and the most obvious to spot.

Clipping polygons can be avoided either by changing the path of the camera or object being clipped, or by changing the camera's size or focal length. In many cases, it may simply be a matter of changing the path of the camera, or adding more keyframes, to avoid clipping the object.

Camera Targets

Animating a camera is typically not as sophisticated as character animation. Camera movement may be as subtle as panning slightly to follow the subject or as animated as trailing an fighter plane through a maze of asteroids. Whatever the reason, when moving the camera through the scene, the viewer gains a better perspective of the entire scene, and may actually feel more a part of the action than a spectator.

Animating a camera can be difficult enough, but how can we keep the camera pointing at the subject when both the subject and the camera are moving? The answer to that puzzling question is to use target objects.

A target object is no different than other objects. In fact, the target object is any object, including Null objects, contained in the scene. An object which uses another object as its target object will always point to the target object. Regardless of where the target object moves to, the object aimed at it will automatically rotate in its position so that it is facing its target object. For animation, targets are a must for keeping the camera in line with the subject.

Targets work on objects, cameras, and lights. This means that any object can use any other object in the scene as its target object. A spotlight can follow a dancer as it moves across the stage, or all the heads on a group of toys can be made to watch another toy as it moves across the scene. **In Figure 9-10, we can track the spotlight as it moves across the stage, following the clip**.

FIGURE 9-10 As the clip moves across the stage, a spotlight which has the clip as its target will follow it across the stage.

TIP: To make an object follow it's target for a limited time only, use either a Null object or an invisible object (if Null objects are not available) as the target object. *Check if invisible really works.* Using a Null object, you can actually pull the camera through the scene by the target Null. When the camera (or any other object) needs to follow another object, set the coordinates of the target identical to that of the object which is to be followed for the specified frames. When the target is to change, or the focus is on infinity, move the Null object off of the object being followed.

TECHNIQUE: Steps for Creating a Target Object

1. *Take aim:* Select the object looking for a target. While some programs allow you to aim any object at any other object, some programs only allow you to aim lights or cameras at other objects.

2. *Assign target:* Different animation systems have different targeting commands, yet they are essentially the same. Typically, a "Target" or "Point At" command is selected through a menu or a icon palette or button. Selecting this command will normally present the user with a list of objects to select as a target, or the user may be asked to select the target from the scene by actually clicking on the object.

3. Once the target has been selected, the object which is aimed at it will follow the target's every move.

TIP: When aiming objects (not cameras or lights) at other objects in the scene, be sure of the object's orientation. If the object is incorrectly oriented, the back of the object may be pointing at the target instead of what you thought was the front.

An object may have only one designated target at any one time. Some animation systems allow an object to have one target for the duration of the animation, while other systems allow for multiple objects over time, but only one target at any one time.

Safe Areas

Once the camera settings are in place and objects are animated, we are confronted with the final task of keeping the action on screen. Due to the difference in pixel aspect ratio, animation created on a computer and played back on a television monitor may run off the screen. Objects near the edges of a computer screen will be cut off during television playback.

When rendering animation to be played back on videotape or in broadcast television, you must be sure that the image is within the television safe areas. The safe areas are the areas in which you are ensured that the text and objects will be completely on screen, without risk of being cut off due to the NTSC or PAL video resolution.

The television safe areas consists of two rounded rectangles centered on a screen with dimensions of 640 x 480 pixels.

The outer rectangle is the safe area for action, or objects in motion. This rectangular area has the dimensions of 580 pixels wide x 486 pixels high. The innermost rectangular area is for text and titles and has the dimensions of 520 pixels wide x 380 pixels high.

Some rendering packages offer a display option which will display an outline of the television safe areas during scene layout. To ensure your objects will be seen on a television monitor, be sure that they are within the appropriate safe area. **Figure 9-11 illustrates the safe areas outline**.

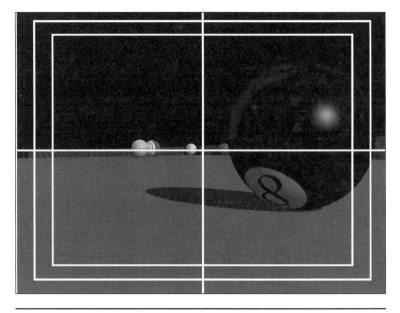

FIGURE 9-11 Use the safe areas display to ensure that objects will not get cut out of the frame when playing back an animation on television monitors.

Rendering
Scenes

10

Choosing a Rendering Algorithm

After the models have been built and animated, its time for you to take a break and for the computer to do its part of the job, rendering. Rendering is the process of compiling all of the object, texture, and lighting data to create a visual image. All of the surface textures will be applied and shadows will be calculated, if needed. This is all part of the rendering phase, and before we let the computer do its part, we must decide what type of rendering algorithm we are going to use.

Deciding on a rendering algorithm is an important decision. Animation, color printing, computer output, television, and movies all require different parameters when rendering images. Compression/decompression

(Codec) algorithms must be chosen, and the quality of each Codec varies.

Some Codecs produce low-quality output, but take up very little disk space. Others produce the highest quality output when quality outweighs rendering time. Knowing what each compression algorithm and rendering algorithm has to offer makes it easier and more efficient for you to choose one when rendering your scene.

Although computers used in 3D modeling are getting faster all the time, the time factor is still important when creating 3D art. Same-day service in this industry does not exist. Rendering time can easily exceed modeling time, especially if you have only one machine on which to do your rendering. Give yourself plenty time to render and choose the most appropriate algorithm the first time, so you can avoid rerendering.

TIP: Whenever rendering, especially animation, try to use off-peak computer hours. Since the rendering process is very CPU intensive, it is best to render at a time when the computer would otherwise be idle, such as overnight. Although some rendering packages will allow you to render in the background, it is best to let the animation render un inhibited. Overworking the system is a sure way to send it crashing.

Wire Frame Rendering

The wireframe mode is the simplest method of rendering available. Although you may not have thought of this as a rendering algorithm, by definition it is. In most modeling software, the wireframe mode is the default mode of displaying objects as they are modeled. **Figure 10-1 shows a model viewed in wireframe mode**.

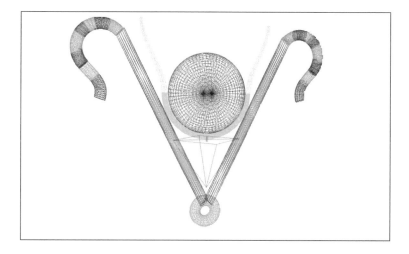

FIGURE 10-1 The wireframe mode has been the standard view for modeled objects ever since viewing a model became possible. Wireframe models show only geometry data and motion. No other attributes of the scene are available.

Using a wireframe mode of rendering has the distinct advantage of speed. When viewing an object in wireframe mode, all other rendering effects are disabled. No surface attributes are visible and no lighting effects can be distinguished. This is not the type of algorithm to use when presenting proofs to a client, but it is ideal for modeling and scene setup.

The wireframe mode may also be used for viewing a quick preview of motion. An animation rendered in wireframe mode may take only a few minutes, while the same animation fully rendered may take many hours or days.

Used primarily for the default display mode in most computer systems in the past, the wireframe mode may soon be replaced by shaded graphics modeling (SGM). With the advent of OpenGL (PC) and QuickDraw 3D (Mac) previewing in a shaded mode is quickly being implemented with some software packages such as Caligari trueSpace (PC) and Strata StudioPro (Mac).

Hidden Line Removed Rendering

Similar to wireframe rendering, the hidden line removed rendering mode also reveals an object's geometry in the most basic form. The hidden line removed mode does exactly what its name implies; it removes hidden lines. Still a wireframe view of the models, this algorithm treats all objects as if they were solid and removes the hidden lines. Although all objects are drawn as solids, surface attributes are not rendered in this low-level rendering algorithm. **An example of a hidden line removed view is pictured in Figure 10-2**.

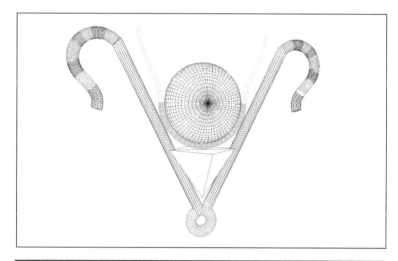

FIGURE 10-2 In hidden line mode, all objects are rendered as though they were solid, although no surface attributes are rendered (including transparency).

In this case, less is more. Fewer lines are drawn, yet this mode takes longer to calculate than wireframes, because the computer must decide which lines are in front and which are behind and object. The hidden line removed mode makes it easier to distinguish between object surfaces without the overhead of rendering surfaces. While this mode is faster than all other modes of rendering (other than wireframe), the output quality is still only good enough for object and animation previews.

Flat Shading

Revealing more surface information than the hidden line algorithm, the flat shaded mode will show differences in surface colors. Flat shading mode is the best choice for a rough preview of stills and animation. Lighting is limited to illumination of polygons only. Each polygon receives only one light source and, as a result, is rendered as a single color. Although there is no shading on individual polygons, the group of polygons making up an object's surface can portray some sense of shading across many polygons.

Flat shading is fast, but faceting is very obvious on the surfaces of objects, as is evidenced by the image in Figure 10-3. Because of its speed, this is a good choice for rendering animation previews when a solid surface is needed. Shadows, transparency, reflectivity, and texture maps are not supported when rendering with a flat shading algorithm.

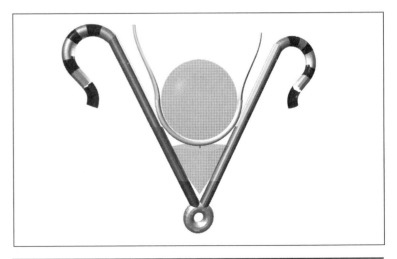

FIGURE 10-3 While the flat shaded mode is fast, it produces faceted objects and does not render shadows.

Gouraud Shading

While the flat shaded and wireframe modes are preview modes, Gouraud shading algorithm is the lowest level of quality renderers. Gouraud shading uses intensity interpolation to render an object's surface. Working with the vertices of a surface, the Gouraud method utilizes the normals at the shared vertices of the surface to calculate the shading across a surface.

Although Gouraud shading produces a very smooth surface, there may be some discrepancies around vertices that fall directly within the specular highlight. **Gouraud is a fast rendering algorithm which will render lighting effects on object surfaces, but will not render shadows (see Figure 10-4).**

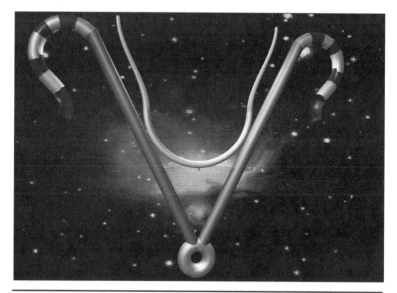

FIGURE 10-4 Gouraud shading can produce smooth shading, although texture maps are not rendered and reflection and refraction are not supported.

Phong Shading

A step up from the Gouraud shader is the Phong shading algorithm. Named after the developer of this rendering technique, Phong Bui Tong, Phong shading is a normal vector interpolation shader. This shader will evaluate the position of the vertices of a surface and the associated normals and interpolate an entirely new set of normals across the object's surface. The new set of normals is then used to calculate the intensity of each pixel used to depict the object's surface.

Because the Phong technique calculates every pixel's intensity on a surface, environment mapping and surface mapping are supported with this rendering algorithm (see Figure 10-5). This makes Phong a viable alternative to the lengthy process of ray-tracing.

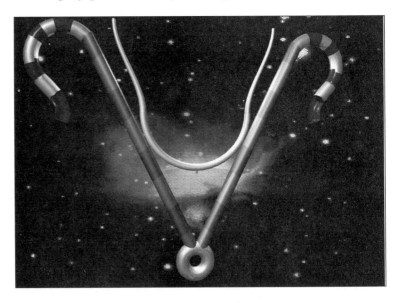

FIGURE 10-5 Phong shading can produce realistic images, due to its texture mapping abilities.

Many animation systems such as Electric Image Animation System use Phong shading as their primary or best rendering algorithm. Phong shading is very fast and can create very convincing images due to its excellent texture mapping support. Because of its speed, Phong shading is very useful when rendering long animation sequences.

Some drawbacks with Phong shading are that it may not handle reflective surfaces very well and refraction is not supported. While this may seem to present a problem, it can be overcome with the use of reflectivity maps and a little more involvement from the artist.

During animation, the eye is more forgiving because objects are in motion and cameras are moving. Using Phong shading on the animation will be more than adequate for most uses, while ray-tracing can be saved for single frame images, such as a magazine cover. Overall, when rendering animation, the time saved rendering in Phong shading can easily be much less than if ray-tracing were used.

Ray-Tracing

Although the Phong rendering algorithm is very accurate at rendering surface detail, it lacks the light tracing ability which makes ray-tracing the star of rendering algorithms. Second only to radiosity in realism, the ray-tracing algorithm produces very realistic and high-quality output. Named after the way it treats light, ray-tracing traces reflected light back through the scene to its source. **By following the rays of light backward from the camera, the ray-tracing algorithm can calculate reflections, refraction, transparency, and realistic shadows (see Figure 10-6). This** allows for excellent reflections as well as accurate transparency and refraction. Other than interobject diffuse illumination, nearly every aspect of real light is taken into account.

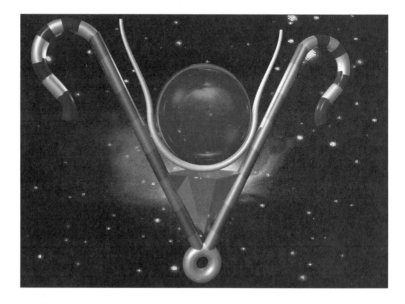

FIGURE 10-6 Ray tracing will accurately portray light, transparency, refraction, and reflection in an object.

Ray-tracing's big disadvantage is that it is slow. Due to the intense amount of calculations needed to accurately portray all light sources, ray-tracing can be very costly in the sense of time. Every light source added to the scene will exponentially add to the rendering time since the light source may affect every object in a scene.

Each rendering program has its own set of standards for the amount of light rays produced by a light source. It is the ray-tracer's job to analyze each one of them until it reaches the light source or the reflective recursion limit or the transparency recursion limit.

To keep the ray-tracing algorithm from running wild when chasing light rays, many rendering packages allow the user to configure the ray-tracing parameters. By changing different rendering values prior to rendering, one can change the quality of the output to suit the current needs. To limit the number of times a ray of light is traced through objects, the reflective, transparency, and refractive recursion limits must be set. Although a default value is set for these parameters, you may need to adjust them to fit the needs of the scene. Scenes with many reflective or transparent objects should adjust these numbers accordingly. For more information on the recursion limits, see the sections below or consult your software's user manual.

Radiosity

To carry the effects of ray-tracing a step further would require radiosity. Radiosity picks up where ray-tracing leaves off. **While ray-tracing follows rays of light back to their source, picking up reflections and refraction along the way, radiosity goes one step further and detects inter-object diffuse illumination (see Figure 10-7).**

FIGURE 10-7 Radiosity can detect the subtle levels of light reflected from other objects. Very CPU intensive, this algorithm is not for wimpy machines.

Interobject illumination is the effect of scattered light off of an object's surface. First developed at Cornell University, radiosity produces photorealistic renders by calculating all of the light on all surfaces. As you may have guessed, this rendering algorithm requires lots of rendering time and RAM. In fact, many machines cannot handle radiosity as a viable means of production output.

Strata StudioPro offers an experimental radiosity algorithm which works very well, yet they make no apologies for the amount of time it takes to render. A warning dialog is presented when choosing radiosity, informing users that this rendering algorithm is not for weak computers.

RayPainting

To incorporate the accuracy or Phong shading or ray-tracing with the artistic style of a hand drawn or painted image, Strata StudioPro currently offers a rendering algorithm called RayPainting. RayPainting works like ray-tracing by calculating shadows, reflections, etc., but will render the image using user-configurable brush sizes and stroke types. The type of paint and medium are also user selectable. Not a postprocess, but incorporated into the rendering itself, objects appear to have brushstokes which follow the object, not the image. **Figure 10-8 illustrates the use of RayPainting on the same example used in the previous rendering algorithms**.

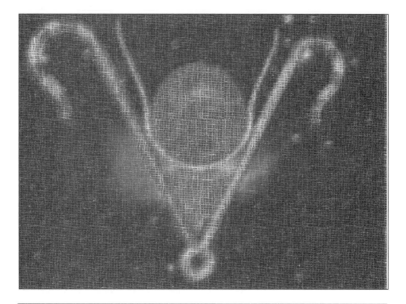

FIGURE 10-8 RayPainting in Strata StudioPro can provide very interesting effects on a rendering. RayPainting supports all ray-tracing qualities in addition to rendering the image using a user-configurable brushstroke, paint type, and medium.

Antialiasing

Regardless of the rendering algorithm you use, it is desirable to have smooth edges and curves. To create smooth edges out of square or rectangular pixels, rendering software uses an effect known as *antialiasing*. **When a straight edge is rendered on an angle other than the horizontal or vertical, there is a stair-stepping effect which occurs due to the shape and size of the pixels (see Figure 10-9).** By antialiasing the edge, it appears smoother. Two popular antialiasing methods create a smooth edge by averaging the pixel color or by supersampling.

FIGURE 10-9 Aliasing or stair-stepping occurs along curved and diagonal edges due to pixel shape and size.

Using the pixel averaging method, the color of a pixel on the edge of a line or curve is averaged with the surrounding pixel colors. **The pixel is also given an influence factor that correlates with the percentage of the pixel occupying space along the mathematically true edge of the line (see Figure 10-10).**

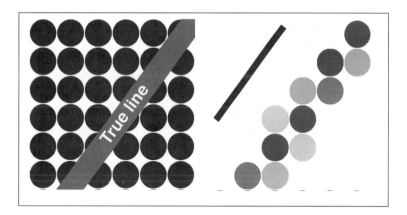

FIGURE 10-10 The top pixel is about 75% along the true line, while the bottom pixel is only about 20%. The color of the top pixel will therefore have a 75% influence of the color of the edge, while the bottom pixel will have only a 20% influence of the edge color. In this example the bottom pixel will be more of a light gray, while the top pixel will be closer to black.

Adaptive Sampling

Adaptive sampling is a method of antialiasing also known as *edge detection*. During the rendering process, the image is analyzed for edges. Edges are determined by the color differences in neighboring pixels. If, after analysis two pixels fall below the color difference threshold, they are ignored. If they are above the threshold value, they are antialiased.

Adaptive sampling allows the user to control the rate of antialiasing used on an image. By changing the level of detection, the user can create rough draft images or finely antialiased images. The level of adaptive sampling is controlled by the sampling threshold.

Sampling Threshold

Used with adaptive sampling, the *sampling threshold* controls the amount of antialiasing performed on an edge. Images with a lower sampling threshold will produce a sharper, more antialiased edge. Conversely, a higher sampling threshold will produce a coarser edge, showing more of the stair-stepping effect which occurs in computer-generated images. Lowering the sampling threshold will also increase the rendering time, since more edges will be found, resulting in higher antialiasing.

Although there are different algorithms for antialiasing, the following describes the procedure for Newtek's Lightwave 3D. Using the default setting of eight in the sampling threshold box, Lightwave will check the green values of two neighboring pixels. If the difference in the two values is greater than eight, the red value is checked. The pixel will be antialiased if the difference in the red values is twice the sampling threshold or higher. If the difference in values is within the threshold, the blue value is checked. The blue value must be four times the sampling threshold for antialiasing to occur. If the difference between the pixels falls within the threshold on all three of the color values, the pixels are not antialiased. The actual antialiasing is done by averaging the color values between the two pixels to create a smooth edge. **Figure 10-11 illustrates the difference between two edges which were rendered with different sampling threshold levels**.

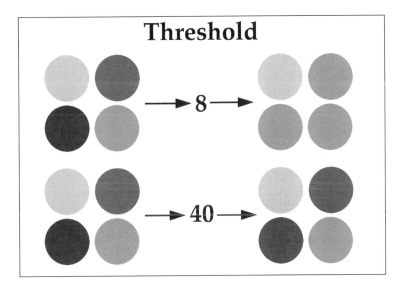

FIGURE 10-11 Using different sampling thresholds, various levels of antialiasing can be achieved. A lower sampling threshold will produce a smoother curve.

Supersampling

Slightly different from the adaptive sampling method of antialiasing, the supersampling method used in Strata StudioPro creates a smooth edge by increasing the resolution of the image and interpolating the pixels back to the specified image size. By increasing the resolution, supersampling actually has more data associated with each pixel. **A supersample value of three (used in Strata's Extra Smooth option) will generate a 3 x 3 grid of pixels around each pixel (see Figure 10-12).** This produces an image with nine times the information of a nonantialiased image for each pixel. When the image is displayed on the screen, it is displayed at the proper resolution, because the extra resolution information for each pixel is interpolated down to make one pixel, resulting in a smoother image.

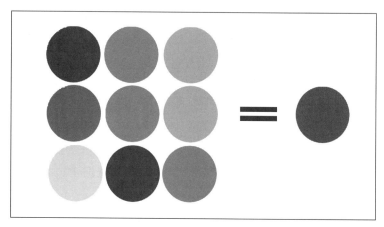

FIGURE 10-12 A supersampling factor of three will generate a 3x3 grid around each pixel, increasing the information for each image to nine times the size of the final image. The final image is comprised of pixels which have been interpolated down to one pixel from the additional high-resolution information.

Alpha Channel Support

While the rendering algorithms and antialiasing methods are utilized at render time, alpha channels are created at render time to be used for postproduction. Very often in graphic design or image manipulation, images and film are composited with other images or backgrounds to create special effects. We have all seen the effects of image compositing. Used extensively in movies, the effect is achieved by blocking out a background, then superimposing a different background in its place. In computer graphics, the same effect is achieved digitally, through an integrated 8-bit image called an *alpha channel*.

The alpha channel can be used to display many types of information. From depth of field and color to individual object geometry and background information, the alpha channel has many uses and is employed in many different ways by different software programs and artists.

Background Alpha Channel

The most basic of alpha channel support is the background alpha channel. **When this option is selected, the image is rendered without a background map, while the background is rendered as a single color, usually black (see Figure 10-13).** The image will however, have an alpha channel attached to it which can be used for image processing in any quality image processing program. The alpha channel contains a mask which depicts where objects do and do not appear. By using the alpha channel in a program such as Photoshop, you can easily extract just the objects in the scene to paste over different backgrounds.

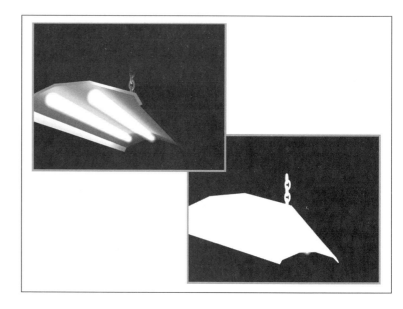

FIGURE 10-13 Using a background alpha channel, a rendered scene can easily change backgrounds by compositing the image into others.

G-Buffering (Geometry Buffer)

Carrying the concept of alpha channels to extremes, a new format introduced by RayDream could prove to be very beneficial for postproduction. The new format, called G-buffering, renders alpha channels for various types of image information. **When rendered using the G-buffer format, images will render individual alpha channels to hold information on pixel color, object masking, distance in scene (great for depth of field effect), normal vectors, 3D position, and surface coordinates (see Figure 10-14).**

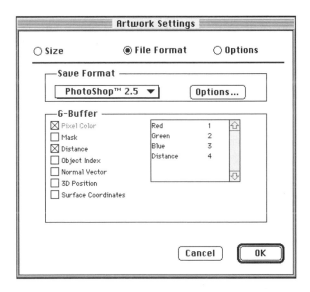

FIGURE 10-14 The G-buffer format in RayDream Designers' rendering options may prove to be a new standard in 3D image processing. The flexibility of this format makes it easy to change lighting or add depth of field in postproduction.

While this is a relatively new format, it presents many options for image processing. Using the alpha channels in an image processing tool such as Photoshop can be a real benefit when adding different effects or compositing images. Lighting can be altered in an image through the use of the normals vector channel, or you can create a depth of field effect by using the distance channel with some added Gaussian blur.

Automated Postrendering Options

Unlike the options which aid in image manipulation, these rendering options are used to direct the software to create some postrendering effects, before the image is written to disk. Such effects as shadows, motion blur, and lens flares, are created by the rendering software when directed to do so. These effects are global to the entire animation or image and must be explicitly employed to create the effect.

While these effects are created by the software, some of the features have numeric data associated with them which directly affects the degree of the application. Many of these effects are also applied after the image is rendered, but before it is saved to disk. All of these effects will increase rendering time, some substantially and some very little. While the availability of each feature varies with the software packages, so does the feature's applicability. Some are useful very often, while others may be seldom used.

Shadow Maps and Ray-Traced Shadows

Adding shadows is one of the options which is used often, but not every time. Rendering a realistic scene involves many things, one of which is shadows. As a light source's rays shine outward, they are reflected and absorbed by different types of surfaces. Solid objects absorb more light than transparent objects. Light that is absorbed by an object casts a shadow on objects which are in the same light path.

In the real world, we don't think too much of shadows. In the 3D world, shadows are very CPU intensive. Every shadow, just like every light source, adds a significant amount of rendering time to the overall rendering process. Rendering algorithms such as Gouraud and Phong do not provide shadows and, therefore, shadows must be calculated by ray-tracing or radiosity.

Shadows produced from ray-tracing will typically be hard-edged shadows, while shadow mapping produces more realistic, soft-edged shadows (see Figure 10-15). Most programs which allow shadow maps will do so only on spotlight sources. Electric Image Animation System and RenderMan offer an option for soft-edged shadows. Strata StudioPro offers a soft edge on spotlights which can achieve a similar effect.

FIGURE 10-15 Ray tracing (left) produces hard-edged shadows, while shadow mapping will produce more realistic, soft-edged shadows.

TIP: Use shadow maps for as many objects as possible, memory permitting. Shadow maps are faster, but require more memory. If you must choose only a limited number of objects which can use shadow maps, select the main subjects of the scene. Lesser shadows can be retouched via a postrendering process, if necessary.

Motion Blur

Motion blur is only needed when there is motion, and typically only when the motion is very fast. To the human eye, objects which move very fast appear blurry as they move across our field of vision. On film, moving objects appear blurry when the object is moving faster than the shutter speed. In computer rendering, there is no real motion and the objects are just rendered at their new location at every frame. When watching a computer-generated animation with moving objects, it will appear unnatural if fast moving objects do not appear even slightly blurry. By default, objects in computer-generated animation are always rendered clear and crisp. To make an animation appear more realistic, motion blur can be added to the rendering process. **The resulting image (see Figure 10-16) will make the animation more convincing when objects move rapidly within view.**

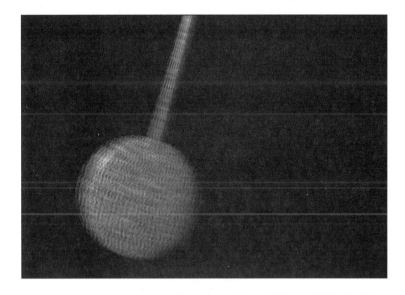

FIGURE 10-16 Adding motion blur makes an object's motion seem less jerky and more convincing to the eye.

To solve the motion blur problem, many animation systems have added features which allow for moving objects to be rendered with a motion blur. To create the effect of motion blur, the object is blurred slightly in the direction of the movement. Adding motion blur to an object can increase rendering time significantly and should only be used when necessary.

TIP: Use motion blur sparingly, due to the increase in the CPU load. Objects which are closer to the camera are candidates for motion blur, while distant moving objects may not need motion blur.

Field Rendering

Unless the majority of your output goes to videotape, field rendering is used even less than motion blur. Field rendering enables the rendering software to create two fields of information for each frame rendered instead of one. For animation with lots of horizontal motion, objects will appear to move more smoothly, because there are, in a sense, 60 frames per second of playback. This option is best suited for animation that is designed for video playback, because of the video interlacing not found in traditional film.

To understand how field rendering works, you have to understand the way a television or computer monitor's images are drawn (see Figure 10-17). The screen is divided into two fields with each field consisting of either the even or odd rows of pixels. Without field rendering, every other row is a duplication of the previous row. This is why lines which are a single pixel thick will flicker on a television monitor. With field rendering turned on, both the odd and even rows of pixels are given information. When the field-rendered image is played back on a video monitor, motion will appear smoother, because there is twice as much information for each frame.

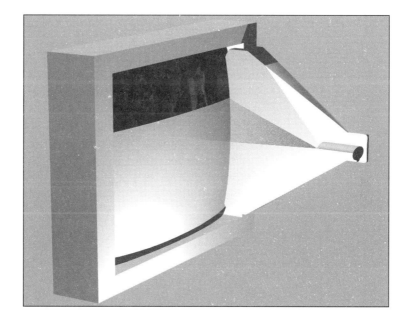

FIGURE 10-17 The color guns inside the computer monitor or television set move very rapidly across the screen to create an image.

TIP: Field rendering has no effect when playing animation back on film. This feature is designed for video playback only. Using field rendering will increase the rendering time, but will not result in a better image for nonvideo players.

Depth of Field

Unlike the motion blur that is used extensively in animation, depth of field is prevalent in still images. Depth of field is described as the area in which the camera is no longer in focus. If you look at photographs you will notice that objects in the image do not have the same amount of focus, especially as the distance between the objects increases. Objects in the foreground can be in focus, while objects in the distance, or background will be out of focus. This can also work in the opposite way, with the background being in focus while the foreground is out of focus. This phenomenon is caused by the type of lens used to produce the image. **Figure 10-18 shows an example of objects rendered with a depth of field**.

FIGURE 10-18 Depth of field will cause objects which are not at the focal distance to be slightly out of focus. Using depth of field can give an image the illusion of being a photograph instead of a computer-generated image, because computers will typically render an image in perfect focus throughout the image.

In computer-generated images, there is no real distance between the objects, so the objects always get rendered in focus. Even though rendering software uses simulated cameras with different lens sizes, they are considered perfect cameras, with everything always in focus. The problem is that this can sometimes produce images which are unnatural looking. To create a more natural image, we must create depth of field.

Depth of field is affected by the camera's lens size, focal distance, f-stop, and film size. To simulate this on a computer these controls must be adjusted. The focal distance is the distance at which the camera is in perfect focus. This can be adjusted to include objects either near or far from the camera. The f-stop controls the amount of light allowed to enter the lens. The less light allowed to enter the camera, the greater the range of focus. Objects not within range will appear blurry or out of focus.

Focal Distance

Depth of field is controlled by a number of factors, one of which is the focal distance. The focal distance determines the distance in which the camera is in perfect focus. Objects located at this distance will appear clearest and sharpest in the image. Normally, this distance is set to include the most important object in the scene, although it is sometimes intentional to do otherwise.

The focal distance can be used to draw attention to certain objects within the scene. By setting the focal distance to a subject in the background, attention may be drawn to distant mountains or skylines, as opposed to the objects in the foreground.

TIP: When setting the focal distance, you can use the visibility distance formula to determine the distance between the camera and an object.

F-stop

The f-stop setting, like the focal distance, also affects the depth of field of an image. The F-stop controls the amount of light which is allowed to enter the camera by changing the size of the aperture on the lens. The more light allowed to enter the camera, the smaller the range of focus, thereby creating depth of field. Typical aperture settings are 1, 1.4, 2, 2.8, 4, 5.6, 11, 16, 22, 32, 45, 64. The larger the number, the smaller the aperture and consequently, the smaller the amount of light that reaches the film (either real or simulated). As you may notice, each successive f-stop setting halves the size of the opening of the aperture and amount of light entering the camera.

To create a narrower depth of field, select a lower f-stop setting. To widen the depth of field and have more objects in focus, set the f-stop setting to a higher number.

Recursive Properties

While the automated postrendering options are settings on the camera itself, the recursive properties are settings which really affect the way light is handled by the camera. For effects like reflectivity and transparency, a ray of light must be traced back to its source from the camera lens.

As light is followed back to its source, it encounters the different objects which had reflected it toward the camera lens. In the real world, light is scattered off of many objects until the falloff and decay cause the light to no longer be seen. In a virtual world, it is possible for light to be bounced back and forth into infinity. Each reflection or level of transparency is another set of calculations the computer must solve. To avoid rendering shutdown, a recursive limit controller is used. By changing this rendering parameter, you can achieve a set of reflections or transparency which is appropriate to the scene.

Reflectivity Recursion

One method of saving time in rendering is to set a low limit for the reflectivity recursion. Typically the limit is set to a default value of one. This will allow only a single reflection of the same object on a neighboring object's surface. If you were constructing a house of mirrors, this setting would obviously not be sufficient to create the effect of infinity mirrors. To get the best effect, increase the recursion limit by one or two at a time. Use the lowest possible value to create the desired effect, since this can increase rendering time significantly.

Transparency Recursion

Just as important to the rendering process as reflectivity recursion is the transparency recursion setting. As light is traced back through the scene, it may pass through objects which have transparent surfaces. To create a realistic image, the light must stop somewhere. A setting of six will trace through six surfaces before giving up. In scenes where there may be lots of transparent objects, such as a house of glass, the recursion level may need to be raised. **If the ray-tracing algorithm reaches the transparency recursion limit before all transparent surfaces have been rendered, the remaining surfaces will appear black, due to the lack of light reaching their surface (see Figure 10-19).**

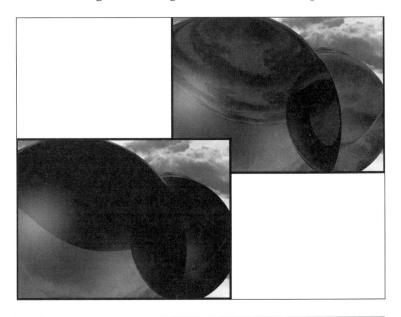

FIGURE 10-19 As you can see, setting the transparency recursion to a low number such as two will not be sufficient through all of the surfaces. Typically, the default setting will be enough, but occasionally, the recursion level must be raised to accommodate multiple layers of transparent objects.

Rendering Effects by Algorithm

	shadows	surface maps	smooth shading	transparency	refraction	reflectivity	inter-object illumination
wireframe							
flat shaded							
Gouraud			●	●			
Phong		●	●	●		●	
raytracing	●	●	●	●	●	●	
radiosity	●	●	●	●	●	●	●

Quick Reference for Choosing a Rendering Algorithm

Rendering Choice Quick Reference	
Modeling	wireframe, flat-shaded, hidden line Shaded Graphics Modeling (SGM)
Quick Preview	hidden-line, SGM, Gouraud shading, Z-Buffer
Good Preview	Gouraud, Phong, Z-Buffer, Preview Raytrace
Animation	Phong, Raytracing (with caution)
Stills (video)	Phong, Raytracing, Radiosity
Printing	High Resolution settings, Phong, Raytracing, Radiosity

Rendering Queues and Batch Queues

When doing production work, be sure that the rendering package you purchase has the ability to set up rendering queues or batch queues. This allows the user to set up a number of scenes to be rendered, start the rendering process, and walk away. The renderer will automatically render a scene or animation, save it to disk, and start the next rendering job automatically.

Since rendering varies greatly with the size of the image and the complexity of the scene, the rendering queue allows you to leave the system alone overnight or for the weekend without having to load each image to be rendered.

Although the rendering queue does not render the image faster, it does allow you to leave the computer unattended while it does its work. Some rendering packages also offer a networking capability in which the rendering queue can be used to render images over many machines. Networking packages are offered for Strata StudioPro (RenderPro), Lightwave 3D (ScreamerNet), 3D Studio, and Electric Image Animation System (Renderama) to name a few. You should check with the individual software vendors for any package you intend to purchase. **Figure 10-20 is a shot of the rendering queue from Strata StudioPro.**

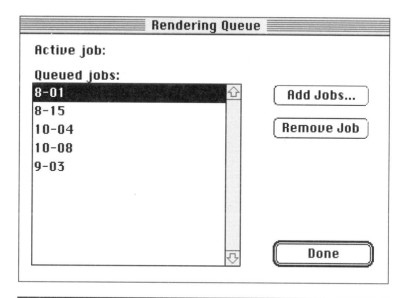

FIGURE 10-20 Using a rendering queue allows multiple animations or images to be set up for rendering, unattended. Load the queue with the suspended rendering files, and they will render one by one until completed or until the process is interrupted by the user.

TIP: Estimating your production time accurately is crucial when bidding on a contract. By keeping a log of actual rendering and modeling times for every project or model you work on, you will build a reference which may help determine accurate modeling and rendering times for future projects.

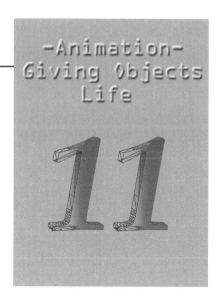

-Animation-
Giving Objects
Life

11

➤ Animation

Animation is the process of giving life to inanimate objects. By animating 3D objects, we can create the illusion of reality. What makes 3D animation stand out is the fact that objects will look real, yet they can be made to stretch, break, disappear, or morph into other objects. While animation is more difficult than 3D modeling, the special effects possible with 3D graphics are limited only by the imagination.

Lifelike and realistic animation is not a trivial task. In actual practice, animating an object may prove to be more difficult than creating the object itself. To animate an object, values in the various properties of an object are changed through the use of *keyframes*. Keyframes are specific frames in which an object property has been explicitly described. Keyframes can be created for any animatable property of an object, light, or camera.

Like its two dimensional cousin, 3D animation is created by rapidly displaying many frames in successive order, each image slightly different from the previous image. Because the frames are displayed at a high rate of speed (30 frames per second), the images blend together to give the appearance of smooth motion.

Although the basic premise of animation is the same, 3D animation has some major advantages over 2D cell animation. Because it is digital, 3D animation can suffer many edits and unlimited layer compositing with no degradation in image quality. This alone becomes extremely beneficial, especially during animation. When building a 3D scene, you need build it only once. From one scene, you may add any number of cameras, and set them at any viewing angle. Once the scene is built, you can create many different perspectives on the same animation by simply setting up another camera and rendering the scene. Once the scene has been built and the cameras set, the computer will do all of the work in creating the images. It is this type of versatility which makes 3D animation a viable alternative for visualization and special effects.

Animation is an exciting and wonderful art form. Just as creating computer models to look just right took some time, you can expect animation to also take some time to master. When you think you have a particular animation skill perfected, move on to a more difficult task, such as realistic organic movement, such as with people, animals, and liquids. Animating computer objects can captivate and frustrate you for many years to come, so sit back and enjoy the adventure.

Animatable Properties

To animate an object, you must be able to change its property values. Almost every property associated with an object can be animated. Some software does not provide a means for animating every property, while others do. Typically, the low to midrange animation packages will offer many animatable properties, but not all. It is the high-end systems which allow for all properties to be animated as well as additional special effects.

Typically properties which are animated are listed in Figure 11-1. While these properties are the most common animatable properties, there are many others. When purchasing an animation system, be sure you know what features you want before you spend the money on an animation package which does not suite your needs.

Object Properties

Position   Texture
Rotation   Shape   Scale

Light Properties

Color   Direction   Intensity

Camera Properties

Position   Target   Focal Point

FIGURE 11-1 While these are the most common animatable properties, they represent only a few of those found in high-end systems.

369

For true quality animation, you will need the best possible animation software you can afford. Depending on your needs and your budget, this can vary greatly. Some animation packages can cost as little as a few hundred dollars, while others can cost as much as several thousand dollars.

TIP: When purchasing an animation system, or a modeler for that matter, it is pretty safe to say that you get what you pay for. While there are many midrange animation systems on the market, to build high-quality output for production work, you need high-end animation systems. Programs such as Electric Image Animation System (EIAS) will run faster and produce very high quality, all at a reasonable rate of speed.

Animation Methods

When creating a 3D animation, two basic methods which used to animate an object's properties: keyframing and event markers. Both use similar methods, although event-based animation is more favorable because separate time lines can be created for each object within a scene.

Keyframe Animation

A very simple and effective method of creating animation is through the use of keyframes. Every animation has a minimum of two keyframes. A keyframe is a frame in which some property of an object has changed. For example, a pendulum which swings back and forth needs only three keyframes, one at the left swing, one at the top of the right swing, and one just slightly before the top of the left swing (for the returning swing). Each keyframe created is associated with the object which created it. Any particular frame in an animation can be designated a keyframe for one or multiple objects or properties.

Every property which can be animated can create its own set of keyframes. Keyframes from different properties may share the same keyframe location in the sequence of frames, such as a keyframe at frame 15 in which an object is rotated 45° and is also moved 2 inches along the positive X axis.

When a keyframe is created, the computer compares the values of two successive keyframes for each property and creates the in-between frames for that object. *Tweening* is the process of generating the frames in-between two keyframes. **In Figure 11-2, a keyframe was added to the pendulum object at frame 0 and frame 15. Frames 1 through 14 were generated by the computer through calculation.** In the case of the pendulum, the rotation was set from +45° in keyframe 0 to -45° in keyframe 15. If no tension, continuity or bias was set for either keyframe, the pendulum will swing -6° per frame. To make this look more realistic, we must add tension, and bias to the keyframes (discussed in later sections).

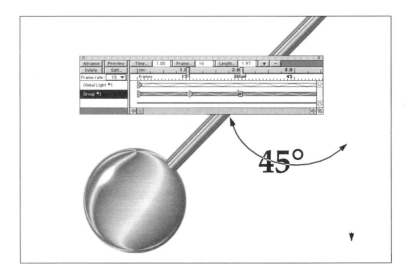

FIGURE 11-2 To make the pendulum swing, we start the object at a rotation of +45° and create a keyframe at 0. With an off-center pivot point, we set the rotation to minus 45° and create a keyframe at frame 15. The object will swing from left to right over the course of 15 frames a distance of minus 6° per frame.

All animations, must have keyframes to set the motion. Some programs such as Strata StudioPro and Vision 3D will create an automatic keyframe when an attribute is changed on an object. Others, such as Lightwave 3D require you to specifically create a keyframe. In either case, the keyframe is a marker which tells the computer that a certain property has changed for that object. When the animation is rendered, the object property (such as size or position) will gradually change during the time span between the previous keyframe and the current keyframe. Any of the animatable properties can be used to create a keyframe in animation.

Event-Based Animation

Event-based systems are very similar to keyframe systems, except that they are based on time lines instead of numbered frames. **The event time lines display event markers, frame number, frame rate, and time (see Figure 11-3).** Event-based systems provide for very sophisticated animation since each object can have its own time line. In the pendulum example, we could use a jewel hanging from the pendulum which is rotating slightly at its own pace.

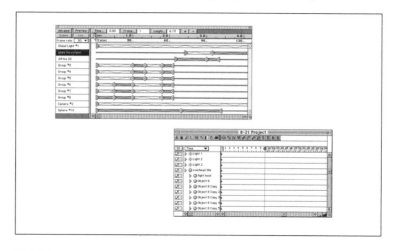

FIGURE 11-3 Event-based animation systems use time lines which give information about various controls at specific instances in time. These time lines are from Strata StudioPro and Electric Image Animation System 2.5.2.

In the same way that keyframes tell the computer about specific properties, event markers also describe the condition of an object's properties. In event-based animation systems, each object property also creates an event marker for that object. At any point in time, there may be many event markers from several objects.

EXERCISE - A Simple Animation

Using the pendulum example, we will animate the pendulum to swing back and forth. The pendulum will swing from side to side using a cycled animation sequence. This will keep the pendulum swinging throughout the course of an animation.

1. *Load the pendulum:* You may either load the pendulum object or create your own. Regardless of whether you use the model provided or your own creation, be sure that the circular end and the arm are designated as a single object or grouped together. **The pendulum object is called pendulum.dxf and is located in the objects directory**.

2. *Check the pivot point:* The pivot point of the pendulum object must be centered over the end of the top end of the pendulum arm **(see Figure 11-4). If the pivot point is anywhere else, the object will not swing properly. If the pivot point is not at the top end of the pendulum object, move it so that it is located in the same position as the X in Figure 11-4**.

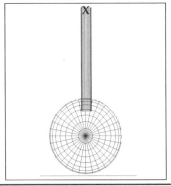

FIGURE 11-4 Be sure the pendulum arm (rectangle or cylinder) and weight (sphere) are a single object or a grouped object, and that the pivot point is located at the top of the arm, denoted by the X.

3. *Set keyframe or event marker 0:* While keyframe 0 is
created automatically, you must recreate it when
you change a property from its original or modeled position. Since we are going to rotate the position of the pendulum, we must reset keyframe 0 or
the first event marker *after* the rotation. Select and
rotate the pendulum object 45° along the Z axis.
**Your pendulum should look similar to the object
in Figure 11-5**.

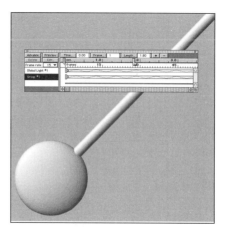

FIGURE 11-5 Rotate the pendulum object 45° along the Z axis to position your object as the pendulum in this image. This will be the starting
position for the pendulum, so you must also set the first event marker or
keyframe 0 after positioning the pendulum.

4. *Create motion:* Select and rotate the pendulum
object minus 90° along the Z axis. This will position the object at the top of the other side of the
pendulum's swing. Create a keyframe or event
marker after completing the rotation. Typically, in
event-based animation systems, an event marker is
created automatically when an animatable object
property has been changed.

5. *Preview the animation:* Since we have created two keyframes or event markers, we have technically created an animation. Use whatever preview method your system uses to preview the motion. The pendulum should swing from the left to the right. Save your work, we will return to this animation later.

We have just completed a very simple animation, although this animation can use additional information to make the motion of the pendulum swing more naturally. The later sections on Tension, Continuity, and Bias will use the pendulum animation to achieve a more realistic motion.

TIP: When animating objects with complex geometry or high polygon counts, you may substitute the objects with boxes. By using a box primitive, you can reduce the polygon count significantly. This will make screen redraws quicker during the animation process. Simply replace the boxes with real geometry when the motion is complete and render as normal.

Linear Keyframes and Event Markers

Whether you are using keyframes and event markers, each can be designated as linear or spline. By setting a keyframe or event marker to linear, motion will be restricted to a straight path as it enters and exits the keyframe. A linear event marker causes rigid motion and is not typically used when animating characters. It is more useful when animating mechanical objects which move along a single axis at a time, than with more organic animation. **Figure 11-6** illustrates the difference in the motion paths after the event markers were converted to linear.

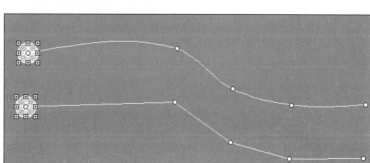

FIGURE 11-6 Notice the difference in the path of the two spheres. Each has an identical motion path, yet the lower sphere's path had all of its event markers converted to linear.

Spline Keyframes and Event Markers

By using spline-type keyframes and event markers, the animator has complete control over the action at each keyframe. Spline markers can control tension, continuity, and bias, which can dramatically affect the way an object moves through that particular keyframe or event marker. Typically, a spline motion path is one which flows into and out of each event marker or keyframe it encounters. Just like objects which are created using splines, the appearance is very smooth.

Along any motion path, there could be any combination of linear and spline event markers. The use of the different types of markers is up to the animator. **Figure 11-7 shows two identical paths with some markers designated linear and some spline**.

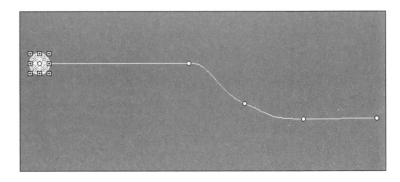

FIGURE 11-7 By setting the event markers to linear in the beginning and end of this animation path, the object will flow on a straight path until it reaches the second event marker, which is set to spline and starts the beginning of the curved motion. By making the event markers during the curved motion splines and the ends linear, we get a smooth motion through the curve while the object will approach the final event marker along a straight path.

Tension

Because real objects normally do not move in a linear fashion, animated objects can sometimes appear to be jerky or unnatural in their motion, if no tension is applied. Objects moving from point A to point B in 30 frames will do so with equal force applied to all 30 frames. The problem is that the laws of physics do not work that way. Objects take time to build up speed and to slow down. A common problem seen with beginning animators is that objects are animated to move instantly, from 0 to 60 in one frame and then stop on a dime. To make objects accelerate and decelerate in a realistic fashion, we must add tension to the keyframes which start and end a motion.

Tension is added to an object's keyframes, not the objects themselves. Tension values usually range from -1 to +1 and may be set to any value between. A tension of 0 is considered normal or no tension. Adding more tension to a keyframe will cause the object to slow down as it approaches the keyframe (moving less with each frame as it approaches the keyframe) and accelerate as it leaves the keyframe. Using negative tension will cause the object to accelerate as it approaches the keyframe and slow down as it leaves.

Keyframe Tension

Positive - object slows gradually as it approaches the keyframe.

Negative - objects speed up as they approach the keyframe.

Zero - no tension, object speed unaffected by keyframe.

FIGURE 11-8 Use a traffic light to remember how to control tension. At high tension, i.e., equivalent to a red light, objects will slow to a gradual stop as they approach the keyframe. Yellow is negative tension, objects will speed up as they approach the keyframe. Green equals no tension, the object will continue on its path according to the keyframe without changing speed.

Using tension can be compared to the way traffic signals control the roads (see Figure 11-8). A red light signifies high tension, a yellow light means negative tension, and a green light means no tension. Each keyframe would have its own traffic signal. As an object approaches the keyframe, it looks at the traffic signal (keyframe tension control). If the light is green (no tension), it continues on its way, following the keyframe instructions. If the traffic signal is yellow (negative tension), the object accelerates toward the keyframe (just like in real life). If the object sees that the keyframe traffic signal is red, it begins to slow down so that it will approach the keyframe with a gradual slowing (no skidding).

While adding tension to keyframes will slow the object smoothly, the time between the keyframes remains the same. The difference is in the amount of movement given to the object per frame. When no tension is added, the object will move the same distance for each frame between the keyframes. Positive tension will cause the frames to move a smaller distance each frame as the object approaches the keyframe. The amount of slowing depends on the tension and the number of frames between the keyframe with tension and the previous keyframe.

TIP: Add tension to smooth motion on an object. Tension will create a more realistic slowing or acceleration of objects as they enter and exit keyframes. Tension works on any animation attribute, such as movement or rotation on any axis.

Continuity

In addition to adding tension to an event marker or keyframe, continuity can also be added if the marker is designated as a spline. Spline motion paths are used so that animated properties may transcend gradually, or fluctuate in value along a smooth curve, since objects in the real world do not move like robots along a linear path. Continuity is used to break the smoothness of the motion path for sudden action, such as a basketball hitting the rim or the backboard when missing the basket. **Figure 11-9** illustrates a motion path in which the continuity of the path has been broken.

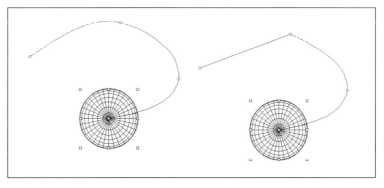

FIGURE 11-9 Breaking the continuity of a motion path is useful when the object must change direction immediately, as in a collision with another object.

As the basketball flies through the air toward the basket, we can observe a smooth spline path (with tension), until the ball hits the backboard or the basket. At that time, the ball will radically change direction (assuming we don't make the basket). When working with spline motion paths, continuity must be broken to achieve a sudden change in direction.

By breaking the continuity at the keyframe, the ball can have smooth motion until it hits the keyframe. As the object leaves the keyframe, the motion path can send the object sharply in another direction. To break the continuity of a keyframe, use a negative value. Using a positive continuity value on a keyframe may cause the object to overshoot or float around the keyframe. Continuity values range from -1 to +1 with a value of 0 being equal to normal or unbroken continuity.

TIP: Positive continuity is almost never used. For most cases, a value of minus 1 will break the continuity of the keyframe without excess object motion.

Bias

While continuity and tension control the way an object moves through a keyframe or event marker, bias is used to control tension and continuity. The bias adjusts the emphasis of the keyframe. The bias setting can be used to place the emphasis of the tension either before the keyframe (negative bias) or after the keyframe (positive bias). By changing the bias, we can cause the object to anticipate the event marker as it approaches, or overshoot it by adding a positive bias. **Figure 11-10 illustrates identical motion paths except for the bias applied to the lower path**.

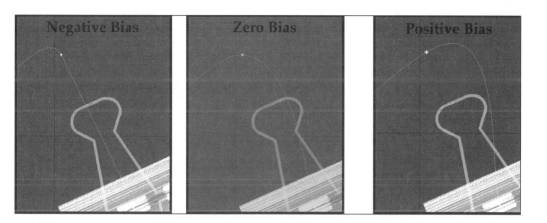

FIGURE 11-10 Adding bias to the motion path will cause the tension to favor one side of the keyframe or event marker. Negative bias will cause more tension to be placed before the keyframe, while positive bias will cause the tension to be placed after the keyframe or event marker.

Birth and Death Events (Instant Dissolve)

While most keyframes or events describe a motion type, the birth or death event marker is quite different. This feature enables objects to disappear from a scene if no longer needed or if not needed at the start of an animation. **You may choose to use this effect when animating something such as soap bubbles floating around the room and popping, while new bubbles are generated (see Figure 11-11).**

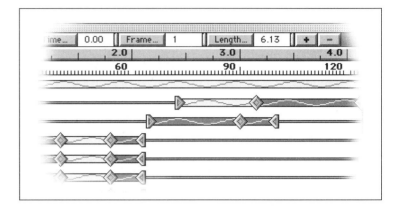

FIGURE 11-11 The use of birth and death events can make objects appear and disappear throughout an animation. Objects may die and be born again as often as needed.

By setting a birth event, the object will instantly appear at the frame which contains the birth event. Similarly, the object will disappear when it encounters a death event. Since birth and death events are instantaneous, you may choose to use a dissolve instead to have an object appear over time. By causing an object to disappear through the use of a death event, the object's geometry is no longer considered during rendering until it encounters a birth event. Objects may have multiple death and birth events during a single animation.

Motion Paths

In order for objects to move through a scene, a motion path must be assigned to the object. Motion paths can be imported or created within the scene. Some motion paths are very complex, while others are as simple as moving one inch to the left. Once an object has moved, a motion path is created for that object. The motion path describes the way an object moves or rotates, as well as any changes to other animatable properties. While the motion path typically is visible in animation software when an object is selected, it does not render. **Visible motion paths are used as a means of visualizing the object's history of direction and movement (see Figure 11-12).**

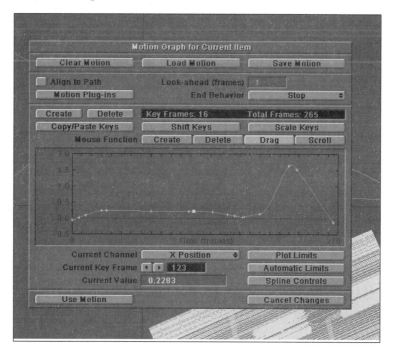

FIGURE 11-12 Motion paths dictate how an object moves through a scene. Motion paths may also be used for nonmoving attributes, such as scale. The visible path shows how an object changes over time.

A motion path can be predrawn and imported into a scene (or drawn into the scene if the software provides), or it can be created by setting keyframes as the object is moved around the scene. Once created, a motion path can be edited to fine-tune an object's movement.

 TIP: The words *keyframe* and *event marker* are used interchangeably in this text, although they are slightly different. When the difference in the two is a factor, it will be explicitly explained.

Motion Paths Through Keyframes

Since all moving objects need motion paths, a path can be created by simply moving an object and creating keyframes at various times in the motion. When creating a motion path from keyframes, simply drag the object around the scene, creating keyframes along the way, as you also advance the time line marker. If your animation software does not use a time line, use keyframes at each position where the action changes, advancing the keyframes at the desired rate (normally 30 frames per second). **Use keyframes anywhere the object changes direction or motion stops in order to keep the action flowing correctly (see Figure 11-13).** You may need to add multiple keyframes through the curve to keep the object from floating beyond the curve.

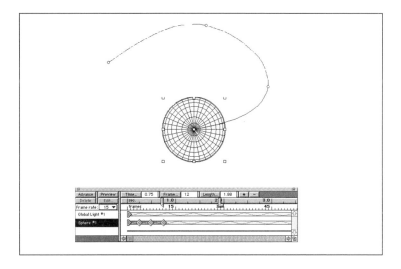

FIGURE 11-13 By moving an object through the scene, keyframes can be created along the way to create a motion path. Once the path has been established, it may be edited for fine-tuning.

TIP: When there is stop-and-go motion in an object, be sure to add a keyframe to mark the end of the stop period. If an object is to move for 15 frames, stop for 5 then move again for 15 frames, there must be 4 keyframes, an initial starting keyframe (frame 0), end of first motion (frame 15), end of stop (frame 20), and end of second motion (frame 35). Although it may seem obvious to place the keyframe at frame 20, putting in the stop motion keyframe is often forgotten, especially when the distance between motions is a hundred frames away.

Motion Paths from Splines

Although a viable method of motion path creation, keyframing the motion is not as accurate and transportable as spline motion paths. Spline motion paths are created through the use of existing line segments or splines. Although they must exist before the object is assigned to it, a spline motion path can be drawn specifically for the use of a motion path. This is a powerful alternative to creating each keyframe by manually moving an object.

Using a spline for a motion path is also very useful when keeping objects aligned with other models during animation. Suppose you were to animate a roller coaster as it moves along the tracks. Manually scripting the motion path through the use of keyframes could prove to be very tedious. The alternative would be to use a preexisting spline. By using the same spline that was used to create the track (assuming it was created by extruding or sweeping along a path), you could attach the roller coaster car to that same path, and it would follow the tracks exactly! **Figure 11-14 illustrates how the same path can be used to create an object and a motion path**.

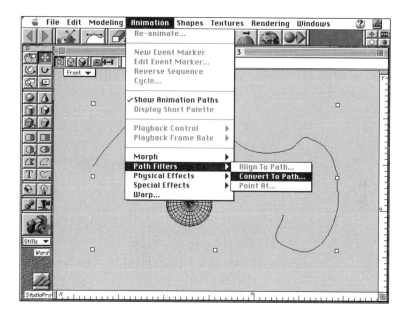

FIGURE 11-14 Motion paths can also be created through the use of 2D lines. Objects can be associated with the path so their animation movement will follow the path. Using a predrawn path is useful when the path of an object will be very intricate or needs to be very precise around other objects.

Animating Cameras

Although cameras are more sensitive to motion than other objects, motion paths will work equally well in animating a camera. The ability to animate a camera is a very powerful tool which should be a major consideration when purchasing an animation system. Perspective is what sets 3D graphics apart from other aspects of visual production. By animating the camera, we can get a better impression of perspective. Flying around objects and moving freely about the scene show the viewer that these objects are real, and have depth and volume like real objects do.

There are many times when a camera is animated during an animation and there are times when it is not. While adding a motion path to a camera is the same as adding motion to any other object, camera motion paths which do not flow smoothly will quickly become apparent when rendered.

When animating cameras, one must be very careful to keep the camera motion smooth and on target with the subject of the frame. As a camera becomes animated, it may begin to drift from the subject, or its motion may get rough as it passes through keyframes. Some techniques are available to combat camera motion problems.

 TECHNIQUE: Animating a Camera

- *Use target nulls:* By targeting the camera to a null object, the camera can focus on different subjects at different times during an animation. This is very convenient when the camera is moving through a scene with lots of scenery. The target null must also be animated ahead of the camera to dictate what the camera will be "looking at" as it moves through the scene.

- *Parent the subject:* By attaching the camera to the subject, the camera can be made to follow an object through a scene. This works very well when the camera is made to chase an object through a complex scene, because you need only animate the motion of the subject and the camera will follow.

- *Limit camera banks:* As a camera moves through the scene, you may want to limit the ratio of the bank, as a camera goes through a turn. Unless, you are trying to simulate an IMAX airplane ride, excessive banking on turns can be disturbing to the viewer.

- *Use low or no tension:* As the camera comes upon a keyframe with tension, the camera may get pulled in a different direction than the current flow. By removing the tension or setting it very low, the camera will flow smoothly through the keyframes. Because the camera is the viewer's eyes, any small disturbance in movement will immediately distract the viewer.

Timing

Whether animating an object or a camera, through splines or keyframing, timing is very critical for creating a realistic scene. Timing applies to all objects, including cameras and lights (if animated). While there are no set rules on timing, there are some basic guidelines. It is always important to keep you audience interested, whether you are animating an engine component, corporate logos, or the next *Toy Story*. Keeping the audience's interest can be a matter of timing.

TECHNIQUE: Timing Guidelines

- *Thirty frames per second:* When creating animation, the typical rate of full motion video is 30 frames per second. What this means in an animation is that objects which appear in camera view for less than 30 frames will very likely be missed by the viewer. This of course, will depend on the object and the animation, but it is something to keep in mind before rendering.

- *Keep object motion smooth:* Keep the pace of the motion consistent with the action. Animated objects should not jerk suddenly, without reason.

- *Keep camera motion smooth:* Camera motion should flow smoothly. The camera should almost never have a jumpy motion (unless it is intended to look as though it was hit by something). When panning, the camera should pan slow enough so that the entire scene can be established. Follow an object as it crosses the field of vision. If it does not stay in the frame for at least three seconds, the pan may need to be slowed down.

- *Let it be read:* When important text is in the frame, it should be visible for at least 4 seconds for simple text. This is only when the text is intended to be read, such as a label or header for an upcoming sequence.

Hierarchical Animation Objects

A number of objects are used exclusively as animation helpers. These objects are called *hierarchical objects* because they are parented to or they become associated with, other objects. The use of parents and targets is immediately appreciated when animating complex motion. While parents can be used to control the motion of objects, the target objects can be used to control the direction in which an object is facing. Some hierarchical aids are not really objects, but positions in space, such as the null object, while others, such as the target objects, may be other objects already located in the scene.

Null Objects

A primary hierarchical animation object is the null object. Null objects are not really objects, but placeholders that are used to represent a position in space. Nulls are used primarily as target objects or parent objects for other objects during animation. Null objects do not have surface or size properties and will not render. See the sections on *Target Objects* and *Parent Objects* to learn how to use null objects effectively.

TIP: Null objects are used because they have no geometry and will not render. If your software does not have null objects, you may also use a simple cube which has been assigned a 100% dissolve. An object that has been 100% dissolved will not render at all. If you do not have a dissolve feature, you may use transparency, but be sure to turn off all visible properties (specular, luminosity, reflectivity, refraction, diffuse color, and glossiness) because even though the object is invisible, some of these surface properties may render.

Target Objects.

Unlike null objects, which are never real objects, a target object can be a preexisting real object in a scene. When creating an animation, movie, or photograph, it is normally favorable to keep the subject in view of the camera lens. To keep the subject within the sights of the camera lens, we can make the subject a target object. When an object has been designated the target of the camera, the camera will continue to look at that object regardless of its position or the camera's. While each object can have only one target, an object may be the target for multiple objects at any one time.

In the illustration in Figure 11-15, three positions of the camera have been composited to show how the camera reacts when targeted to the subject. As you can see, the camera will always be "looking" at the target object. This is very useful when the subject or the camera are not stationary during an animation. Without the use of a target object, it would be very difficult to keep the camera focused on the subject, if it were to move in a nonlinear fashion through 3D space.

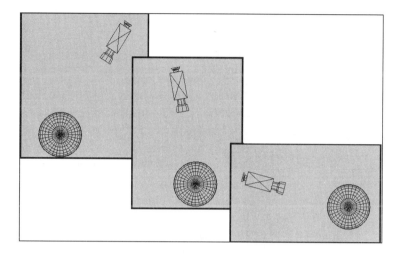

FIGURE 11-15 In this image, the camera position at three locations has been composited to illustrate a point. Notice how the camera is always pointing at the sphere.

Using a target object for the camera is a very powerful tool. This lets the animator concentrate on where the camera is going, not what it needs to look at. There are times, however, when the subject of the animation changes during the course of the animation. During a flyby over a proposed resort development, for example, the camera may want to focus on the waterfall as you enter the resort, then move on to show amenities such as the pool, tennis courts, and living spaces. Since many packages do not allow you to change the target, a null object can be used to allow you to change the subject, without changing the target of the camera.

TRICK: Use null objects as targets when the subject is going to change through the course of an animation or when the camera is animated. By using a null object as the target, you can adjust the position of the null to create a more aesthetic frame. Because the camera will point directly at the object's pivot point, there may be times, as the camera approaches the object, when that angle will be incorrect. When a target object is used, the target can be dollied back to correct an improper angle on the subject.

The key to using targets effectively is to choose the correct target object. Many times, using the subject itself as the target can lead to an improper or bad camera angle. The trick to getting a good camera angle while keeping the subject in frame is to use a null object as the target. Simply place the null object at the center of the subject as the camera approaches. This will ensure that the camera is pointing directly at the subject. By using a null object as the target, the angle of view on the subject can also be adjusted to create a favorable image.

By using a null object for the target, the camera can pan from side to side, or appear to "look around" while on a fly-through, simply by animating the null object along a path similar to that of the camera. By placing the null object near various key objects during the animation, it can appear as though the target object is changing through the course of the animation. By using the null object as a target, the camera will always point directly where you want it to, without having to animate the camera rotation in addition to its motion.

TRICK: While using a target object is great for cameras, they are also very useful when animating other objects. The eyes and head of a character model can be targeted to a colorful beach ball, for example, and the head and eyes will turn to watch the ball as it goes by. This effect adds a nice touch of realism to the animated character.

Parent Objects

In animation, the target object is used to keep another object facing it. Parent objects, however, are used to control the relative position of two objects. Parenting of objects allows the animator to establish a relationship between two objects. One object is the parent, and the other is the child object. Unlike the real world, parents are chosen in the 3D world. Object properties are not required to establish a parent-child relationship. Parent-child relationships are established to keep together objects which have some logical connection. Parents can be children and children can be parents, but parents cannot be children of their own children.

The characteristic motion of a parent-child relationship is relatively simple. The child object can be animated without restriction or without affecting any other objects (unless it is a parent object also). **The parent object, while not restricted in its movement, will affect all of its children with it's motion (see Figure 11-16).** The child objects are free to have their own motion paths, which will always be followed, but when the parent object also has a motion path, the child objects will inherit that motion as well as maintaining their own.

FIGURE 11-16 While the child objects are free to move about on their own, they will also inherit the motion of the parent object.

A real-life example of a parent-child relationship between unrelated objects could be the example of sea gulls and fishing boats as they return from a day at sea. If you do not live near the coast, or have never seen a returning fishing boat, this may take a little imagination. In this example, the boat is the parent object and the seagulls are the children objects.

As the fishing boat appears with the day's catch, seagulls will swarm around the boat like bees around a hive. The boat will navigate the inlet, choosing whichever path it feels necessary. This is the motion of the parent object. The seagulls are free to fly anywhere they please, and they do, diving and swarming around the boat. Because they are the child objects (and hungry), the seagulls will follow the path of the boat until it reaches the docks. In a sense, the seagulls are slaves to the motion path of the boat. This is what a parent-child object relationship does in animation. Objects can move freely about the scene on their own, but when the parent object moves, all of the children will also move also, following the same path as the parent, while maintaining their own individual paths in relation to the parent.

Inverse Kinematics

One of the newest hierarchical animation classes to enter the scene in the last couple of years is *inverse kinematics*. To create a model which has fluid motion and realistic motion in related parts, the model must be created with kinematics in mind. A kinematics model is one in which the pieces of related groups, such as the pieces of a leg or arm, are built to accommodate realistic movement and motion. The realistic movement is possible through a hierarchical element chain of the parts of the limb. Applying inverse kinematics makes the entire limb work as though it were real.

A feature once only possible on mini and mainframe computers, inverse kinematics is now being offered in more and more desktop packages, such as Electric Image Animation System 2.5 and Lightwave 3D. **Inverse kinematics allows the animator to link existing objects to create lifelike movement through the use of parent-child object relationships (see Figure 11-17).**

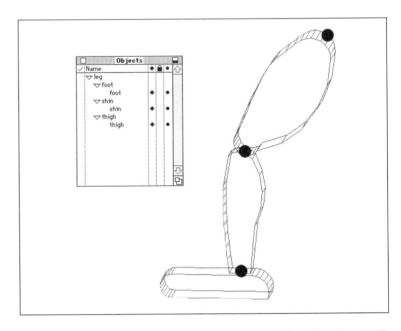

FIGURE 11-17 This figure shows a basic leg hierarchy for inverse kinematics. For models such as a hand, the parent-child tree would be more complex due to the fingers.

Inverse kinematics (known as IK) works by establishing a chain between multiple parent-child links. This is the old "leg bone connected to the hip bone" scenario. By linking the parts of a leg, creating the limits and locations of the joints, the leg can be made to act like a real leg when walking. The use of inverse kinematics makes animation so much easier, because the technology is built in. You need only build the model, create the joints, and define the basic movement.

Animation Output

After all of the keyframing and motion have been set, the textures applied, and the cameras positioned, an animation is ready for rendering. An animation is created by rendering a series of sequential frames, which when played back in a fast, logical order, appear to give the image motion. When creating an animation, the individual frames can be rendered separately, then compiled using a utility program, such as Adobe Premiere, or the frames can be rendered into a single file movie, such as QuickTime or AVI.

TIP: For the highest versatility when rendering an animation, render the output to a series of single images (one for each frame). While this may take over a megabyte for each image and the animation must be built separately, it allows for greater quality and postproduction work, if desired.

Rendering to single frames can be very beneficial when creating animation for various types of output. Once all of the frames have been rendered, building multiple copies of the animation at various quality levels will take less time than rerendering the entire animation. Even if the animation were to be played on multiple platforms, the individual frames can be converted and built on each of the native platforms needed. Different output options require different hardware, software, and memory configurations, which may not be available for or suitable to every platform. Having the flexibility to accommodate the different needs will save time in the long run. Converting files is typically faster than rerendering.

Animation Output Options

While every major platform has the capability to play back animation, the formats available for each platform vary. While the graphics world tries to struggles for a standard digital format, NTSC (United States) and PAL (Europe) remain the standard formats for television and broadcast. If your output will be for a computer monitor, as in the form of a CD-ROM or multimedia presentation, your limitations on output are dictated by the power of the computer in which it will be played. For broadcast, animation will have to be recorded to tape and played back on television monitors, requiring that the animation is set to NTSC or PAL color and size standards.

One of the major problems with the NTSC standard is that it was initialized years ago, before today's high-quality images were possible. As a result color is limited, and intense blues, yellows, and especially reds will bleed horribly if not corrected before recorded to tape. Programs such as DeBabelizer (Equilibrium Technologies) can color correct an image or animation before it is sent to videotape.

Another problem with NTSC video is that the actual displayable area is smaller than that of a computer monitor. The size of NTSC video is actually 720 x 486 pixels, but the size of video which is sent to the screen is actually only 640 x 480 pixels. Due to the curve of the monitor and the housing, the screen size can vary significantly. To keep all important video on-screen, television safe areas have been established. While these areas are smaller, they ensure that the action and titles will always appear on screen and not along the edges. The safe areas for NTSC video consist of two rounded rectangles on a 640 x 480 pixel screen. **The** inner rectangles' dimensions are 580 x 430 pixels and 520 x 380 pixels (see Figure 11-18).

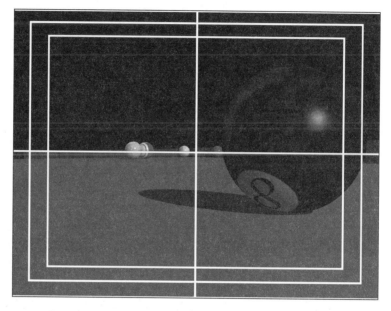

FIGURE 11-18 The television safe areas for NTSC video. All text must appear within the innermost circle, while all action must be inside the outer rectangle. Anything outside the outer rectangle is at risk of being cut out of the visible range.

PICS

This Macintosh format, introduced by MacroMedia™ (formerly known as MacroMind™), uses the resource fork in a single file to store the sequential frames of an animation. While this format does have the advantage of extracting individual frames from the file, there are a couple of problems with this format.

The PICS format has the distinct problem of not supporting files larger than 16-megabytes. When the format was designed, Macintosh file systems could not support files with more than 16-megabytes in the resource fork. Depending on the codec used during rendering, most animation can easily and quickly exceed the 16 megabyte file size. To use this format, the animation would have to be rendered in small chunks. For a 15-second animation run at 30 frames per second and a 640 x 480 pixel resolution at 24 bit, this could mean at least 30 different animations to hold all of the frames.

Another problem with the PICS format is that it cannot play back at real time. To achieve smooth close to 30 frames per second playback, the entire file would have to be loaded into a RAM buffer.

QuickTime

While the PICS format creates a single file of all self-supported frames, QuickTime frames must be kept intact to be viewed. QuickTime was originally created as an extension to the Macintosh operating system, which is now available for Windows™ operating systems. When first created, movie playback was postage sized and chunky. Today, QuickTime can support 640 x 480 pixel real-time playback. The QuickTime architecture supports still images, text, sound, and MIDI as well as animation. A number of QuickTime codecs support both lossless and lossy compression.

A lossless compression/decompression (codec) technique saves all data associated with an image, but results in slower playback. The QuickTime animation and image formats are lossless codecs. When using either of these techniques, total image quality will remain intact, but playback speed will be reduced.

A lossy codec will reduce the image quality for the sake of greater compression and quicker playback. Many of the lossy codecs have controls which allow the user to choose between various levels of quality, compression, and speed. Cinepak, a lossy codec, can support full screen (640 x 480 pixel) playback at 30 frames per second.

A list follows of the various QuickTime codecs:

- *Video compressor:* This codec is best suited for compression and capture of analog video. Moderate- to high-quality playback can be achieved from both CD-ROMs and hard disks. While alpha channels are not supported in this codec, the entire image is saved from frame to frame, which causes large file sizes, yet enables repeated passes for postproduction work. Compact video format, an extension of the video format, is optimized for 16-bit color and will provide better compression ratios and dithering than the standard video compressor.

- *Animation:* The animation compressor has multiple modes, ranging from black and white output to various levels of grays to millions of colors. Compression is achieved by saving the difference between successive frames. For this reason, the entire QuickTime movie must be intact when image editing. For 3D rendering, the most popular settings are "Millions of Colors" and "Millions of Colors +". The "+" means that the compression technique will save the frames in addition to an alpha channel. This is extremely useful for compositing background images into video, yet the file size is large and the playback is slower. At the highest setting, the animation codec is a lossless compression algorithm, preserving all image information intact. The lowest setting will produce a lossy compression, achieving a higher data compression ratio.

- *Cinepak:* This compressor is very popular with CD-ROM developers because animation files are small and playback is extremely fast. Cinepak can support full-screen (640 x 480 pixels) playback at 30 frames per second. The drawbacks are that it takes up to ten times longer to compress the animation and a lot of image information is dropped during compression. This codec also offers a data rate controller, which enables comparable playback on slower systems.

- *MPEG:* One of the newest codecs, MPEG compression requires the use of a decoder board when creating and playing MPEG-encoded files. Because the compression and decompression are done through the use of hardware instead of software, this codec can achieve high quality with fast playback. The only drawback is the required hardware. Systems without the MPEG hardware cannot play files created with MPEG encoding.

- *None:* This is a noncompression compression algorithm. Using the none compressor will produce files with the least degradation. Unfortunately, the playback is extremely slow and the file size is extremely large. When recording an animation in this format, you must be sure you have ample disk space. This format is highly useful when quality is the primary concern and disk space is not an issue.

- *Photo JPEG*: JPEG format is excellent at storing still images. JPEG accelerator boards are available which come with their own compression software, which enables greater playback and compression abilities.

QuickTime VR

One of the newest and exciting formats of QuickTime is the QuickTime VR format. **QuickTime VR format is a panoramic format which encompasses a 360° view in every frame (see Figure 11-19)**. Using this format with a QuickTime VR interface, game developers can create animation clips which allow the user to look interactively in any direction, as well as up or down, seamlessly. This is a very new and exciting format which shows lots of promise for interactive CD-ROM games.

FIGURE 11-19   QuickTime VR format will render each frame as a panoramic view. When coupled with a QuickTime VR interface, the animation becomes interactive, providing the viewer with the opportunity to view the animation from virtually any angle.

AVI

Unlike QuickTime, which is available on both Macintosh and Windows platforms, AVI animation is only playable on Windows systems. Users of the Windows™ operating system on PCs may be familiar with .AVI files. These are animation files which can be played from the standard Windows Media Player. When rendering to the .AVI format, the user is prompted for a compression technique. Depending on the codecs installed on the machine, the codec list could vary. Some of the common codecs used in .AVI files include Cinepak compression and IBM's Indeo format. Files may also be rendered without compression, as in the QuickTime None option. The following is a list of .AVI options:

- *Compressor:* Use this field to choose from the codecs installed on the system. Only installed codecs will be visible.

- *Compression Quality:* This field will affect the quality and the compression ratio of the animation file. Choosing a higher number indicates a higher quality image, resulting in a lower compression ratio. The higher the quality, the lower the compression ratio, and consequently, the larger the animation file.

- *Keyframe every:* This field enables the user to control the number of keyframes used when saving the animation file. The higher the value inserted in this field, the lower the quality of the animation. For best compression, set the "keyframe every" value to 1. The "keyframe every" setting does not alter the frame rate of the animation, but it does control how many frames will be saved and how many will be generated as "tweened" frames. A setting of one will save every frame, while a setting of 2 will cause the system to save every other frame, while saving only the difference between the keyframe and every other subsequent frame.

- *Data Rate:* As in the QuickTime Cinepak files, the data rate can also be controlled in some .AVI codecs. By changing the data rate, the animation can be made to play back at a comparable speed on slower systems.

- *Configure:* This button will present a second control panel for setting other parameters if required by other software or hardware.

FLC

Like the AVI animation type, the FLC animation is also a PC based format. This animation codec creates 8 bit animation files which can be played in either DOS or Windows™. Since the color depth is limited to 8 bits, only 256 colors can be displayed in a single frame. This format does however have options to build a more colorful animation for systems which have a better display than 256 colors. The following fields are available options when rendering to a .FLC file:

- *Universal color palette:* Checking this box will use the default 8-bit color palette when saving the animation file.

- *Create palette on first frame:* Checking this box will force the system to create a palette (of 8 bits) from the first frame in the animation. This works well if the same colors are used throughout the animation. New colors will not translate as well using this setting.

- *Create palette for each frame:* Checking this box will cause the codec to create a new palette for each frame in the animation. This feature allows for more than 256 colors to be displayed throughout the course of the animation. This option does not translate well on systems with an 8-bit color display.

- *Dither frames:* Using this feature creates a smoother transition through gradient colors which have a tendency to create a banded look on 8-bit displays. As in all dithered output, artifacting or noise may occur in the image.

Intersecting Geometry

In all of the confusion of moving and rotating of objects and cameras in a scene, objects are bound to run into each other. Some collisions may be as subtle as an object barely clipping a wall when turning a corner, or as blatant as a car driving through the side of a house. Since objects will not bounce off each other like real objects (unless collision detection is applied), object geometry will intersect as the two objects pass through each other. Intersecting geometry not only becomes very noticeable when rendered, but it can also cause problems with some types of renderers. **When animating multiple objects, it is important to be sure that objects do not pass through (or intersect) each other's** geometry. When working in wireframe mode, it is not always obvious from a single viewpoint as to whether two objects are intersecting (see Figure 11-20).

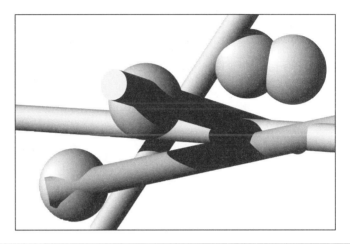

FIGURE 11-20 Objects that pass through other objects that are supposed to be solid can quickly spoil the illusion of realism in an animation. Check all animation paths from multiple angles and render some still images at questionable intersections.

When looking for unintentional object intersection, be sure to check from multiple views. In areas that are congested, create a couple of low-resolution still images to check that the objects are not passing through each other. This may tend to be a tedious process on longer animation, but it is a necessary evil for quality control. Using shaded graphics modeling really benefits here, because object intersection is noticed at the modeling stage, and not after time has been devoted to rendering. Nothing takes away from the realism of an animation like objects that pass through each other when they are supposed to be solid.

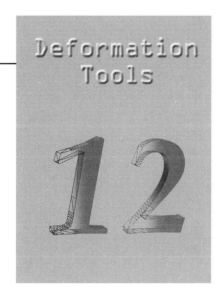

Deformation
Tools

12

→ Metamorphosis/Morph

One of the hottest and most popular tools in 3D animation is the ability of one object to morph into another. It's been used in videos, commercial advertising, and many other forms of animation. Object Morphing enables the animator to transition between different related shapes. Morphing can be used to create changing objects, pouring liquids, or many other special effects. **Figure 12-1 shows how a cube can be morphed into a sphere**.

413

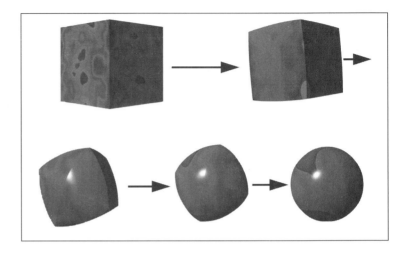

FIGURE 12-1   Through morphing, changes can take effect over time through a smooth transition, instead of an instant change.

Morphing two or more objects is best when the morph is undetectable by the viewer. By using different objects in the morph chain, the change can be so subtle that it looks as though the object is real and not a morph. If a special effect can be applied and not detected, it means that the animator did the job of convincing the audience that the object was real, and not the work of special effects.

Morphing Points

The simplest method of morphing is morphing points. Objects which are morphed from one shape to another require that both objects have the same number of vertices or points. **Using this method, an object's vertices are tracked from one position to the morphed position (see Figure 12-2).**

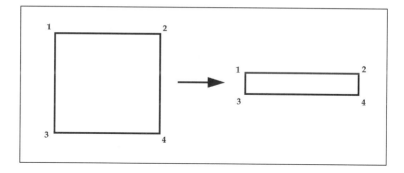

FIGURE 12-2 Using vertices to morph an object can produce very convincing morphs between objects.

While this can produce very effective results in morphing, it can become tedious ensuring that the vertices are positioned correctly in both objects. Vertices that are not positioned correctly will result in an incorrect morphing sequence.

 TECHNIQUE: Morphing Object Vertices

- *Use same points:* When morphing objects which have the same number of vertices, it is best to use the same points to create all morph targets. Create the points and order from top to bottom or vice versa. Use the same ordering when creating each morph target in the series to ensure the correct morphing sequence.

- *Use plenty of morphs:* Creating a complex morph sequence may require that more than two objects be created. Depending on the type of morphing, there may be several morph targets. The correct number of morph targets is directly related to the type of object and morphing which is to be animated. For a smoother morph, you will need to add more morph

targets. Be sure to make changes over curved surfaces gradual to avoid "jumping" morphs.

TIP: When morphing requires that objects have the same number of
vertices, it is best to create the original and the morph target out of the
same set of points. The order of the points is also a consideration and
should be consistent between the two objects.

Spline Morphs

While morphing points from one position to the next
works well, spline morphing works even better. This type
of morph will morph any ordered spline object into any
other ordered spline object. Just like all morphing features,
the beginning and ending morph shape must be created.
The benefit of a spline morph is that the object being morphed retains a smooth appearance through the entire
morph, without creating all of the in-between morph targets required when morphing vertices. To use the spline
morph feature, the objects must be true, ordered spline
objects. **Figure 12-3 shows an example of an object being
morphed using the spline morph method**.

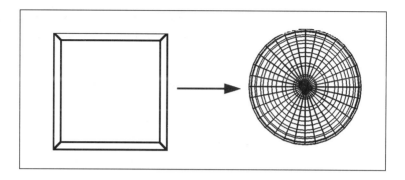

FIGURE 12-3 Spline morphs provide seamless morphing with minimal effort during the morphing process. Both objects in the morph must be ordered spline objects.

Particle Morph

When spline morphing or point morphing are not possible due to the object's construction, particle morphing can be used. Objects which are not spline objects or not of the same number of vertices can be morphed through the use of particles. In the particle morph feature, the object is automatically subdivided into particles by the software, then the particles are morphed into the target object. Although the morphing process is not as smooth as morphing between explicit objects, it can be used very effectively for many morphing effects. **An example of Strata StudioPro's particle morph is show in Figure 12-4**.

FIGURE 12-4   Using Strata StudioPro's particle morph, objects are exploded then rebuilt to create the new object.

Metaballs, Blobs, and Globs

They are called blobs, globs, blobbys, and metaballs, but they really are just another form of deformation. This type of deformation is produced by a group of spheres, each of which has its own deformation influence area. The influence level is used to build a mesh between the two spheres as they approach each other's area of influence. The effect is similar to the way that drops of mercury are drawn to each other. As the two spheres move toward each other, they will reach out to join with the other sphere. **The reaching and the joining is the work of the metaballs function and is dependent on the amount of influence given to the group (see Figure 12-5).**

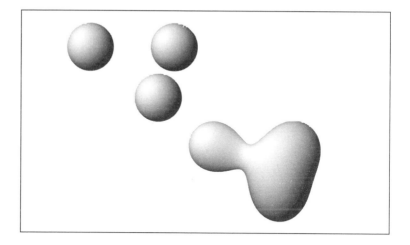

FIGURE 12-5 Spheres are given an influence level which causes geometry to join them as they enter the field of influence. The higher the influence given, the farther away the influence will affect the spheres.

How Metaballs Work

Even though the metaball feature is a type of deformation, it is really used to build objects, not deform them. The deformation comes from the fact that all metaball objects are constructed of spheres. Because of the influence of each sphere on all the surrounding spheres, the shape becomes much more organic looking than just a group of spheres. The geometry will reach toward the spheres, resulting in a smooth form which looks very organic.

The influence surrounding each sphere can be compared to gravity. The closer one gets to the center of the object, the more gravity there is. As we move away from the center, the effect of gravity lessens. When two metaball sphere move toward each other, their gravity influences the two surfaces. **The result is a pulling of the surface toward the area of equal gravitational pull (see Figure 12-6).**

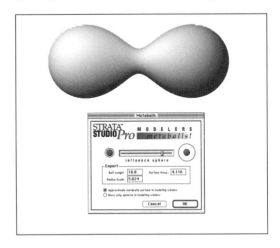

FIGURE 12-6 As we can see in this image, the geometry between the two spheres is gravitating toward eachother. The area between the two spheres has an equal gravitational pull, causing the geometry to be stretched. The scale of the blob dictates how big the blob is at the center of the sphere.

The methods used by the programmers who created the different metaball features may vary, so a general explanation is given here. It must first be understood that metaballs or blobs works primarily with spheres. In many cases, nonperfect spheres will be made perfect by the metaball function. While spheres can be of different sizes, perfect spheres are used to easily determine the influence area on each object.

While the use of metaballs can create some stunning effects and models, use this feature cautiously. Metaballs are memory and CPU intensive and could really bog down a system. Compound the system slowdown with the learning curve of controlling the influence of the spheres and you've got a real aspirin muncher of a day on your hands. With the right attitude and expectations, frustration can be avoided, and some very interesting modeling and animation effects can be achieved.

TIP: Be cautious when attempting to create objects with metaballs without substantial amounts of RAM. Having anything less than 40 megabytes of RAM can lead to slow screen redraws and long rendering times.

TECHNIQUE: General Metaball Parameters

While this explanation covers the basics behind metaballs, there are some fine points which vary between the different metaball and blobby extensions. To fully understand how your particular function works, you may need to read and reread the manual. As with all tools, experimenting and trial and error are the best teachers.

- *Influence or blob threshold:* This controls the amount of influence or attractiveness the spheres have on each other. A higher setting will creates a larger area of influence, thereby joining more blobs together.

- *Blob scale, radius scale:* These affect the size of the polygons and spheres used in the metaball feature. Changing the scale will directly affect the scale of the blob created.

- *Specific controls:* There are specific controls for each of the different metaball features. While most features have a default setting that enables the metaball function to work with a minimal number of parameters, each of the functions also has

421

"Expert" settings which are best explained in the user's manual.

Animating Blobs

Metaball and blobby functions cannot only be used for building objects, they can be used for animation effects as well. The metaballs feature is very adept at creating special effects such as flowing water or gelatinous effects like in the movies *The Abyss* or *Terminator 2*. By animating the spheres and applying the correct influence (not always an easy task), very convincing results can be had. An effect such as the cyborg in *Terminator 2* can be achieved by using a metaballs function in animation.

To animate the metaballs, all of the spheres used in the metaball (or blob) must be created and animated before the metaball or blobby feature is invoked. Once the group is animated and the metaball feature applied, the influence each sphere has will show up during rendering. The fact that an exact model is not always shown prior to rendering is what makes this function somewhat frustrating.

Since metaballs are a very CPU-intensive feature, most midrange modeling software does not normally include this feature. Programs such as Electric Image Animation System and Strata StudioPro include this feature as part of the standard package, while 3D Studio makes this feature available as a plug-in called MetaReyes from 4D Vision.

Splines

Although they are used as a basis for construction, splines are also deformation tools. Splines are a very powerful, yet simple concept used in the development of organic objects. Splines work the same way that Bézier curves work in 2D illustration. By applying tension to the spline, you can accentuate or diminish the curve created by the spline. In very basic terms, a spline is a linear group of points which runs horizontally or vertically through the object in which it resides.

Points in the spline object are also given individual influence levels which are used when editing points on the object's geometry. **By changing the influence level, a point can be used to create a smooth curve, or sharp spikes, as seen in Figure 12-7.** When creating organic shapes, this feature becomes extremely important and beneficial.

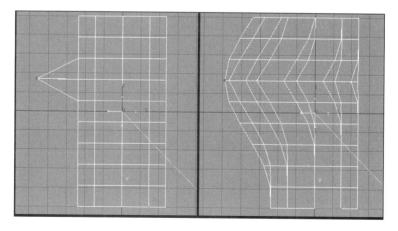

FIGURE 12-7 By changing the gravity or flex of the points, you can create sharp spikes or smooth depressions or bulges.

The power behind spline objects is that they tend to produce very smooth curves with very little effort, unlike polygonal modelers. **By changing the control points on the spline which runs through the object's vertical or horizontal axis, you can change the shape of the object as though it were made of rubber (see Figure 12-8).**

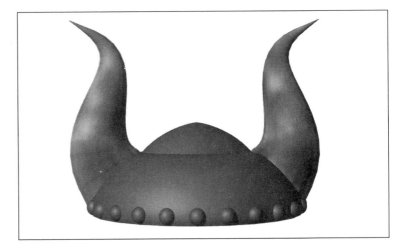

FIGURE 12-8 Moving the control points on a spline object can change the entire shape of the object. Creating this Viking horn was as simple as moving the spline control points. Because of its curves along different axes, this shape would not have been created as easily without the use of splines.

A number of different types of splines are available in the various modeling packages on the market. Many programs use B-splines or Catmull-ROM splines, while other, more sophisticated modelers offer a variety of other spline types, such as the powerful NURBS-type spline. Of all the modelers I have come in contact with, Pixel Putty Solo offers the widest variety of spline types—nine in all. A list of different spline types and the specific splines associated with those types follows.

TECHNIQUE: Spline Types

- *Linear:* A linear spline is the most basic spline type. Points on a linear spline are joined with segments which run directly to each point. A linear spline has sharp edges and tends to look faceted when creating curves. At least two points are required to create a linear spline.

- *Interpolating:* An interpolating spline uses the points as a connector for geometric segments and therefore causes the segments to intersect at each point. Unlike the linear spline, the interpolating spline is able to create smooth curves, although they tend to be more constricted than an approximating spline. While only two points are needed in a linear spline, at least three are needed to create a curve. Typical interpolating splines include Catmull-ROM and Hermite splines. Tau splines are interpolating splines with tension and bias parameters, normally found in approximating splines.

- *Approximating:* The approximating spline offers the most versatility and control over curved objects. When creating an approximating spline object, the points are used to control the tension of the spline, and spline geometry may not necessarily intersect the points themselves. Approximating splines create smoother curves than other spline types, since all of the points used through a curve influence the way the curve is drawn. B-splines, tensed B-splines, and beta splines are all examples of approximating splines.

Using Spline Objects

Any of the spline types can be used to create different objects and shapes. Spline objects can be created either from primitives or from two dimensional splines. Using a spline primitive as a starting point, the splines which make up the object can be manipulated into any desired shape. Spline objects can be subjected to the same deformation and transformation tools as polygonal objects and, for the most part, can handle them better. Deformations and morphing are especially suited for spline objects, which handle these types of tools very well.

Because spline objects handle curves very well, there are especially easy to manipulate into organic objects. Using gravity controls and spline tension, different types of curves can be created with the spline object.

Mesh and Patch Objects

Splines can be used in many ways, each serving a specific type of object construction. All spline objects are created of a spline mesh that has been modified to create the specific spline primitive. A spline mesh is equivalent to 3D cloth. The threads of the cloth are splines which run through the entire mesh. Splines may be added to either the horizontal or vertical edges of the spline mesh, the way threads are added to create more material. Spline mesh can be used to create many organic shapes, such as waving flags and rippling water.

A mesh object, sometimes called a spline patch, is a surface constructed of horizontal and vertical splines along the same plane. In programs such as Pixel Putty Solo, where all objects are spline objects, a spline mesh is created internally then reshaped to create the requested primitive (cylinder, sphere, etc.). Along both the vertical and horizontal axes, there are any number of parallel splines. The splines which make up the mesh surface may be of any spline type. Even splines along the same axis may be of different spline types.

Spline mesh is subject to the same rules and characteristics of standard spline objects. The mesh object may also be changed through the use of any available tools which are applicable to spline objects, such as Boolean operations and deformation areas. **A spline mesh is pictured in Figure 12-9**.

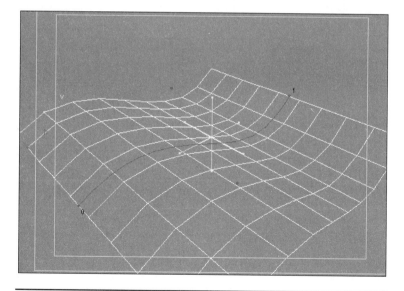

FIGURE 12-9 A spline patch starts out flat, yet through a series of geometric operations, may become virtually any shape by manipulating the splines.

Deformation Areas

While splines and metaballs are the building blocks used to construct objects, deformation areas are used to change the shape of objects which have already been constructed. A deformation area is an area in 3D space which, when intersected by a linked object, will cause the linked object to become deformed to the relative shape of the deformation area. This type of special effect is very useful in animation such as a balloon, squeezing through a keyhole, or a liquid flowing through a funnel. When the object first begins to enter the deformation area, it will begin to take on that shape. As the object moves through the deformation area, it will be reshaped as though it was clay being pushed through a press. **Figure 12-10 illustrates a sphere which has been pushed through a deformation area**.

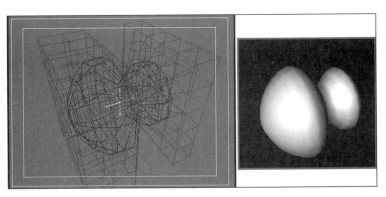

FIGURE 12-10 Deformation areas are extremely useful in cartoon-type animations. Characters and objects can easily be deformed as they enter the area. On the serious side, deformation areas can be extremely helpful when animating organic forms, such as liquid.

TIP: Deformation areas are extremely useful in character animation. When creating objects which are to be deformed, use spline objects or create the object with triangulated mesh to give the object a smooth deformation.

TECHNIQUE: Creating a Deformation Area

- *Create the deformation area:* To create a deformation area, your animation package must have a deformation function available. If it does not, check to see if a plug-in version is available from a third-party vendor. In most cases, the deformation area is simply a mesh cube used to define an area in space.

- *Deform the area:* Using standard modeling tools, change the deformation area to the desired shape. The deformation area is not rendered, but the object passing through it will take on its shape as it passes through the points in space taken up by the deformation area.

- *Link deformable objects:* Typically, objects which use the deformation area need to be linked to it. Once linked, any object which passes through the deformation area will be deformed. As the object leaves, it will return to its original shape.

- *Animate the objects:* Objects can be animated as normal before and after they pass through the deformation area. Deformation areas can be used very effectively for creating collision effects, such as a ball bouncing on the floor. Using a deformation area on the floor, the ball will automatically appear to squash under its own weight.

Postproduction Morphing and Deformation

While morphing and deformation are not offered with every modeling and animation package, there is an excellent alternative. There are products on the market which specialize in postproduction effects. One of the finest postproduction morphing tools I have ever used is Elastic Reality by Elastic Reality, Inc. This tool offers postproduction effects for both still images and animation. For a complete review of Elastic Reality, see Product Reviews in Chapter 13.

3D Studio

Autodesk Inc.
2320 Marinship Way
Saulsalito, CA 94965-9910
Voice: (800)879-4233
Fax: (415)491-8398
Platform: DOS

A long time leader in PC-based 3D modeling and animation, Autodesk's 3D Studio is still considered the powerhouse of the PC. With high-powered modeling capabilities as well as complex animation, 3D Studio continues to aid in the production of high-end animation.

One major advantage to 3D Studio is the plug-ins feature. Immense plug-in support by third-party vendors make this product an ever changing and evolving system. This allows the user to add additional functionality as the need arises, while continuing to use a product that is familiar, once learned. One of the largest complaints about 3D Studio Release 4 is that it does not run under

Windows. This is still a DOS-based application and the interface is very different from that of standard Windows applications. Getting past that, however, and into the meat of the program will lead to some powerful modeling and animation.

Modeling

As with any high-end modeling software with lots of capabilities, it is easy to become overwhelmed by the myriad dialog boxes and menu items, and 3D Studio is no exception. 3D Studio ships with a tutorial manual which is close to 500 pages, and it is very detailed with respect to how to accomplish a particular task. Without the manual, the learning curve on the 3D Studio may be quite high.

3D Studio provides spline tools, Booleans, and lofting tools. The lofter is also used to create lathed objects by duplicating a profile around an axis to form the ribs. This technique does seem cumbersome, yet it is effective. The strength is being able to edit the objects through spline paths used to loft across.

Texture

Assigning and creating materials in 3D Studio is more comforting than the modeling mode. Textures can be created through a variety of property settings found in most texture creation software, with a sample window at top to show the result of the settings.

3D Studio supports procedural textures and image maps which can be imported into the texture itself. There are no less than 50 controls on the texture screen. One of the different aspects of texture usage is that the textures are all stored collectively in a materials library, as opposed to separate files. At first this seems slightly restrictive, but it does allow you to store textures with more meaningful names, because they are not restricted to the eight character file naming convention enforced by the DOS operating system.

Lights

The standard light types (ambient, distant, point, and spotlight) are all present in 3D Studio. Lights are added to a scene (by default, a scene in 3D Studio has only ambient light) and moved into position. Multiple lights are allowed and are treated like objects which can be moved through the normal transformation controls. With spotlights, the Show Cone toggle button will display the cone of light to show which areas of the model will be illuminated by the light source. This does not, however, make the light visible when rendered.

Cameras

Like lights, there may be multiple cameras present in a single 3D Studio scene. This is a tremendous benefit when modeling and creating animation. While only one camera may be used at a time for rendering, it does provide additional perspective on the scene layout.

Camera controls are also pretty standard. Lens size, field of view, and camera roll may be set directly through the camera dialog. A nice feature in the camera settings is the calculate button. After a field of view angle is set, pressing the calculate button will calculate the correct lens focal length for that field of view. There are also stock lens sizes supplied which will have preset parameters.

Rendering

3D Studio has four main modes of rendering called flat, Gouraud, Phong, and Metal. While the first three may be familiar, since they are used by other programs, the Metal setting is used to render reflective surfaces not found in the Phong rendering.

Rendering controls include antialiasing, shadows, background image controls, and other resolution and output options. The resolution and output options encompass a wide variety of options including rendering fields, pixel size, and rendering alpha channels.

Atmospheric conditions (read fog) can also be incorporated into the rendering process. This will produce a linear degradation of the image until the fog completely engulfs objects in the distance.

Animation

There are some very high-end animation capabilities incorporated into 3D Studio, including parent-child links. The basis of animation is handled through keyframing through a visual spreadsheet type of setup. This aids in visually being able to see what is happening in a designated time period.

When creating an animation, keyframes can be adding along a time line and then edited, or moved to another place in time. This approach makes changing complex and choreographed animation much simpler than the traditional keyframe only method.

Documentation/Learning Curve

The documentation supplied with 3D Studio is extensive. Including the tutorial, there are well over 1500 pages of documentation. Very extensive reading and patience is needed, especially for the beginning 3D modeler. Even for those who have experience, and would like to leaf through the book to find a particular command, the learning curve is still somewhat high.

While learning 3D Studio will take some work, the tools are there for creating amazing models and animation. This tool, though somewhat difficult, will bring pleasing results to those with the fortitude to push through the extensive reading and tutorials.

addDepth

Ray Dream, Inc.
1804 N. Shoreline Blvd.
Mountain View, CA 94043
(800)846-0111
Platform: Windows

For desktop publishing, and slide and multimedia presentations, addDepth can quickly turn text, corporate logos, and 2D art into 3D objects. Not considered a modeling tool, addDepth is mainly for presentation graphics and printed material to create a quick 3D "look" to traditional flat objects, such as text and logos. For creating graphs and pie charts that are visually more exciting, addDepth is the tool to use.

Because addDepth is not a 3D modeling package, it is easier to use and produces quicker finished images. This, of course, does not come without limitation. Objects are limited to producing an extruded version of flat art. The 3D object can then be rotated to create a more pronounced 3D look and add more perspective to the piece.

addDepth provides a number of preset presentation types to get you started and is fairly easy to understand. The object controls let you easily edit artwork and settings, using the familiar drawing tools used in most vector art drawing programs. Shading settings can also be changed, allowing the simulated light to come from any angle.

Once artwork has been created, it can be exported to an EPS file, which makes it easily imported into any number of page layout programs available. For 2D production with a little more pizzazz, addDepth is a great tool. It is really the first step toward getting into 3D art, without the learning curve normally involved in creating 3D objects.

Elastic Reality

AVID Technology
Metropolitan Technology Park
One Park West
Tewksbury, MA 01876
Voice: (508)949-2843

One of the hottest visual effects currently being used is object morphing. This effect is being incorporated into video, film, and other 3D work to create stunning effects. For postproduction work, I know of no other morphing tool which has the power that is so readily available in Elastic Reality. Elastic Reality has been used in big Hollywood films such as *Forest Gump* and *Stargate* to create astonishing visual effects. Because it works with shapes, and not points, image morphing is easier and faster.

What makes Elastic Reality stand out above other traditional morphing programs is that it incorporates standard line drawing tools, such as Bézier curves, to outline areas which are to be morphed, instead of a point to point correspondence between two images. Elastic Reality works equally well with still images or animated sequences or video. Animated objects can be morphed into other moving shapes without degradation to the motion. This alone is a very powerful capability which is already making it a highly prized tool among advertising agencies and special effects houses.

Although the power behind Elastic Reality is the main reason it was used in Hollywood films, it is also very easy to use. Bézier curves are used to designate areas of morphing as well as exclusionary areas. There are also controls to vary the effect of the morph, transparency, and the degree and speed at which it is implemented. Being able to control varying degrees of morphing with different parts of an image is another strong point of Elastic Reality morphing control.

Whether building 3D models or desktop publishing, Elastic Reality is another one of those tools the professional visualization artist should not be without. It is very easy to use, since the tools are already familiar, and the interface is very intuitive and the layout is clear. All of the power and ease comes with a surprisingly low price tag (less than $250 for a Macintosh) for such an innovative tool.

436

Electric Image Animation System 2.5

Electric Image Incorporated

117 East Colorado Blvd., Suite 300

Pasadena, CA 91105

Voice: (818)577-1627

Fax: (818)577-2426

Platform: Macintosh, PowerMac

There is not much to say about Electric Image Animation System that has not already been said. This outstanding program has a long list of professional credits behind it in both movie and television, including *Terminator 2: Judgment Day* and NBC's *Dateline*. Although it carries a price tag in the neighborhood of $7500, this system can quickly pay for itself. With fantastic lighting effects, animation plug-ins, and a fast rendering engine, Electric Image Animation System (EIAS) is my choice as the premier high-end animation system.

Modeling

EIAS is capable of importing nearly 30 different model types. This allows models from virtually every 3D program to be imported into EIAS. Although models are not constructed in EIAS, text can be built, complete with beveled edges, inside of EIAS.

While models cannot be built in EIAS, they can be assembled there. Object hierarchies and groups can be established within EIAS or the established hierarchy of the model may be preserved during importing.

Texture

While not a modeler, EIAS does handle texture application very well. In fact, while EIAS allows the user immense control over every facet of texture application, the controls are laid out in such a way as to not be intrusive. Applying textures is relatively simple, even for the novice user. For those with more specific texture needs, EIAS has complete controls for creating complex textures through compositing existing images and textures to create new textures.

Lights

In 3D modeling and animation, the two most important factors are textures and lighting. Electric Image Animation System handles both of these aspects superbly. Memory permitting, EIAS can handle the calculations involved for millions of lights. While this number may possibly never be reached in a typical scene, EIAS is no ordinary animation system.

Electric Image Animation System, has five different types of lights, including a camera light and a tube light. The camera light is a neat idea, because it creates a light attached to the camera, so that light will always shine on the scene directly in front of the camera. Unlike nearly every other rendering package on the market, EIAS can render visible lights, including volumetric light shafts.

Cameras

EIAS supports a single camera used to view the scene. The camera can be animated or aimed at objects as they move around the scene. I particularly like the implementation of camera transformations. Using a three-tiered process, the camera can be moved and rotated in a single window with one tool. Depending on which part of the camera object you click on, you can either change the view direction, the distance, or the position of the camera.

Rendering

Electric Image Animation System can produce very realistic images very quickly. The rendering algorithms are highly optimized for both speed and quality. Use of a Phong shading algorithm produces very fast and accurate results, while shadows and reflection can be accurately portrayed.

When creating an animation, speed is always a consideration. Since 30 frames per second is a standard rate when creating animation, frame counts can skyrocket very quickly. Because of its speed, EIAS makes animation possible where it may not have been feasible without EIAS, simply due to the number of frames requiring rendering.

Animation

Animation is what EIAS was designed to do. There are many animation capabilities which make it the perfect solution. There are particle systems, inverse kinematics, object deformation, and many other special effects, such as metaballs. Sounds can also be synced up with the animation to further enhance the quality of a final rendering.

Objects which are imported into EIAS can have splines attached to them, allowing for character animation on a model that may not have been designed to do just that. To really experience the poise and grace of Electric Image Animation Systems, you must see what it can do in person. For anyone involved in 3D animation, this complete tool set can do at a fraction of the cost what UNIX-based systems are doing.

Documentation/Learning Curve

Electric Image Animation System 2.5.2 is like no other program I have used. There are extensive options and tools, and it takes time to learn the ins and outs of this program. Included in the package are a reference manual, tutorials, and supplemental volumes. Like anything worthwhile, although it may take a while to become an expert, EIAS is laid out in such a manner that you can begin rendering in a few minutes. Because there are so many tools, it will take some time for a user to reap all of the extensive rewards waiting at the end of the Electric Image Rainbow.

form•Z Render Zone 2.7

auto•des•sys Inc.
2011 Riverside Drive
Columbus, OH 43221
Info: (614)488-9777
Fax: (614)488-0848
Platform: Macintosh, PowerMac

With more tools that many other programs combined, form•Z is one good solids modeler. This software package includes floating-point precision, multiple layers, and just about every tool imaginable for creating virtually any 3D object. With both a drafting and modeling mode, form•Z can be used for modeling projects of every caliber, from playful characters to CAD accurate product and architectural design. In the latest release, form•Z RenderZone, rendering capabilities are integrated into the software package. Now, models can be built, textures created and applied, and the scene rendered all through one integrated package.

While form•Z is one of the most pricey modeling software packages on the Macintosh market, it does perform very well. With an extensive tool set and precise control over object creation, form•Z will quickly become the modeler of choice for 3D professionals looking for complex modeling capabilities and accurate object design.

Modeling

As the primary function of form•Z, the modeling is very accurate and controllable. Each tool has its own set of default options which can be set to fit the need or left as is. The modeling environment may also be changed to any possible viewpoint and any scaling. The views can also be saved and added to the view menu for future use and a customized interface.

The interface is slightly different from the typical Macintosh interface, adding additional functionality to the palettes. Numerous tear-off palettes (about 23) can be collapsed, moved around, or left on the main palette. Although the number of palettes is more than you will find in most modeling programs, they are laid out nicely and in good order. Palettes can also be removed from the main palette until needed, to keep the interface from overwhelming the less experienced modeler.

A unique benefit of form•Z is that it offers a 3D modeling and 2D drafting mode. Objects of both types may be moved between the modules. The modeling module is used to create 3D objects while the drafting module is used to create 2D design using two dimensional tools. Objects can be imported into the drafting module to use 3D objects in a two dimensional design and vice versa. Overlap occurs in the tool sets between the two programs, but some tools are unique to the different modeling modes. Together the integrated modes are extremely useful for engineering and design.

Some of the modeling tools available in the modeling module include standard tools such lathe, extrude, and sweep tools as well as the more advanced sweeping (probably the best I've seen anywhere), Boolean, and rounding tools. There are also a number of mesh tools for manipulating and creating C-mesh objects.

form•Z also uses layers and hierarchical groups, which make object construction easier and more organized, especially when building complex objects and scenes. Groups and layers can then be exported to a number of file types such as DXF, RIB, 3DGF, 3DMF, and FACT. The FACT file format is the format used in Electric Image Animation System and allows form•Z to integrate smoothly, keeping object hierarchy and applied textures intact during transfer.

Although the abundance of tools and options may at first seem intimidating to the inexperienced user, it is easy to warm up to form•Z after spending a little time getting to know the interface. form•Z RenderZone is a world-class high-end modeling system that enables 3D artists to be limited only by themselves, and not their software.

Texture

Not to be outdone by the modeling aspect of form•Z, the texture creation and manipulation portion of the software is equally manageable. Called *surface styles*, textures are created by editing 16 primitive surface styles, with dozens of accurate textures to draw parameters from, such as metals, organic, stone, and synthetic categories.

The texture attributes are logically laid out, with a preview that is updated automatically, every time a parameter is changed. The preview is also configurable for the shape it renders and the number of passes used to create the preview.

When choosing an attribute to edit, the user may choose from a list of surface types, such as marble, wood, etc., or from a predefined surface from one of the categories of materials. Once the surface property has been chosen, it may be used as is, or edited further to accommodate the need. Image maps may also be applied to surfaces to use as color, transparency, and bump maps.

One of the best integration of two programs is the relationship between form•Z and Electric Image Animation System (EIAS). Models created in form•Z can be saved directly to EIAS format, and the texture information remains intact. When working toward high-end output, using these two high-end packages will give you the best results you can get in the business, without compromise.

Lights

As with most modeling packages, form•Z offers multiple lights within a scene. Although the tools are not as extensive as the tool set offered through the modeler, they are adequate for illuminating a scene. form•Z offers distant, point, and spotlights (as well as ambient light controls). The lighting controls allow you to configure standard issues such as color, intensity, and shadows.

The shadow control is a nice feature, in that either ray-traced or shadow-mapped shadows can be applied to light sources independently. The shadow-mapped style of shadows will produce a softer shadow than the ray-traced shadow and form•Z also has controls to set the amount of softness desired on the shadow. With this type of control, different light sources can cause different types of shadows, which can be used very effectively when creating scenes with realistic lighting.

442

One of the only drawbacks with the lighting in form•Z RenderZone, is the inability to apply color textures to a light source. Since there are ways around this, I see it as only an inconvenience, and not a showstopper. One feature which I think is great with the lighting controls is the ability to give a light a visible glow. This effect will give the light a visible cone or sphere shape depending on the light type. Glowing lights are especially effective when they are used in places where the source of the light is seen and not implied, such as with a lightbulb or candle flame.

Cameras

In addition to adding lights to a scene, one must be able to view the scene from various perspectives. In form•Z, there are no cameras per sé, but there are provisions for different views. Virtually a view from any angle can be set and rendered through the view palette and the view can be set to be axonometric or perspective projection.

Because a scene is seen through a view and not a camera, there are some limitations, such as lens size, which may not produce the desired effect directly. While form•Z is a premiere modeler, its rendering capabilities are still being developed and while perfectly suited for scene rendering, they are not intended for special effect and animation rendering.

Rendering

Scenes can be rendered in form•Z using eight different techniques, including wireframe and ray-tracing. There are numerous options which you can select for higher or lower quality images for previewing or final production. Environment maps and effects, such as fog, can also be applied to the scene.

Rendering can also include realistic shadow effects through shadow mapping of various degrees, as well as the hard-edged shadows of ray-tracing. Rendering also supports reflections, transparency, and refraction for creating realistic glass and metals.

Animation

form•Z does not support animation and objects cannot be animated within form•Z. For many users of form•Z, an animation system such as Electric Image Animation System is used because of its seamless integration of form•Z models.

Documentation/Learning Curve

form•Z has many options for its tools, providing the user with absolute control over model creation. While this control is an outstanding feature, it does not come without a learning curve. form•Z ships with five manuals (900+ pages of documentation), plus a 206-page tutorial manual. The quick reference guide is 24 pages in length. Although this documentation seems extensive, it is needed to cover all of the options of the software. The best part is, you can work with some of the options and work up to others.

In short, the learning curve to form•Z is not bad. Once the basics have been learned, modeling comes very quickly. As one uses form•Z more, the strength of the program becomes quite evident and appreciated.

Infini-D

Specular International
479 West Street
Amherst, MA 01002
Voice: (413)253-3100
Fax: (413)253-0540
Platform Macintosh, PowerMac

Infini-D from Specular International is a popular 3D product which is capable of producing 3D modeling and animation from concept to delivery. Both 2D and 3D graphics professionals are turning to Infini-D to incorporate their 3D ideas into 2D presentations because of the ease with which files may be transferred. Images created in 2D programs, such as Adobe Illustrator, can be imported directly into Infini-D to be given three dimensional treatments, then exported back out to image manipulation software for compositing. Not to be confused with an illustration tool, Infini-D offers modeling, rendering, and animation capabilities.

Modeling

Infini-D has some interesting features for creating objects. While the approach is somewhat different, it is effective nonetheless. There are tools for creating free-form objects as well as extrusion, bevel, and lathe tools. There is also a terrain tool, which creates terrain and other predefined objects such as a rippled surface, blackhole, and the Mandelbrot set for terrain generators.

While many of the basic modeling commands are available, excessive tools are not present. This may be a blessing for the beginning to intermediate modeler who does not want to be inundated with lots of options and modeling parameters. The advanced 3D modeler may use the free-form modeling workshop to create more complex objects.

Textures

Using the same easy to understand operation as in the modeling workshop, Infini-D makes texture creation and application easy to understand. Many procedural textures are shipped with Infini-D and all are fully editable. Image maps and QuickTime movies may also be applied to surfaces or combined with other textures.

One feature I found very interesting is the surface composer. This feature allows one to create a new surface shader from a combination of other surfaces. One surface can be used to create the bump, while the other defines the color, and so on. Layering effects are also possible, making the entire process of texture creation an art in itself.

Lights

Infini-D incorporates the three basic light sources (ambient, point, and spotlights) into a scene. You may add as many lights as memory permits, although increased lighting will lengthen rendering times. Lighting controls include color, intensity, and light type.

Infini-D has the ability to alter the color of a light over time. Through the animation procedure, a light can animate its color from one point in time to another. This feature can create some nice effects during animation.

Cameras

Like lights in Infini-D, you may add as many cameras as memory permits. Cameras may be named, which I find a very handy feature. Cameras can be positioned anywhere in a scene and may have any one of a number of lens types. Infini-D includes a number of presets such as the micro, fish-eye, and the super telephoto. Supplying preset camera lenses is always a nice feature. There is also a custom setting for those who like to set their own lens size parameters.

Like all other objects, cameras can be animated or made to point at a specific object or point in a scene. This is a very handy feature when creating animation and tracking a moving object.

Rendering

Because of the ray-tracing algorithm and the ability to render lights and shadows, Infini-D can produce very photorealistic images. While ray-tracing images can produce the most realistic results, it is not the only shader provided. In addition to ray-trace and wireframe modes, objects can be rendered with flat, Gouraud, and Phong shading. Shadows are capable with both the Phong and ray-tracing rendering algorithms.

Animation

Animation is controlled through a device called a "Sequencer" in Infini-D. The Sequencer is used to edit the event marker of the animation. Event markers are created by adding snapshots of an object in motion.

The overall features in the animation or Sequencer palette are useful. Controls for previewing an animation produce a wireframe preview of the animation sequence rather quickly. The palette approach used in the Sequencer is becoming popular with more and more programs, and although I do not know who initiated the idea, Infini-D incorporates it very well.

Aside from the standard animation, Infini-D also has a morphing feature which will morph two shapes regardless of the point count. The only hitch is that the objects must be from a similar modeling tool (i.e., two lathe objects). I like this feature, because morphing can become very tedious with two objects created from two separate sets of points.

Documentation/Learning Curve

While the documentation is not as extensive as in other programs, this is primarily because it is not needed. Included with the manual is a tutorial that takes the user through the various tools of the software. Since the interface is simple to understand and implement, extensive documentation is not really necessary, and we can always save a few trees.

The overall learning curve for Infini-D is minor. Anyone with 3D knowledge should have no trouble understanding the tools. For beginners, there is some insight into the art of modeling and animation, but it may be best to purchase third-party publications for modeling information.

MetaReyes 3D Studio Plug-In

4D Vision
4800 Happy Canyon Rd., Suite 250
Denver, CO 80237-1074
Voice: (303)759-1024
Fax: (303)759-0928
(800)252-1024

One of the truly most unique plug-ins to enter the market is the MetaReyes plug-in. This plug-in creates only spheres, albeit lots of them. The concept is to create lots of spheres to create the mass of the object, then converge the spheres so that they mesh to form a single object. This gives the shape a very organic and realistic look. Very realistic dinosaurs and human figures can be created using MetaReyes, as well as animating liquids.

The MetaReyes plug-in, when installed, works with 3D Studio. The plug-in ships with documentation which also explains the concept behind MetaReyes. Learning the concept of blobby balls, or *metaballs* they are sometimes called, is actually harder than learning the tool. The best part is that the tool is incorporated into 3D Studio, so there is no new software to learn.

Of the different plug-ins available, this one comes highly recommended. Since the MetaReyes can be animated, creating flowing water and animating very organic shapes is infinitely easier using MetaReyes under 3D Studio.

Pixel Putty Solo 1.6

The Valis Group
Tiburon, CA
(800)VALIS 04
(415)435-5404
Platform: Macintosh, PowerMac

One of the best modelers to hit the market, Pixel Putty Solo is a NURBS and spline-based modeler, supporting nine types of splines. Through an intuitive interface, objects can be created rather quickly through editing of the spline primitives or through the use of spline mesh.

Pixel Putty Solo has some very powerful modeling features including Boolean operations, displacement mapping, and free-form deformations. Version 1.6 also provides inverse kinematics and real-time capture of motion data.

With its speed, powerful spline capabilities, and low price tag, Pixel Putty Solo is one modeling tool every 3D modeler should have in his or her toolbox.

Modeling

Pixel Putty Solo offers the basic primitives, all created with a spline mesh construction. The spline types of any object can be changed to any of the nine supported splines, allowing the artist to control the low-level construction of objects. Even the amount of flex of gravity can be adjusted for each individual point or spline through the use of the Flex slider.

Pixel Putty Solo also supports a lathe tool, lofting, extrusion, path extrude, deformation areas, and a disrupt tool which is great for adding noise to an object's geometry.

While Pixel Putty Solo does not currently offer some tools found in other software packages, it does have some nifty tools and is about the best free-form spline-based modeler in the Macintosh market. Its powerful spline capabilities with definitely fill the void found in many other modeling packages, regardless of their price.

Texture

While shaders are supported in Pixel Putty Solo, there is no means of image mapping directly in Pixel Putty Solo. Use of a program such as ResEdit, will allow you to access the PICT resources within the shader to change or add an image. Some cool shaders are supplied with Pixel Putty Solo, and creating your own variances of those can be achieved through the "Shaders..." dialog.

Pixel Putty Solo also ships with a program called Shader Maker, which converts shaders to a Pixel Putty-usable format. While Shader Maker does allow you to change parameters on shaders, it does not provide a means of previewing the edited shader from within Shader Maker.

Lights

Multiple lights are allowed in Pixel Putty Solo and the three standard lights (distant, point, and spot) are available, as well as ambient light. While visible lights are not supported, there is a shader provided which can be used to produce a visible light, although the edges are not transparent enough to be totally convincing.

Cameras

Although multiple lights are supported in Pixel Putty, only a single camera is available through Pixel Putty Solo. This camera cannot be deleted or duplicated, but the standard settings can be changed, such as camera position, field of view, and f-stop. The camera object can be animated just like any other object in Pixel Putty Solo.

Rendering

When viewing a scene through the provided camera or having that window visible, a preview can be rendered. To render quality stills, you need a rendering engine, such as Pixar's Mac RenderMan, which integrates nicely into the Pixel Putty "Render Setup" menu option.

Models created in Pixel Putty Solo can be exported to DXF, RIB, and 3DGF files. When exporting models which don't support free-form deformation, the Multi-Frame DXF option can be used to export a DXF file for each frame in the deformation or animation. This can prove to be a very handy feature for use in object morphing.

Animation

Although Pixel Putty Solo has a very low price tag, some of its features are very high end. Objects can be animated through deformation areas, with twists and bends and inverse kinematics (IK). Through the use of IK, complex character animation can be achieved, and Pixel Putty Solo has the right tools needed for character animation.

Adding animation keyframes is intuitive and also allows the animator to control the attributes which are to be key at a particular keyframe through the keyframe dialog. Once the object is animated, a flipbook wireframe animation can be generated very quickly to preview the animation.

Documentation/Learning Curve

While the documentation does provide five tutorial examples for modeling, animation, and inverse kinematics, the overall documentation is on the brief side, although over 300 pages of large print text is included with the software. This should not be a deterrent, because where the documentation may be sparse, the intuitiveness of the software allows for a minimal learning curve into the world of spline and free-form modeling.

Ray Dream Designer

Ray Dream, Inc.
1804 N. Shoreline Blvd.
Mountain View, CA 94043
(800)846-0111
Platform: Macintosh, PowerMac, Windows

While Ray Dream Designer 3 is primarily a 3D illustration program, Ray Dream Designer 4 has moved into a whole new realm from previous versions of the product. Ray Dream Studio includes four separate packages for creating and animating in 3D. The animator includes sophisticated tools such as inverse kinematics and object deformers. The 3D illustration package had been beefed up by adding better camera controls, unlimited lights, and optimization for 32-bit operating systems. Ray Dream Designer is available for Macintosh and Windows 95 platforms. Due to press deadlines and release dates, I was unavailable to review Ray Dream Designer 4, but offer this review of Ray Dream 3.1.2.

Modeling

While Ray Dream Designer 3.1 does not offer the sophisticated tools of the high-end modelers, it does provide the essentials needed for beginning 3D modeling and illustration. Tools such as extrusions, twisting, sweeping, and lofting are provided as a means of construction, and can be used with a minimal amount of training.

One unique concept provided by Ray Dream Designer is the Modeling Wizard. For a beginning modeler, this little feature can take the beginning modeler through the steps involved in creating the various types of objects, such as sweeps and lathes. While there is not a whole lot of control through the Modeling Wizard, it does provide the beginner with information about the steps required to create various types of objects.

Textures

While texture development is not as sophisticated as in some of the higher end packages, Ray Dream Designer does allows for some unique texture applications. In addition to applying a shader to an object's surface, you may also paint directly on the object's surface, with the 3D paint tool.

Ray Dream allows the artist to create various shaders through the use of their editable procedural textures such as wood and marble. Shaders can also be combined by mixing components of different shaders to create new shaders.

Lights

Multiple lights can be added to a Ray Dream Designer scene. The standard distant, point and spotlights are provided, as well as the standard controls. Gels are supported and, although not as powerful as other gel capabilities, bit-mapped images may be incorporated into customized gels.

Cameras

While multiple cameras are supported, controls on the type of lens and zoom factor are minimal. While this may limit the experienced 3D modeler, the smaller set of camera controls is adequate for the beginning modeler who is just getting his or her feet wet when working with camera controls.

Multiple cameras may be positioned anywhere in the scene and are easily selected from the object tree window, which is part of the modeling interface. While the camera controls are minimal, the use of multiple cameras is a major benefit for the beginner who may require many views of a scene under construction.

Rendering

Ray Dream Designer offers the artist two modes of rendering: preview and artwork mode. The preview and artwork modes provide for images of varying resolution and quality. The two modes are made distinctive so that variations in rendering techniques may be tried using the preview mode, while a setting is maintained in the artwork (or quality) rendering.

Ray Dream Designer offers both ray-traced and Z-buffered rendering techniques, with the ray-tracer producing very nice results. The ray-tracing option renders realistic shadows, reflections, and refraction.

An interesting rendering option is Ray Dream's own G-buffering option. This option will capture other pertinent information, such as depth of field, object masking, and surface position in alpha channels attached to the final rendering. The alpha channels are extremely useful in image compositing and graphic design and layout.

Animation

Ray Dream Designer 3 does not provide for animation, but Ray Dream Animator, part of the Ray Dream Studio, does provide for some sophisticated animation tools such as inverse kinematics and deformation tools. Ray Dream Studio and Ray Dream Animator were unavailable for review at press time.

Documentation/Learning Curve

Because it is less feature laden, Ray Dream Designer is easy to use. For the beginner it is a great tool for becoming familiar with 3D modeling concepts. For the price, there is no better bargain for beginning modelers. While the documentation is not very extensive, it does offer enough to get the artist going.

With its inexpensive price tag, Ray Dream Designer 3 is a nice way to start 3D modeling without spending the big-budget money normally associated with 3D modeling. With Ray Dream Studio hitting the market with increased functionality, users of Ray Dream Designer 3 can make the transition into advanced techniques rather painlessly, with an interface and concepts they already understand, without paying a very high price tag.

Strata StudioPro Blitz 1.75

Strata Inc.
2 West St. George Blvd., Suite 2100
Ancestor Square
St. George, UT 84770
(800)Strata3D
Platform: Macintosh, PowerMac, Windows

Since its arrival on the 3D scene in the late 1980s, Strata has been dedicated to creating user-friendly modeling and animation software and has once again hit the mark with Strata StudioPro Blitz 1.75. Although the tool set and functionality are very similar to version 1.5.2, the Blitz interface and rendering engine are faster, because they take advantage of QuickDraw 3D and Power Macintosh RISC chip technology.

By incorporating QuickDraw 3D technology, StudioPro Blitz offers shaded graphics modeling (SGM), rendering a nice smooth shaded rendering in real time. This type of modeling offers greater control when assembling scenes, creating models, and applying textures.

One of the greatest features of StudioPro Blitz is the integrated modeling and animation package, which allows the artist to build the models, assemble the scene, and render the animation in one seamless package. The animation is controlled through an event-driven time line for greater flexibility and control over object choreography.

StudioPro Blitz also offers many animation output formats including Virtual Reality Modeling Language (for 3D Web browsing) and QuickTime VR format. While these formats are relatively new, they show great promise for the world of 3D interactive entertainment.

Because StudioPro Blitz is reasonably priced, user friendly, and has one of the best ray-tracing algorithms in the business, this is an excellent package for all-around modeling and animation.

Modeling

Strata has been offering some advanced tools in its modeling package since the early versions of StudioPro. Some of the tools have been refined in the Blitz version, such as the skinning tool (which offers the choice of spline or polygonal object creation).

Blitz offers all of the traditional basic 2D and 3D editing and derivation tools, such as the 2D and 3D sculptor, lofting, lathing, and extrusion. Also offered as part of the standard package are more advanced tools such as the sweep, Boolean, and Metaballs tools.

Textures

While texture control is something which has plagued many 3D modeling packages, StudioPro Blitz makes it very accommodating. Strata offers the capability to create a variety of textures including procedural and animated textures. I found StudioPro to be one of the most intuitive interfaces for creating and applying textures to objects.

Using a visual approach to texture application, texture maps are easily applied or changed, and can be previewed quickly through the preview window that is integrated into the texture pallet. Textures may also be saved and imported to and from disk.

Through third-party venders, texture plug-ins are available including ripples and clouds textures which are completely customizable.

Lights

StudioPro Blitz offers the three traditional light sources (distant, point, and spot-lights). While visible lights are not possible in this version, StudioPro offers some other very powerful lighting features such as gels and soft shadows.

Through the use of gels (which are like textures for lights), you can simulate off-screen geometry and create multicolored lighting effects with a single light. This is a nice feature when creating scenes with unusual lighting demands or when adding implied geometry, such as the leaves of a tree overhead.

Multiple lights can be applied, with memory being the only limit on the number of lights added to the scene.

Cameras

In addition to multiple lights, StudioPro also accommodates the use of multiple cameras. This feature make animating and rendering much easier, since multiple views can be planned simultaneously, without having to keyframe a single camera over time.

Camera lenses are also animatable in that the size of the lens can change over time, as well as the position and rotation of the camera as it moves through a scene.

Rendering

One of the strongest points of StudioPro Blitz is its rendering abilities. By far one of the best ray-tracing algorithms in the business, StudioPro is capable of producing high-quality, photorealistic images in a reasonable amount of time. The ray-tracer provides realistic reflection and refraction, with realistic color and lighting effects.

One of the unique rendering abilities of StudioPro Blitz is that it also has stylized rendering effects which can be applied automatically as part of the rendering process. Called RayPainting, this effect allows the user to set various parameters to create an image which looks as though it was hand sketched or painted, and not computer generated. This stylized feature is great when incorporating the image as a base for design and other graphic applications.

Animation

Using an event-based animation palette, animation keyframes can be easily moved along the time line. Tension controls are also readily available and easy to use. Individual objects or groups of objects can be classified as shapes and animated independently of the main animation time line. This aids in creating complex animation paths where many parts are moving in sync, yet independent of each other.

Animation can be output in QuickTime and PICS file format for the Macintosh. As of this printing, the Windows version had not been released.

Documentation/Learning Curve

While the documentation is adequate for getting started, Strata provides excellent technical support and also instructional classes in beautiful St. George, Utah. Having been through the four-day course, I have experienced first hand the genuinely sincere, friendly, and eager-to-help attitude which is so predominant at Strata Inc. The courses range from beginning to advanced sessions in both modeling and animation.

Although the instructional classes are both entertaining and instructional, the software is by no means difficult to learn. Because of the intuitive interface design and the implementation of the tools, the learning curve is probably the lowest of any program in its class.

TextureScape

Specular International
479 West Street
Amherst, MA 01002
Voice: (413)253-3100
Fax: (413)253-0540
Platform: Macintosh, PowerMac

A neat little tool to come along from Specular is TextureScape. In 3D modeling, texture and lighting are the most important aspects of creating a realistic or convincing image. Texture creation can, at times, become a very time-consuming hurdle, especially when the texture needs to be tiled across a surface seamlessly. TextureScape handles tiling of textures effortlessly.

A relatively simple program to use, TextureScape offers very powerful texture capabilities. The basic premise is to apply colors and characteristics to a two dimensional PostScript shape. Adding layers of different shapes and patterns can create very realistic textures, as well as some really funky ones. The best part is that the textures are always seamless and resolution independent.

TextureScape can also morph between multiple textures and create animated textures. Both of these options work well and can be used to produce nice random-type textures such as cloud sequences or cobblestones.

TextureScape is a great addition to any 3D modeler's toolbox, and comes in at under $200. When seamless tiled textures are needed, this tool hits the mark dead-on. The learning curve is low and the price is reasonable.

trueSpace 2.0

Caligari Corporation
1933 Landings Drive
Mountain View, CA 94043
Voice: (415)390-9600
Fax: (415)390-9755
Platform: Windows, Amiga

One of the bright new stars in the PC market is Caligari's trueSpace. This program has evolved over the past couple of years into a strong modeling package. Version 2.0 offers real-time shaded rendering while modeling by taking advantage of the PC's OpenGL capabilities. Caligari's trueSpace 2.0 offers many features including object deformation, Boolean operations, and inverse kinematics. While offering features found in some expensive programs, trueSpace 2.0 has remained an inexpensive product for any production house or individual.

Modeling

Navigating and creating objects in trueSpace is accomplished largely through an icon interface. Floating palettes allow access to the various tools and texture attributes, and allow objects and the camera to be moved around the scene. Most of the icons are easily understood, but some of them (such as the point editing icons) can be misunderstood.

The modeler is strong and has many tools for object sculpting and deformation. For creating organic models, these tools can quickly become a best friend. Other tools provide bevels, sweeps, lathes, and extrusions. The object deformation tools enable an object to be deformed initially or during animation.

Textures

Creating materials and textures for objects in trueSpace is a truly unique experience. To start with, the interface used to build the materials or textures is very graphical and there is constant feedback with every attribute that changes. The attribute layout is fairly standard, yet completely icon driven.

The unique part of trueSpace's materials interface is that objects can be painted by surface, polygon, or even by vertices. This can create some very complex texturing on objects, rather easily. The only drawback is that the icons for each type of paint tool are easily misunderstood.

Overall, the material generating capabilities are unique and effective, although only three procedural textures are supplied with trueSpace 2.0. Photoshop and other third party-plug-ins can be incorporated into the material creation process and it even ships with some Kai's Power Tool plug-ins.

Lights

trueSpace supports three of the four common lights: distant, point (called local), and spotlights. Ambient lighting is not supported by trueSpace and must be simulated through a material's ambient glow attribute. Multiple lights are supported and the default setup consists of several light sources.

Lights have limited controls; one can change their position, direction, color, intensity, and shadows. In many cases this is sufficient, but complex lighting strategies with colored gels and gobos are not supported. Fortunately, there are ways of creating this same effect through cutouts and transparent objects.

Cameras

Like lights in trueSpace, cameras have limited controls. Camera controls are limited to position, rotation, and zoom factor. This is somewhat limiting, but the next release may contain more camera control.

Multiple cameras are also supported, which is a nice benefit considering the otherwise lack of camera control. Cameras may also be made to point at other objects in a scene or to always look ahead when animating.

Rendering and Animation

Although trueSpace offers 3D rendering technology for real-time rendering during the modeling phase, the final image rendering modes are somewhat slow. Fortunately, there are three rendering modes: Flat, Phong, and Metal mode. While the Flat mode is the fastest, there are no highlights rendered, and is not high enough quality for a final rendering. The Phong and Metal modes can be used to calculate reflective lighting and surfaces, but they are slow.

When rendering a preview of a scene, trueSpace fortunately has provided a means of rendering select objects in the scene. While this can speed up preview rendering times, it does not help when the entire scene is rendered for the final image.

While the rendering time may be long, the time needed to keyframe an animation is not. Objects can be animated manually by repositioning and recording the frame or through the use of spline paths for motion. Textures, background, fog, cameras, and materials are all animatable, which proves to be a nice feature in trueSpace.

Documentation/Learning Curve

While some aspects of trueSpace are simple to understand and implement, others are not. The modeling tools in this version are greatly improved from the previous version, with some new inclusions, such as the deformation tool. The documentation comes with a tutorial manual, which is helpful, but the reference manual is vague at best. It seems as though the software is aimed at the beginning and intermediate modeler market, yet the manuals do almost nothing to explain some of the key concepts of 3D modeling.

Glossary

A

algorithm - the step-by-step description of a logical procedure. In the case of rendering, it is the procedure for interpreting geometry and color date for image creation.

alpha channel - a channel used in image processing for creating a selection area. Alpha channels are typically 8-bit, gray-scale images.

animation - a series of images displayed on-screen quickly, with each successive image slightly different from the previous to create the illusion of movement.

antialiasing - a procedure which removes the jaggies, or stair-stepping effect of drawing a diagonal or curved line using square or round pixels. Antialiasing takes the average of the neighboring pixels to determine what color the pixel in the direct line should be.

asymmetrical - nonmirrored on opposite sides along an axis. A sphere is symmetrical, while an organic object such as a plant may be considered asymmetrical.

attenuation - in lighting, the rate at which a light decays. Light sources will have a falloff distance in which the user specifies a distance (in units) for which the light "falls off" or does not appear to illuminate an object's surface.

axis - one of the three imaginary lines (X,Y,Z), used in 3D space to determine the position, movement, and rotation of an object.

axes - reference to more than one axis.

B

Bézier curves - a type of point used in creating complex curves with a minimal number of points. A Bézier curve uses handles to control tension through the vertices of a curve.

Boolean operations - a procedure used to affect the interactive geometry of two objects. Although more than two objects may be used in a Boolean operation, cleaner geometry may result when using only two objects with complex geometry.

bounding box - an imaginary box which completely encloses all of an object's geometry. The bounding box is used to represent the object's geometric limits and when used instead of object geometry, results in faster screen redraws.

bump map - a gray-scale image used in textures and shaders to create artificial surface geometry. A bump map is processed at render time and is used to create artificial surface normals on an object's surface.

byte - a digital measure of memory consisting of 8 bits. In digital imaging, varying numbers of bits are used to store color information for each pixel.

C

camera - an object used to view and render a scene. In many 3D programs, the camera object is very similar to real-world camera characteristics. Cameras can be animated and lens sizes can be changed to create a variety of image effects.

camera view - the view as seen through the lens of the camera. When rendering through a camera, all objects seen through the camera's view will be rendered.

child object - an object which has been parented to a parent object. A child object can be moved or animated freely, but will also move in relation to a parent object when the parent object is animated, moved, or rotated.

clipped polygon - a polygon which has intersected the rendering camera's lens. Clipped polygons appear as irregular polygons flush against the viewport or camera lens.

color map - an image which has been used to determine how color is placed on an object through the use of a shader or texture. Color maps can be up to 24-bit color or gray-scale images.

color picker - a dialog box used to display a range of color from which the user can select a color value. Colors may be changed by changing red, blue, and green color values.

constrain - to keep from certain movement. Constraining an object on the Y axis will only allow movement along the Y axis and will not allow the object's X or Z values to change.

coordinates, absolute - position of an object based on the coordinate system of the current modeling or rendering package. Coordinates are based on horizontal, vertical, and depth values using the X, Y, and Z coordinate system respectively.

coordinates, relative - the X, Y, and Z coordinate system used to describe the distance or movement of an object in relation to its current position.

coordinates, world - the X, Y, and Z coordinate system used to describe the location of objects throughout the entire scene. World coordinates are absolute to the modeling or rendering environment.

D

default - the choice used by the software when no choice is made by the user. Usually factory set, the default assures that some value is used wherever data are needed.

dialog box - a window which appears to request information or alert the user of an action or error which has occurred.

diffuse color - the true color of an object. As most objects will have a slight variation in color in extreme light or dark, the diffuse color is used to determine what the primary color of the object is in normal lighting situations.

E

end cap - in a modeling environment, end caps are added to objects such as cylinders in order to keep the object from appearing hollow. The end caps are circular polygons used to close up the object. End caps are removable if not desired.

environment - the scene in which the model is rendered. The environment can include such attributes as fog, reflective attributes, and environment maps. In many software packages, the environment is described as either a sphere or cube which encompasses the entire scene.

environment map - an image attached to the environment used for displaying clouds and such so as to give the illusion of an environment other than that which is modeled in the scene.

extrusion - converting a 2D drawing to a 3D object by adding depth. An extrusion can be described as pushing a 2D object through material much like a cookie cutter cuts cookies out of dough.

F

facet - in a 3D modeled object, the polygons used to create the object form facets. Facets are also called faces and are visible in lower quality renderings. When smoothing is turned on for a surface, facets become less visible.

fast boxes - in Strata StudioPro and Vision 3D, fast boxes are a type of view used to view objects in box form only. Other software packages may refer to these as a bounding box view.

flat shading - a rendering algorithm which renders each polygon as a single color without shading. A fast rendering algorithm used primarily for previewing a modeled object.

fractal - a pattern which is mathematically calculated. The fractal design is usually increasingly complex. Fractal examples include the Mandelbrot and Julia set.

G

geometry lines - lines used to connect points in an object. These lines are used to visualize the object's shape and are not rendered.

gigabyte - used as a term for digital storage, it represents one billion bytes. A byte consists of 8-bits. Not long ago, a gigabyte was considered a lot of storage. Today's high-quality graphics demand intense amounts of storage, and a one-gigabyte hard drive is minimal equipment and will fill up fast when creating computer animation.

glow - in rendering, an object may have the appearance of generating its own soft light. Objects which give off light from within are said to glow. Setting the glow factor on a shader assigned to an object will make the object's surface appear to glow. Unless using radiosity, the glow from the object will produce light visible on other objects within the scene.

Gouraud shading - (pronounced "juh-ro"), a method of interpolating the color intensity of polygons from adjoining vertices, instead of a single normal from the center of the polygon. This method produces a smooth shaded surface, although polygon edges may become apparent when the specular setting is medium to high.

H

hidden line - modeling mode used to remove geometry lines which would be hidden if all surfaces were solid or opaque. The object is still drawn in a wireframe mode, though all hidden lines are removed.

hierarchy - tier-ordered relationship of linked objects used in modeling and animation. Hierarchical links are used in inverse kinematics and other complex animation procedures.

I

image map - an image which has been imported into rendering software to be used in a surface texture. Image type is dependent on software, but is typically PICT (Macintosh) or .BMP (PC).

image mapping - the procedure in which images are used to build textures using existing images. The images are then placed on an object's surface according to the mapping orientation.

index of refraction - the rate at which light is bent as it passes through a transparent material, causing objects seen through the material to be distorted.

K

key frame - in animation, a frame used to define the attributes of an object (such as position, scale, or rotation) at a particular point in time.

L

lathed object - a 3D object which has been created through rotating a 2D shape along a single axis, to create a 3D object.

lathing - the process of revolving a 2D object around an axis to create 3D geometry.

light - an object used to illuminate a scene. Light objects include distant, spot and point lights. In most software, the lights themselves are not visible when rendered, only the illumination effect they have on other objects.

M

map - an image used in textures and shaders to be applied to an object's surface.

matte - a nonshiny surface which gives an object a dull surface appearance.

megabyte - a term used to describe digital storage which is equal to 1,024,000 bytes. A full-screen 24-bit image is close to one megabyte of storage.

mesh - a surface type which is typically created from splines or control lines. Mesh surfaces are very flexible after initial creation and can be used to create various objects and connective pieces.

model - a computer representation of a geometric shape. A model can be created of any shape in existence using a variety of tools.

modeling - the art of creating 3D computer models.

morphing - derived from the term *metamorphosis*, morphing is the process of changing one shape into another. Morphing is used extensively in animation to give shapes the appearance of organic movement.

movement - the act of changing an object's position in 3D space.

N

navigation - the ability to change one's position in 3D space successfully.

Null Object - a nonrenderable position in space, used primarily in animation for controlling objects or groups.

O

object - a computer model, light, or camera as it is represented within a scene.

orthographic view - a modeling view in which the perspective has been removed. Orthographic views will show all objects at their relative size, regardless of distance between objects.

P

panning - moving the camera or view from one side of the screen to the other in a horizontal or vertical motion.

parametric - involving parameters. Many tools require data input called parameters.

parent - an object used to control subordinate or child objects. Child objects of the parent can move freely, but as the parent object is moved or rotated, the child objects will follow.

perspective view - a view in which perspective can be observed. Perspective views are used when rendering or modeling to give the scene its 3D appearance.

Phong shading - a rendering algorithm which uses interpolation to shade the surfaces of polygons.

photorealism - a term used to describe images which are computer generated, but look as though they are photographs of real objects.

PICS file - a Macintosh format used to store animation images in an uncompressed format. PICS files can also store an image's alpha channel, but the entire animation is limited to 16 megabytes.

PICT file - the standard Macintosh file format for single images. PICT files can retain 24 bits of color and an additional 8 bits for an alpha channel.

pixel - a shortened form of picture element, a pixel is the smallest colored dot on a computer monitor.

primitive - the basic 3D model building blocks. The primitives are spheres, cubes, and cylinders. While some software includes a cone as a primitive, it is possible to create a cone by converging the points on one end of a cylinder.

procedural texture - a texture or shader which is defined mathematically instead of through the use of image maps. Procedural textures are beneficial because they typically are created to run through an object's geometry as opposed to applied to the surface. Using a procedural marble texture on an object will cause the texture to flow around curves and bumps, as though the object were cut from a block of the material.

R

ray tracing - a rendering algorithm used to create realistic lighting effects on objects. The most computer-intensive rendering algorithm, second only to radiosity, ray tracing can create very realistic reflections and refractive effects.

reflectivity - a property of an object's surface which causes an object to reflect an image, such as a mirror.

render - the process used to create the final image of a 3D model. Depending on the type of rendering algorithm chosen, lighting effects, textures, reflections, and other visual properties will be calculated by the computer.

rendering algorithm - methods of rendering images. Different rendering algorithms are utilized for speed or image quality. The rendering algorithm chosen will directly affect the way an image is produced from a model.

rotation - spinning an object on an axis. Rotated objects are revolved around their pivot point along a selected axis.

rounding - the process of using fillets to create smoothly joined corners on objects. This process creates a more realistic object through a smoother transition over edges.

S

scale - to change the relative size of an object. Scaling can be performed on any or all of the axes at one time.

scene - an orderly collection of objects used to create an image or animation.

screen redraws - the time it takes for the computer monitor to recalculate the visible geometry on the screen.

sculptor (3D) - used by some programs to push or pull points on an object as though it were made of clay.

shading - the process of calculating the color differences on an object's surface. Degrees of shading vary, as in the difference between flat shading and Phong shading.

shapes - a classification of objects which are self-supported. A shape classification in some programs allows it to be stored as an entire entity containing motion, texture, and geometric proportions.

shininess - an object property which controls the way specular light is reflected from an object's surface.

specular highlight - the hot area on an object's surface which receives the most light. The specular highlight is typically the color of the light source which it is reflecting, except in metals, which use a specular highlight the color of the metal.

spline object - an object which is constructed of splines or spline mesh.

surface - the collection of polygons which make up the visible portion of an object. The surface is what receives the textures and shaders applied to an object.

surface properties - attributes used to change the appearance of an object.

symmetrical - of similar geometry along a single axis. Primitives are symmetrical, while organic objects are typically asymetrical.

T

three dimensional - also known as 3D; having height, width, and depth.

toggle switch - a button or switch which has only two states; on or off.

tools (3D) - functions which are used in software for the creation or manipulation of object geometry. 3D tools may be used for creating, animating, or postproduction of objects, light, or images.

transformation - changing an object's position, rotation, or scale.

transparency - a surface property which allows light to pass through a surface. Transparency can range from the very opaque to completely invisible.

two dimensional - having only width and height.

V

vertical plane - the axis which runs from top to bottom (along Y axis).

view - a perspective of a model or scene.

volumetric - having volume or substance. Volumetric lighting is light which seems to have a sense of solidity to it, such as light which passes through thick fog or smog.

W

wireframe - a modeling mode generally used in most modeling software. A wireframe model is created by drawing lines from every vertex to its adjoining vertices. In a wireframe model, all object geometry is visible.

world coordinates - in 3D space, a coordinate system which enables the software and the artist to establish an exact location for objects, lights, or cameras.

Index

About the CD-ROM

3D Graphics
Tips, Tricks, and Techniques

David Kalwick

The CD-ROM packaged with this book contains demo versions of some of today's leading 3D modeling and animation software for Macintosh and PC platforms; such as form•Z by auto•des•sys, Infini-D by Specular International, 3D Studio 4.0 by Autodesk, ElectricImage by Electric Image Inc., and Strata StudioPro Blitz by Strata Inc. Also included are 3D models and images, all of which were created using the various software available on the CD-ROM.

System Requirements

While this CD is a dual platform CD, software will run only on the platform for which it is intended. Although each demo is intended to run on the most basic systems, with most requiring either DOS, Windows, or a Macintosh operating system, higher memory and system requirements may be necessary for performing some functions.